Josef Gugler, Hans-Jürgen Lüsebrink, Jürgen Martini (Hrsg.)

Literary Theory and African Literature.
Théorie littéraire et littérature africaine

Beiträge zur Afrikaforschung
ISSN 0938–7285

*Herausgegeben vom Institut für Afrikaforschung
in Verbindung mit dem Sonderforschungsbereich 214
"Identität in Afrika" der Universität Bayreuth*

Band
3

LIT

Josef Gugler, Hans-Jürgen Lüsebrink, Jürgen Martini (Hrsg.)

Literary Theory and African Literature.
Théorie littéraire et littérature africaine

LIT

Diese Arbeit ist im Sonderforschungsbereich 214 "Identität in Afrika" der
Universität Bayreuth entstanden und wurde auf seine Veranlassung unter Verwendung der ihm von der Deutschen Forschungsgemeinschaft zur
Verfügung gestellten Mittel gedruckt.

Die Deutsche Bibliothek – CIP-Einheitsaufnahme

Gugler, Josef; Lüsebrink Hans-Jürgen; Martini Jürgen:
Literary Theory and African Literature. Théorie littéraire et littérature
africaine / Josef Gugler, Hans-Jürgen Lüsebrink, Jürgen Martini . –
Münster ; Hamburg : Lit, 1994
   (Beiträge zur Afrikaforschung ; Bd. 3.)
   ISBN 3-89473-693-3

NE: GT

© LIT VERLAG   Dieckstr. 73   48145 Münster   Tel. 0251–23 50 91
                Hallerplatz 5   20146 Hamburg   Tel. 040–44 64 46

ACKNOWLEDGEMENTS

This volume presents revised versions of papers that were first read and discussed at the colloquium "Theoretical Approaches to African Literature" held at Bayreuth University on 15th and 16th June 1990. The colloquium was part of a series of conferences sponsored by the Special Research Programme "Identity in Africa - Processes of its Development and Change" (SFB 214). We wish to express our thanks to the Deutsche Forschungsgemeinschaft for funding the colloquium and the publication of this volume, to Heidemarie Reichert who went beyond the call of duty in organizing the colloquium and preparing the papers for publication, and to our colleagues who contributed to the colloquium and revised their papers for this volume.

The Editors

IN MEMORIAM

RICHARD BJORNSON

CONTENTS

The Editors and Contributors xi

African Literature and the Uses of Theory 1
    Josef Gugler

Literary Theory and Theories of Decolonization 17
    Biodun Jeyifo

Theory and Moral Commitment in the Study of African Literature 31
    Richard Bjornson

Présupposés théoriques et méthodologiques à une théorie de la
    littérature africaine 43
    Georges Ngal

La littérature négro-africaine de langue française: prise de
    parole et situation de communication 63
    Bernard Mouralis

Of Colonial and Canonical Encounters: A Reciprocal Reading of
    L'Immoraliste and *Une Vie de boy* 75
    Eileen Julien

Inhabitable Words: Text, Metatext and Criticism in Yoruba Oral
    Praise Poetry 89
    Karin Barber

A European's Reading of Soyinka's and Osofisan's Theatre Texts
    in 1990 113
    Joachim Fiebach

Ousmane Sembène et Ibrahima Ly: l'engagement politique de
    l'écrivain dans les sociétés postcoloniales africaines 135
    Maguèye Kassé

Politics and Value in South African Literature: Some Thoughts
    on Recent Interventions by Albie Sachs and Njabulo Ndebele: 143
    David Maughan Brown

Questionnements et mises en perspectives 163
    Hans-Jürgen Lüsebrink

THE EDITORS AND CONTRIBUTORS

Karin BARBER is a social anthropologist who has researched and written extensively on Yorùbá culture and thought. She did her Ph.D. at the University of Ifè, Nigeria, during which period she spent more than three years doing field-work in a small Yorùbá town, Okukù. She subsequently taught in the Department of African Languages and Literatures at Ifè for many years, and did further research on Yorùbá popular theatre, oral performance and religion. She has also done comparative work on African popular culture. Since 1985 she has been a lecturer at the Centre of West African Studies, University of Birmingham. Her publications include a study of oral praise-poetry entitled *I Could Speak Until Tomorrow: Oríkì, Women and the Past in a Yorùbá Town* (1991).

Richard BJORNSON was Professor of French and Comparative Literature at Ohio State University. He is the translator of works by René Philombe (*Tales from Cameroon: Collected Short Stories of René Philombe*, 1984), Mongo Beti (*Lament for an African Pol*, 1985), Ferdinand Oyono (*Road to Europe*, 1989), and Paul Hazoumé (*Doguicimi*, 1990). He authored *The Picaresque Hero in European Fiction* (1977) and *The African Quest for Freedom and Identity* (1991) and had completed a book-length study of Mongo Beti when he suddenly died in 1992. His contribution to this volume was to be his very last essay.

Joachim FIEBACH teaches at the Institut für Theaterwissenschaft, Humboldt University, Berlin. He worked at the University College of Dar es Salaam in Tanzania and at the University of Ife in Nigeria. Current scholarly interests: Comparative and historical studies in cultural performances in Europe, North America, and Africa, and in particular theatre, theatricality and audio-visual mediatisation in the 20th century. Relevant publications *Kunstprozesse in Afrika. Literatur im Umbruch* (1979), *Die Toten als die Macht der Lebenden. Zur Theorie und Geschichte von Theater in Afrika* (1986), *Inseln der Unordnung. Fünf Versuche zu Heiner Müllers Theatertexten* (1990), *Von Craig bis Brecht* (expanded and revised reprint 1991).

Josef GUGLER is Professor of Sociology at the University of Connecticut. His previous positions include Director of Sociological Research at the Makerere Institute of Social Research, Makerere University College,

Uganda, and Professor of Development Sociology at Bayreuth University. Research and teaching have taken him to India, Kenya, Nigeria, Tanzania, and Zaïre. To date most of his research and writing has focused on urbanization in the Third World, and in particular in Africa South of the Sahara. At this time he works on a study of literature and politics in Africa.

Biodun JEYIFO is Professor of English at Cornell University. He has taught at the University of Ibadan and the University of Ife in Nigeria, and at Oberlin College, U.S.A. His teaching and research interests are in the fields of drama and theatre, African and African-American literature and cinema, and Marxist cultural criticism and critical theory. Dr. Jeyifo's current research in critical theory focuses on colonial and postcolonial studies. His publications include: *The Yoruba Travelling Theatre of Nigeria* (1984), *The Truthful Lie* (1985), and *Wole Soyinka: History and Mythopoeisis* (forthcoming).

Eileen JULIEN is Professor of Comparative Literature at Indiana University. Her teaching and research have focused primarily on literatures in French from Africa and the Caribbean. She is the author of *African Novels and the Question of Orality* (1992) and is currently at work on studies of New Orleans carnival traditions and of fictions by Senegalese women. She served as President of the African Literature Association in 1990-91.

Maguèye KASSÉ est maître de conférences au Département d'Allemand de l'Université Cheikh Anta Diop à Dakar (Senegal). Principaux domaines de recherches: culture et développement, en particulier à travers les relations germano-africaines; civilisation allemande contemporaine; analyse comparée des littératures africaines écrites. Publications e.a. sur l'image du noir dans l'oeuvre de Leo Frobenius, Ousmane Sembène, Heiner Müller et la réception d'auteurs allemands dans l'Afrique Subsaharienne (notamment Brecht et Goethe).

Hans-Jürgen LÜSEBRINK, professeur de Lettres et Civilisations Romanes à l'Université de Passau (Allemagne), membre associé du Centre de Recherches Africaines de l'Université de Bayreuth. S'intéresse à l'histoire littéraire française du 18e siècle, aux rapports histoire/littérature et aux littératures francophones de l'Afrique noire, des Caraïbes et du Québec. A publié e.a. *Schrift, Buch und Lektüre in der französischsprachigen Literatur Afrikas* (1990), *Die « Bastille ». Zur Symbolgeschichte von Herrschaft und Freiheit* (avec R. Reichardt, 1990) et *Lectures de Raynal. La réception de l'« Histoire des deux Indes » en Europe et en Amérique au XVIIIe siècle* (édité avec M. Tietz, 1991).

Jürgen MARTINI taught English Literatures and Social History at the University of Bremen. Subsequently he was a Research Fellow at the African Research Centre of the University of Bayreuth and at the Humboldt University, Berlin. At present he serves in the Office of the President of the Assembly of Sachsen-Anhalt. His research and publications focus on African and Caribbean literature, in particular on literature for children and young people, and on drama, theatre, and performance. He has translated (with Helmi Martini-Honus) creative writing from Africa, the Philippines, and New Zealand into German.

David MAUGHAN BROWN is Deputy Vice-Chancellor and Campus Principal on the Pietermaritzburg campus of the University of Natal. He was formerly Professor and Head of the Department of English on the same campus of the University. He is the author of *Land, Freedom and Fiction* (1985) - a study of the fiction written about the "Mau Mau" movement in Kenya. He has published essays and articles on the writings of Ngugi wa Thiong'o, including the *Dictionary of Literary Biography* entry on Ngugi; on Achebe and Soyinka; and on East and Southern African popular fiction, ranging from the *Drum* writers and van der Post to Wilbur Smith.

Bernard MOURALIS est actuellement professeur à l'Université de Cergy-Pontoise où il dirige le département des Lettres modernes. Il a enseigné auparavant dans plusieurs universités africaines ainsi qu'à l'Université de Lille III. Il a publié notamment *Les Contre-littératures* (1975), *L'Oeuvre de Mongo Beti* (1981), *Littérature et développement* (1984), *V.Y. Mudimbe ou le Discours, l'écart et l'écriture* (1988), *Montaigne et le mythe du bon sauvage* (1989), *Les Contes d'Amadou Koumba: parcours de lecture* (1991). Il est par ailleurs membre du Groupe de recherches 931 du CNRS, Langues, Livres, Littératures, et secrétaire général de l'APELA (Association pour l'étude des littératures africaines).

Georges NGAL a enseigné dix ans dans les universités zaïroises, ensuite à Middlebury College, puis à Paris-Sorbonne, Grenoble III et Paris-X Nanterre, et enfin à l'Université de Bayreuth. Principales publications: *Tendances actuelles de la littérature africaine d'expression française* (1972), *Aimé Césaire, un homme à la recherche d'une patrie* (1975), *Giambatista Viko ou le Viol du Discours Africain* (roman, réédité 1984), *L'Errance*, Yaounde (roman, 1979), *Césaire 70* (co-auteur et co-éditeur avec M. Steins, 1985), *Un prétendant valeureux* (roman, 1989).

LITERARY THEORY AND AFRICAN LITERATURE
edited by J. Gugler, H.-J. Lüsebrink, J. Martini
Münster/Hamburg 1993, pp. 1-15

AFRICAN LITERATURE AND THE USES OF THEORY[1]

JOSEF GUGLER

> Je me souviens pourtant que jadis, dans cette Afrique qui passe pour classique, le griot était non seulement l'élément dynamique de sa tribu, clan, village, mais aussi le témoin patent de chaque événement. C'est lui qui enregistrait, déposait devant tous, sous l'arbre du palabre, les faits et les gestes de chacun. La conception de mon travail découle de cet enseignement: rester au plus près du réel et du peuple.
>
> Ousmane Sembène, *L'Harmattan*

This volume presents the papers read at the colloquium Theoretical Approaches to African Literature held at Bayreuth University in June 1990. The preceding summer Hans-Jürgen Lüsebrink, Jürgen Martini and I had taught there a joint seminar on literary theory. The experience was unsettling, and we felt the need to develop our understanding of the uses of theory in the study of African literature. We were delighted that all but one of the colleagues we approached accepted our invitation to a colloquium. We were thus able to bring together leading scholars from three continents. And we could bridge the wide gap that usually separates the anglophone and the francophone. Each of our guests presented a paper, and Bayreuth faculty acted as discussants. Our discussions were lively, and all the papers have been revised for this publication.
　　In this essay, based on my introduction to the Bayreuth colloquium, I will discuss three issues arising from our choice of topic:
1. African literature in the singular,
2. the relation of theory to African literature, and
3. theory.

---

[1] This essay is based on my introduction to the Bayreuth colloquium. I wish to thank, without implicating, Koffi Anyinefa, Oumar Cherif Diop, Eileen Julien, Hans-Jürgen Lüsebrink, and János Riesz for helpful comments on an earlier version.

And I will briefly introduce the contributions to the volume as they relate to that discussion.

On the first issue, I suggest that we can meaningfully speak of an African literature in the singular, at least up to this point in time. *African literature*, of course, is a misnomer, since the body of literature so designated usually excludes the literature of Egypt and North Africa.[2] While regrettable in some ways, there are good reasons for that exclusion, and I will not pursue the matter at this time. More accurately, then, the proposition is that much of the literature produced in Africa South of the Sahara[3] -- and by first-generation exiles from the region -- shares characteristics that distinguish it from literatures produced in other regions. I present as evidence:

--- connections to oral literature are common, though I would not go as far as Abiola Irele (56) to assert that oral literature presents the basic intertext of the African imagination;

--- most prose writing was in a realist mode until quite recently -- in the terms of Richard Priebe (2), writers chose the rhetoric of realism to set up a very direct, explicit relationship between their work and their society;[4]

--- African literature tends to focus more on social relations than on individual character -- in fact, much African writing presents itself as a response to pressing political problems, and these problems are approached in their societal context rather than being reduced to an individualistic analysis;

--- a number of political themes connect authors across the continent, across diverse traditional cultures, across two world religions, across the boundaries of the new nations, and perhaps most strikingly, across the divisions imposed on the continent by the colonial powers who brought different cultures, who pursued different policies, and who (arguably most important, because determining the very medium for most African writers and circumscribing their publics) imposed a division of linguae francae on contemporary Africa; and

--- an on-going dialogue within the literature and among the writers.

If distinctions are to be drawn among African literatures, I suggest that the most important division is between the resistance literature of Southern Africa and the literature of much of the rest of the region that did not

---

[2] A notable exception is Mildred Mortimer who relates francophone novels from South and North of the Sahara.

[3] "Africa South of the Sahara" is cumbersome, but preferable to the racist "Black Africa" and the Eurocentric "Subsaharan Africa." Throughout this essay, "Africa" will stand for Africa South of the Sahara.

[4] Kwame Anthony Appiah (149-52) characterizes the first generation of modern African novels as realist and suggests that they have been challenged at a second stage by postrealist novels such as Yambo Ouloguem's *Le Devoir de violence*.

address the struggle for political independence but, rather, the struggle for emancipation from the West and the major political issues arising when the "political kingdom" that independence had promised turned out less than glorious for most of its subjects. This is not to deny that the national contexts in which African writers operate have become quite distinct over thirty years of independence. We will have occasion to discuss the case of Cameroon.

On the second issue, the relation of theory to African literature, there has been an acerbic debate: What theory should be applied to African literature? Must we reject literary theories developed in a different context as Eurocentric? Do we need an Afrocentric means of reading and understanding texts? Can a properly African theory be developed?

The writing of fiction about Africa has been the near-exclusive domain of Africans for more than a generation. Bernard Mouralis, in this volume, details *la prise de parole* of francophone writers. In stark contrast, Western scholars continue to dominate discussions about African literature. Africans are still struggling to make their voices heard; Georges Ngal, in this volume, presents elements of the francophone contribution to an Afrocentric approach to African literature.

The cultural hegemony of the West has had the effect that, as Karin Barber puts it here (90), "Literature in English and French is more conspicuous and more prestigious than literature in African languages; and any written literature carries more weight than any oral text." Barber's work on Yoruba oral poetics makes a major contribution toward redressing the balance. At the same time it undermines the view that literature is a domain altogether separate from other discourses.

The reasons for the Western dominance of the theoretical enterprise are not far to seek. Biodun Jeyifo (1990, 39), for one, has denounced the failure to acknowledge properly "the vastly unequal relations of power and privilege between African and non-African scholars and critics of African literature."

In this volume, Jeyifo takes aim at "the exclusively and prescriptively *Western* monument of High Theory" (18). His attack is twofold: against the cultural hegemony of the West; and against a "theoreticism" that seeks a special idiom the more elaborate and impenetrable the better, a cloistered, reified neo-scholasticism. Thus the topoi of travel and quest can be shown to express distinct aspects of the project of decolonized theory rather than being necessarily contradictory. Jeyifo locates the central contradictions instead in the world capitalist system. Eurocentrism and nativism alike entail a culturalist obscuring of the systemic features of the contemporary world system. Because the periphery is the weakest link in the chain of global accumulation and concentration of economic, technological, and cultural capital in the center, ideas and cultural and political currents that potentially exceed the historical and structural limits of the world system are in the main generated in peripheral social formations. Theories of literature and cultural production in particular follow different trajectories at the central and peripheral social formations and engage different agendas. Most notably, the paradigmatic shift in emphasis in literary theory in the center from author to reader and finally to text is vigorously resisted and contested by major writers, critics, and teachers of the developing world.

Richard Bjornson -- at the colloquium, and in his contribution to this volume, which was completed before his untimely death -- castigated the tendency to dismiss the relevance to contemporary literary theory of the social, economic, political, and economic crises facing the world in general and Africa in particular. Surveying several schools of literary theory prominent at this time, he argued that "non-African literary theory can only serve a maieutic function, facilitating the birth of an understanding with which African literature itself was already pregnant" (35).

Let me turn to the third issue. There has been, as Terry Eagleton (25-26) put it recently, "a really virulent outbreak of theory, on an epidemic scale ... in the literary institutions for the past twenty years or so." Now, I happen to believe that the taste of a sauce can be judged only when it is applied to a dish, be it pudding as far as the British are concerned, or meat, the one and all of Bayreuth cuisine. Or to put it in a more learned manner, and I quote Laurence Lerner (3), "Theory is important, but so are instances: it is only through their embodiment in actual works of literature that literary theories take on meaning." However, to date, there has been little such connection as far as African literature studies are concerned. There is a good deal of writing about African literature, but most of it does not venture beyond presenting that literature. The unease is widespread. Sunday Anozie (11) speaks of the "critical inertia" in African literary criticism. Simon Gikandi (149) complains about the "acute poverty of theory." And Biodun Jeyifo (1990, 35) concludes that the debates that have taken place over the last two decades "have been under-theorized."

I suggest that we may usefully distinguish three modes of addressing literature: explanation, critique, and interpretation. First off, by *explanation* I mean the effort to enhance the reader's appreciation of the text. The very title of Ousmane Sembène's great classic, *Les Bouts de bois de Dieu: Banty mam yall*, may serve as example. The author himself speaks in a footnote of the superstition that makes people speak of "bits of wood" rather than living beings so as not to shorten their life (77). The reader puzzled by the subtitle may further want to know that "Banty mam yall" repeats the French title in Wolof.[5] If the reader has sufficient curiosity to persist beyond these translations of convention and of language, a discussion of the language issue in Africa, in Senegal, in Ousmane Sembène's public role, in his literary oeuvre, in *Les Bouts de bois de Dieu* might ensue. The need for explanation tends to be particularly pronounced where the text is based in an unfamiliar culture, whether it be a foreign contemporary culture or a past version of our own. Not only Europeans but most Nigerian readers are strangers to the world Chinua Achebe magnificently portrays in *Things Fall Apart,* and even for the contemporary Igbo reader this is a world of the past that has become unfamiliar in many ways.

The task of explanation, then, is -- to paraphrase Lodge (360), summarizing Philip Swallow -- to assist in the function of literature itself, to enable us better to enjoy life, or better to endure it. The great writers are men and women of exceptional wisdom, insight, and understanding. Their novels, plays, and poems are inexhaustible reservoirs of values, ideas, images, which, when properly understood and appreciated, allow us to live more fully, more finely, more intensely. But literary conventions change, history changes, language changes, and these treasures too easily become locked away in libraries, covered with dust, neglected and forgotten. It is the job of critics to unlock the drawers, blow away the dust, bring the treasures into the light of day. Of course, they need certain specialist skills to do this: a knowledge of history, a knowledge of philology, of generic convention and textual editing. But above all, they need enthusiasm, the love of books. It is by the demonstration of this enthusiasm in action that the critic forges a bridge between the great writers and the general reader.

A second mode of addressing literature may be called *critique*. First off, the pretense that writing is realist in the sense of presenting an "objective" record, has to be challenged. Beyond that, I have in mind what Robert Scholes refers to as criticism: it "is 'against' other texts insofar as it resists them in the name of the critic's recognition of her or his own values" (38). Scholes's emphasis that fiction, because it deals with types, with representative characters, can be criticized only from a position correspondingly broad, is particularly pertinent. But rather than use the term "criticism" with its confusingly broad range of meanings, I prefer to speak of critique.

Much contemporary critique is a truly humanistic enterprise: it emphasizes equality. Whether the critics raise issues of class, of culture, or

---

[5] *Banti maam yàlla* is the correct orthography and pronunciation according to Papa Samba Diop.

of gender, they are inspired by the central value of the Enlightenment, the quest for equality. *Les Bouts de bois de Dieu*, to stay with this example, inscribes itself in the struggle for social, racial, and gender equality. It memorably portrays the emancipation of the strikers' wives. It dramatically articulates the workers' demand for respect for their language and culture.[6] The class analysis, however, presents a problem. Although it has a distinguished ancestry, it does not fit contemporary Africa all that well. It certainly does not fit the railroad strike in French West Africa in 1947-48. Sembène presents the railroad workers fighting a private company (377), but as a matter of fact the Régie des Chemins de Fer de l'A.O.F. was a para-statal that had legal status and financial autonomy (Morlet, 38). This throws into bold relief a key issue: Who is going to pay the workers' higher wages? The agency will have to raise its charges for shipping agricultural products to Dakar. Who is going to pay? The overseas consumers of those products? The French commercial houses that control the trade? Or, perhaps, the peasants will receive lower prices for their products? Clearly, there can be no stock response.[7]

The conventional reading of *Les Bouts de bois de Dieu* must be critiqued for more far-reaching reasons. When the book is published in 1960, *l'année des indépendances*, as our francophone colleagues put it, a major issue is shaping up. Urban incomes, and in particular formal-sector incomes, have increased substantially. The urban-rural income gap has thus been exacerbated, and rural-urban migration has accelerated. The problem was recognized in a political document, the Arusha Declaration of the TANU, the national party of Tanzania, in 1967. Written by Julius Nyerere, president of Tanzania as well as translator of Shakespeare into Swahili, the key passage is rather poetic:

> Although when we talk of exploitation we usually think of capitalists, we should not forget that there are many fish in the sea. They eat each other. The large ones eat the small ones, and small ones eat those who are even smaller. There are two possible ways of dividing the people in our country. We can put the capitalists and feudalists on one side, and the farmers and workers on the other. But we can also divide the people into urban dwellers on one side and those who live in the rural areas on the other. If we are not careful we might get to the position where the real exploitation in Tanzania is that of the town dwellers exploiting the peasants. (28)

---

[6] The demand for the recognition of African culture and language is directed not only against the French but also against Islam. The novel's subtitle substitutes the Wolof *bant* for the Arabic *xalima* in the traditional expression *xalima maam yàlla* (Diop).

[7] Even where workers of a private company fight for higher wages, the question: who pays? has to be answered to the extent that their company, rather than pay the wage increases out of profits, is able to pass them on to its suppliers and/or customers.

Class analysis is misleading because it misspecifies the forces on both sides of the contemporary struggle in Africa. The struggle is not between the owners of the means of production and the proletariat. It is between those who have usurped political power and the impoverished and the oppressed. The exploiter is Chief the Honourable M.A. Nanga, Minister of Culture, of Chinua Achebe's *A Man of the People*. And his constituents are fully aware of that: they are clamoring not for higher wages but for their cut of the public resources their representatives misappropriate. The oppressor is Mobutu Sese Seko, alias Field Marshal Kamini in Wole Soyinka's *A Play of Giants*, and one of the inspirations for Tonton in Henri Lopes's *Le Pleurer-rire*.

Workers in key sectors of the economy, such as railroad workers, have not been altogether without leverage in this situation. The true victims are elsewhere. They are mainly peasants who have neither voice nor power, whose only options are to withdraw into subsistence farming or to vote with their feet and move to the city. The victims are the hundreds of thousands of peasants who have died from the effects of civil war and drought in Ethiopia, Somalia, and the Southern Sudan.

It is tempting to assume that the critique in pursuit of equality will have an impact such that its object disappears eventually and that we will be confronted with the question Persse McGarrigle asks in *Small World*: "What do you *do* if everybody agrees with you?" (362). But the constellations of inequality will continue to shift. And new social movements will force a recognition of issues of inequality previously conveniently overlooked. Sembène was a pioneer in casting women in an active role, but for most of us men awareness came later, under the impact of the women's movement. There is little prospect that inequality as an object of critique will disappear any time soon. The struggle continues.

The actual problem, of course, is quite different. It is not just a matter of struggling to realize the central value of the Enlightenment against powerful vested interests. Rather, alternative critiques, based on different moral judgments are conceivable and are actually made. It has been a long time since *Lady Chatterley's Lover* was prohibited, but rumblings against "licentious" literature are still heard in some quarters. More threatening, at this juncture, are moral judgments such as that which inspires the death threat to Salmon Rushdie.

A third mode of addressing literature I am reluctant to call "theory." I would rather label it *interpretation*.[8] Literary interpretation, like much of the human sciences, in truth is a branch of history: past events are interpreted, their occurrence made plausible. We endeavor to provide answers to questions about the past: questions about the writer and his or her creation, about publication or performance, about critical reception, about the response of readers or spectators.

Eileen Julien, in this volume, offers an interpretation that connects André Gidé's *L'Immoraliste* with Ferdinand Oyono's *Une Vie de boy*. Her analysis is all the more striking because the later work is made to illuminate the earlier. They are read as parts of a shared world history, a history experienced on very different terms by Africa and Europe.

Interpretation may start out with a biographical approach. To return to *Les Bouts de bois de Dieu*, we know that Sembène's father was a Lebou fisherman.[9] In contrast, we have virtually no information about his mother. We are told only that her husband divorced her when Sembène was still young. How did young Ousmane react to the separation from his mother? He certainly was a difficult young boy. Sent to stay with one of his father's relatives in faraway Dakar, he is soon returned to his father. There follows a happy stay with an older brother of Sembène's mother -- what does our psychoanalyst make of that? But Ousmane experiences another severe loss: he is about 12 years old when his uncle dies. Ousmane certainly continues to be a difficult boy. At age 14 he hits the French headmaster of his school over the head and is dismissed. Now there is a story that his maternal uncle, the first teacher in Marsassoum in 1922, had lost his job because he slapped the local representative of the colonial administration -- what does our psychoanalyst make of the nephew's following in his maternal uncle's footsteps? At age 19, Sembène joined the French Army. Four years later he was the only member of his company not to receive a honorable discharge because he had resisted military discipline. About his experiences in World War II we are only told that he fought as an artillery man in North Africa and Europe -- we are left to wonder how he was affected by the experience of combat. About his participation in the 1947-48 railroad strike we know nothing.

We would want to insert *Les Bouts de bois de Dieu* in the trajectory of Sembène's artistic creation: his early poems, his paintings, his two

---

[8] The term "interpretation" is used by Scholes to cover what I am referring to as "explanation" as well as part of what I am referring to as "interpretation," i.e., the part that is concerned with the writer and his creation.

[9] The biographic information on Ousmane Sembène is taken from Pfaff and Vieyra.

precedings novels. We may want to give some thought to the fact that Sembène is unusual, at least among African writers, in that only his third novel brought the breakthrough. Is it because the autodidact needed to hone his skills? Is it because his political analysis evolved from the individual hero to collective action? Or is it simply that he persisted where others abandoned their literary ambitions after a first autobiographical novel? Persisted because of his strong personality? Persisted because of his political commitment?

Other dimensions, beside the biographical, would need to be recognized. For one, the socio-political context -- inseparable from Sembène's personal experience of racism and of working in France in blue-collar jobs, inseparable also from the perspective the Communist Party he joined in 1950 provided on those experiences. And the literary context would need to be explored. Autodidact, Sembène comes to read a wide range of French literature. *Les Bouts de bois de Dieu* explicitly refers to André Malraux's *La Condition humaine,* and Emile Zola's *Germinal* can be argued a model. An interpretation of *Les Bouts de bois de Dieu* might move on to address the publication of the book and its serialization in a daily paper, its critical reception,[10] reader response, and indeed spectator response to the play based on the novel.[11]

As concerns reader response, the issues raised by Joachim Fiebach and David Maughan-Brown in this volume involve the response of readers to writing that projects a world of stark contrasts between good and bad, without any ambiguities. Joining debates in Nigeria and South Africa respectively, Fiebach and Maughan-Brown come down on opposite sides of the argument. At one level, the persuasiveness of a Manichaean scenario is at issue. At another, whether it is politically opportune to foster or undermine a Manichaean worldview among readers in Nigeria/South Africa at this particular historical juncture.

Scepticism about the political impact of literature is the fashion among academics. The reactions of governments suggest, however, that this skepticism is exaggerated. Ibrahima Ly -- Maguèye Kassé pays homage to him in this volume -- and Téné Youssouf Guèye died from the sequels of imprisonment. Jack Mapanje was languishing in prison as we were meeting in Bayreuth. Wole Soyinka was imprisoned 18 months. Ngugi wa Thiong'o

---

[10] Most recently, Eileen Julien (1992, 68-84) has reclaimed *Les Bouts de bois de Dieu* as one of the great African epics, all the while spelling out how it revises the epic, thematically as well as formally, by projecting significant change and presenting a plurality of agents.

[11] On the serialization of *Les Bouts de bois de Dieu* in *Afrique Nouvelle* in 1967-68 and the play that premiered at the Senegalese National Theater in 1984, see Lüsebrink.

spent close to a year in prison, soon after his release felt compelled to leave Kenya, and remains in exile to this day. Mongo Beti lived in exile for more than 30 years, Nuruddin Farah did not return to Somalia for 17 years. Alex La Guma died in exile.

The case of Cameroon, detailed by Bernard Mouralis in this volume, is instructive. The regime has co-opted the literati, and they are part of the state apparatus to an extent unknown elsewhere in Africa. The government plays an active role in literary production through its publishing house and its control of the press. The writing of books, the publication of books, and the promotion of books are thus all in the hands of government officials. That the rulers of Cameroon should have gone to such lengths, further than any other African country, suggests that the novels Mongo Beti has written in exile, and perhaps even more the periodical he edits in Paris, *Peuples Noirs, Peuples Africains*, are seen as a threat to the regime.

We can thus construct interpretations of individual works, of an author's oeuvre, of a body of literature, or even of African literature in general. I see a challenging task in delineating general characteristics of African literature, general in that they are common, if not universal, in African literature and distinguish it from the literature of other regions -- a challenging task especially of interpreting these characteristics. Let me hazard five generalizations to be explored:

--- why most African prose adopted a realist mode until quite recently;

--- why African writing focused more on social relations than on individual character;

--- why most African writing addressed political issues: the cultural hegemony of the West, neo-colonialism and capitalism, tyranny, the socialist endeavor;

--- why African literature, with but one major exception, did not address the failure of democracy;[12]

--- why African women writers, with but a few exceptions, did not focus on these political issues but, rather, on interpersonal relationships;[13] and

--- why the resistance literature of South Africa shifted from autobiography to novel, to theatre, to poetry.

---

[12] Chinua Achebe's *A Man of the People* is a very important exception indeed, that it should have remained unique in addressing the failure of democracy in Africa all the more startling.

[13] Aminata Sow Fall's *L'Ex-père de la nation* and Miriam Tlali's *Amandla* are notable exceptions to the rule that African women writers tend to focus on interpersonal relationships rather than political issues. Tsitsi Dangarembga's *Nervous Conditions* relates the paternalistic oppressions of the kin group and the settler colony.

But let me turn to the contemporary literary scene. As we embarked on yet another conference on Africa, once again away from African Studies' "true center of gravity on the African continent" (Jeyifo 1990, 46), we were painfully aware of the crisis confronting Africa. Richard Bjornson dramatically emphasized our concerns. I need not go into much detail, a summary of the salient facts will suffice:

--- in economic terms, the performance of the region over the past two decades has been worse than that of any other major world region -- instead of development there has been a decline in real per capita income;

--- in political terms, dictatorships have been more common in Africa than in any other major world region for over a decade;

--- civil society just about collapsed in a number of countries under the sway of savage tyrants, and in countries torn apart by endless civil wars; and

--- the human cost of hunger, civil war, and political repression that African peoples have endured over the past two decades has no parallel in the contemporary world.

"Things fall apart" -- Chinua Achebe took up the anguished cry of W.B. Yeats more than a generation ago. Today, as Maguèye Kassé emphasizes in this volume, the dream of a reassuring traditional Africa can no longer serve. Indeed, pursuing the dream risks furnishing the alibi for continuing flagrant injustices. Nor does the colonial past any longer provide sufficient explanation for the enormous problems confronting Africa.

Today, we witness that things have fallen apart even further, but what is the literary response? I will borrow from David Harvey's recent discussion of *The Condition of Postmodernity* where he sketches four responses to crisis: silence, sloganeering, limited action, or riding the tiger. African literature, confronted with the crisis, in the main has remained silent -- as if a drought were spreading. As Harvey puts it:

> The first line of defence is to withdraw into a kind of shell-shocked, blasé, or exhausted silence and to bow down before the overwhelming sense of how vast, intractable, and outside any individual or even collective control everything is. (350)

There are, of course, notable exceptions to this silence, and I will turn to them in a moment, but compared to the eloquence with which African writers responded to earlier crises, the silence is distressing. African writers initiated the struggle against the cultural hegemony of the West with originality and vigor. Their response to the disappointments that came with independence was swift and trenchant. But while several distinguished authors did address major aspects of the current crisis, each, after his initial thrust, abandoned the task at hand.

--- Mongo Beti's *Perpétue* poignantly conveys how the oppression of neo-colonialism is repeated at every level of Cameroonian society, but the *Remember Ruben* cycle takes us to utopia, and the *Guillaume Ismaël Dzewatama* sequence turns farce in the end.[14]

--- Nuruddin Farah's trilogy "Variations on the Theme of an African Dictatorship" provides us with an illuminating description and analysis of dictatorship, but his subsequent work moves away from such direct confrontation with the politics of the contemporary crisis.

--- Ngugi wa Thiong'o detailed the establishment of a rapacious bourgeoisie and the proletarianization of the peasantry in *Petals of Blood*, but his two subsequent novels tell a different story and fail to address the current crisis adequately, or so I will suggest in a moment.

Let me turn to the second response to crisis Harvey sets out:

> The second reaction amounts to a free-wheeling denial of the complexity of the world, and a penchant for the representation of it in terms of highly simplified rhetorical propositions. Slogans abound, from left to right of the political spectrum, and depthless images are deployed to capture complex meanings. (351)

Now, I could follow the wise course taken by Harvey and not provide any example, leaving you to apply such indictment to whatever author, to whatever work you do not fancy. But I will stick my neck out. I submit that this indictment applies to Ngugi's *Devil on the Cross* and *Matigari*. This is not the place to present the argument. That my evaluation is not isolated, is attested by Odun Balogun's acerbic criticism of *Devil on the Cross*.

Harvey posits a third possible reaction to crisis:

> The third response has been to find an intermediate niche for political and intellectual life which spurns grand narrative but which does cultivate the possibility of limited action. (351)

The community of Aiyéro provides the striking example, based as it is both in Nigerian reality and in Wole Soyinka's *Season of Anomy*. The trouble, of course, is that the real-life community of Aiyéro is long gone, and that Soyinka's novel does not chart a way out of the crisis.

The fourth response has been, and I paraphrase Harvey (351), to ride the tiger of crisis through construction of a language and an imagery that can mirror and hopefully command it. The magnificent practitioner of that art is Sony Labou Tansi, who gives us with a vengeance that defamiliarization celebrated by some. His *La Vie et demie* may be seen as the literary equivalent of Pablo Picasso's *Guernica*. And much of what Max

---

[14] For a discussion of the great variety of responses to oppression Mongo Beti explores, see Gugler.

Raphael (178) had to say about that painting might be said about the novel as well:

> The reasons for which Picasso was compelled to resort to signs and allegories should now be clear enough: his utter political helplessness in the face of a historical situation which he set out to record; his titanic effort to confront a particular historical event with an allegedly eternal truth; his desire to give hope and comfort and to provide a happy ending, to compensate for the terror, the destruction, and inhumanity of the event.

The trouble with the novels of Sony Labou Tansi is, of course, that they remain the predilection of a small number of aficionados.

The Bayreuth colloqium was exciting, but it also reenforced this participant's skepticism concerning grand theoretical flights of fancy. I suggest that we focus our energies on the tasks I have tried to sketch: to explain, to critique, and to interpret. We can, of course, move on and enquire what theoretical orientations inform our explanation, critique, and interpretation -- as Richard Bjornson reminded us. I readily admit to an eclectic disposition that balks at theoretical straitjackets. We can step up to higher levels of abstraction. Eagleton (24) after all asserts that he has taken us five removes from real life. I manage to count only four removes, even in his scheme of things, but in any case, as we move to higher levels of abstraction, the air gets rather rarefied, the mountaineer becomes weary, and the promised rewards appear, at least to this student of literature, but a fata morgana. I see greater promise in delineating recurrent patterns in African literature and in interpreting these characteristics that establish a distinct African literature.

WORKS CITED

Achebe, Chinua. *Things Fall Apart*. London: Heinemann, 1959.

——————. *A Man of the People*. London: Heinemann, 1966.

Anozie, Sunday O. *Structural Models and African Poetics: Towards a Pragmatic Theory of Literature*. London: Routledge and Kegan Paul, 1981.

Appiah, Kwame Anthony. *In My Father's House: Africa in the Philosophy of Culture*. New York: Oxford University Press, 1992.

Balogun, F. Odun. "Ngugi's Devil on the Cross: The Novel as Hagiography of a Marxist." *Ufahamu* 16.2 (1988): 76-92.

Beti, Mongo. *Perpétue et l'habitude du malheur*. Paris: Buchet/Chastel, 1974.

——————. *Remember Ruben*. Collection 10/18. Paris: Union Générale d'Editions, 1974.

——————. *La Ruine presque coquasse d'un polichinelle (Remember Ruben 2)*. Paris: Editions des Peuples Noirs, 1979.

———. *Les Deux mères de Guillaume Ismaël Dzewatama, futur camionneur*. Paris: Buchet/Chastel, 1983.

———. *La Revanche de Guillaume Ismaël Dzewatama*. Paris: Buchet/Chastel, 1984.

Dangarembga, Tsitsi. *Nervous Conditions*. London: Women's Press, 1988.

Diop, Papa Samba. "Les bouts de bois de Dieu: la lettre et l'allusion." *Le français aujourd'hui, une langue à comprendre, französisch heute. Mélanges offerts à Jürgen Olbert*. Ed. Gilles Dorion, Franz-Joseph Meißner, János Riesz, Ulf Wielandt. Frankfurt: Moritz Diesterweg, 1992. 449-65.

Eagleton, Terry. *The Significance of Theory*. The Bucknell Lectures in Literary Theory. Oxford: Basil Blackwell, 1990.

Fall, Aminata Sow. *L'Ex-père de la nation*. Collection Encres noires. Paris: L'Harmattan, 1987.

Farah, Nuruddin. *Sweet and Sour Milk*. London: Allison and Busby, 1979.

———. *Sardines*. London: Allison and Busby, 1981.

———. *Close Sesame*. London: Allison and Busby, 1983.

Gikandi, Simon. *Reading the African Novel*. London: James Currey, 1987.

Gugler, Josef. "The Quest for the Agent of Liberation: Mongo Beti's Fiction on Tyranny, Neocolonialism, and Liberation." *Culture and Contradiction: Dialectics of Wealth, Power, and Symbol*. Ed. Hermine G. De Soto. San Francisco: EMTexts, 1992. 213-26.

Harvey, David. *The Condition of Postmodernity: An Enquiry into the Origins of Cultural Change*. Oxford: Basil Blackwell, 1989.

Irele, Abiola. "The African Imagination." *Research in African Literatures* 21 (1990): 49-67.

Jeyifo, Biodun. "The Nature of Things: Arrested Decolonization and Critical Theory." *Research in African Literatures* 21 (1990): 33-48.

Julien, Eileen. *African Novels and the Question of Orality*. Bloomington: Indiana University Press, 1992.

Labou Tansi, Sony. *La Vie et demie*. Paris: Seuil, 1979.

Lawrence, D.H. *Lady Chatterley's Lover*. Florence: privately printed, 1928.

Lerner, Laurence. *The Frontiers of Literature*. Oxford: Basil Blackwell, 1988.

Lodge, David. *Small World: An Academic Romance*. New York: Macmillan, 1984.

Lopes, Henri. *Le Pleurer-rire*. Paris: Présence Africaine, 1982.

Lüsebrink, Hans-Jürgen. "Ousmane Sembène und das 'Sprachenproblem' im Senegal: Zur Wahrnehmung und Kodierung von Sprachgebrauch und Sprachkonflikten in *Les Bouts de bois de Dieu* (Roman und Theaterstück)." *Festschrift zum 60. Geburtstag von Carl F. Hoffmann*. Ed. Franz Rottland. Bayreuther Beiträge zur Sprachwissenschaft 7. Hamburg: Helmut Buske, 1986. 203-22.

Malraux, André. *La Condition humaine*. Paris: Gallimard, 1946.

Morlet, Pierre. "La grève des cheminots Africains d'A.O.F." *Servir la France: Revue Syndicale* 37 (1948): 36-42.

Mortimer, Mildred. *Journeys Through the French African Novel*. Portsmouth, N.H.: Heinemann, 1990.

Ngugi wa Thiong'o. *Petals of Blood*. London: Heinemann, 1977.

───────. *Devil on the Cross*. London: Heinemann, 1982.

───────. *Matigari*. London: Heinemann, 1989.

Nyerere, Julius. "The Arusha Declaration" in *Ujamaa -- Essays on Socialism*. London: Oxford University Press, 1968. 13-37.

Ouologuem, Yambo. *Le Devoir de violence*. Paris: Seuil, 1968.

Pfaff, Françoise. *The Cinema of Ousmane Sembene, A Pioneer of African Film*. Contributions in Afro-American and African Studies 79. Westport, Conn.: Greenwod Press.

Priebe, Richard K. *Myth, Realism, and the West African Writer*. Trenton, N.J.: Africa World Press, 1988.

Raphael, Max. *The Demands of Art*. Bollingen Series 78. Princeton: Princeton University Press, 1968.

Scholes, Robert. *Textual Power: Literary Theory and the Teaching of English*. New Haven: Yale University Press, 1985.

Sembène, Ousmane. *Les Bouts de bois de Dieu: Banty mam yall*. Paris: Le Livre Contemporain, 1960.

───────. *L'Harmattan: Référendum*. Paris: Présence Africaine, 1964.

Soyinka, Wole. *Season of Anomy*. London: Collings, 1973.

───────. *A Play of Giants*. London: Methuen, 1984.

Tlali, Miriam. *Amandla*. Johannesburg: Ravan Press, 1980.

Vieyra, Paulin Soumanou. *Ousmane Sembène: cinéaste. Première période 1962-71*. Collection Approches. Paris: Présence Africaine, 1972.

Zola, Emile. *Germinal*. Paris: G. Charpentier, 1885.

LITERARY THEORY AND AFRICAN LITERATURE
edited by J. Gugler, H.-J. Lüsebrink, J. Martini
Münster/Hamburg 1993, pp. 17-30

LITERARY THEORY AND THEORIES OF DECOLONIZATION

BIODUN JEYIFO

1.1

Since the title of this article is "Literary Theory and Theories of Decolonization," perhaps it is only appropriate to start by explaining why I have chosen to represent literary theory in the singular and as a unified formation, even though everybody knows that there are many different schools and approaches in literary theory and what is more, each and all of these diverse schools and approaches have a propensity to proliferate into feuding, schismatic factions. Indeed, taking stock of this aspect of literary theory at the present time, one of Chinua Achebe's luminous proverbs comes to mind: literary theory is like a masquerade dancing; to see it well you don't stand in one place. Thus, properly speaking, in engaging literary theory one should talk of *theories* and reinforce this pluralized enunciation with the image of a carnivalesque parade: classical and post-Marxist Marxisms; Freudian and Lacanian psychoanalytic schools; old and new historicisms; speech act, reader-response and semiotic textual theories; deconstruction and postmodernisms; French and Anglo-American, Western and non-Western feminisms, etc., etc. If this composite profile suggests a gaudy, polymorphous cavalcade, textual confirmation of the profile may be had by recourse to any of the innumerable anthologies and "Readers" on contemporary or twentieth century literary theories. The irruption of theory, and its self-proliferating propensity as it stretches and breaks down disciplinary boundaries and demarcations, is no figment of anyone's imagination.

1.2

And yet I have chosen to represent literary theory in this essay not, as one normally should, as a tapestry of successive, varied schools and approaches, but as a singular, unified edifice, as a monolith more or less. The perspective which compels this deliberate misrecognition comes from the debate and discourses on the decolonization of theory. For within the discourses and counter-discourses in this debate, every single theoretical school or approach is only one layer, one tier in the exclusively and prescriptively *Western* monument of High Theory. This needs to be stated as clearly as possible: the contemporary understanding of theory not only renders it as an exclusively Western phenomenon of a very specialized activity, but also implicitly (and sometimes explicitly) inscribes the view that theory does not exist, cannot exist outside of this High Canonical Western orbit.

1.3

How has "theory" come to be recognized or be recognizable only in terms of this Western exclusivity? This involves, first of all, a powerful, self-authenticating, self-perpetuating inscription of theory in virtually all books, journals and essays on theory as an ineluctably Western production. We may cite a few of the innumerable facts and processes which consummate and perpetuate this inscription. The most influential and widely used anthologies and readers of "literary theory" contain exclusively Western entries, Western theorists and theoretical movements and schools. The very terms "Modern Critical Theory," "Contemporary Critical Theory" or "Twentieth Century Critical Theory" are subliminally presented in these self-authenticating inscriptions as synonymous or identical with "Western Theory." If, relatively speaking, there are a few books and monographs on "non-Western" literary theory (e.g., Chinese, Japanese or Indian), they are either little known and/or deal with premodern "classical" theories and theorists. In sum what we thus have here is the imbrication of discourses on "theory" in age-old Eurocentric intellectual premises and attitudes. Since this is a point that is largely unacknowledged, we can only say, applying a re-understanding of the Marxist theory of ideology, that this is because this "recognition" of theory, which, as we shall presently demonstrate, is a *misrecognition*, has achieved the status of that *naturalization* and transparency to which all ideologies aspire and which only the most hegemonic achieve. Peter Weiss expresses a thought in the play *Marat-Sade* which is pertinent here: people believe and come to accept as self-evident and "natural" what they are told over and over again, what is repeated endlessly as "truth" or "fact." Thus by endless inscription, citation, iteration and reiteration, modern or contemporary literary theory has come to be *naturalized* as an exclusively Western phenomenon.

2.1

To adequately explore this naturalization of literary theory as exclusively Western as properly speaking a *misrecognition*, we would, I believe, have to speak of "theory" as opposed to, or linked in tension in this case with mere "theoreticism." "Theory" in this interfusion would thus be what in most places and contexts it has always been: the power of generalization which permits us to see the connections, the underlying or overarching relations within and between things, and between dispersed, separate phenomena: "theoreticism," on the other hand, is the specialized idiom or jargon through which "theory" supposedly achieves its purchase on the power of generalization. "Theoreticism" in this respect thus entails a vast attempt to *sophisticate* this special idiom or jargon and in contemporary terms the more elaborate or impenetrable the better. The *misrecognition* or *reification* of theory emerges when this sophisticated idiom is taken, in itself, as the end of theory, and when it is imagined that one cannot be "theoretical" unless one speaks and writes in the idiom of this theoreticism. It is a measure of the tremendous success of this misrecognition that, with few exceptions, virtually every critic and theorist now identifies "theory" with this theoreticism, and that we now *know* theory as theory only when we see it in the garb of theoreticism, or when we read or hear in it the accents and the specialised vocabulary of the recognizable discourse of the fraternity and sorority of theoreticists.

It must be stressed that this distinction between "theory" and "theoreticism," between theorists and theoreticists, is not always clear in contemporary writings considered "theoretical." Indeed, one can speak of a *misrecognition* or *reification* of theory only to the extent that theory is now indistinguishable from theoreticism. Stated conversely, this point suggests that theoreticism is now the constitutive abode of theory.

2.2

This understanding or, in our terms, *misrecognition*, of theory is inscribed in varied contemporary institutional and textual practices of very ambiguous effects and consequences: many departments of literature now routinely hire literary scholars under a new category of job description of "theorist"; the faculty of many literature departments are deeply divided by factional distinctions between "theorists" and "non-theorists"; books, journals, conferences, seminars, workshops and graduate courses are devoted exclusively to "theory"; "theory" is now a recognized genre of writing which not only distinguishes the "theorist" from the mere "critic" but also from the author or artist. In "Travelling Theory," an important essay which touches on aspects of the institutionalization of this misrecognition of theory, Edward Said has highlighted the extreme cloistering and self-cocooning of self-constituted "theorists" in the academy. It is with respect to this factor that one can describe this misrecognition of theory as primarily an *academicist* phenomenon, as indeed a sort of neo-scholasticism.

2.3

Ordinarily, it would be enough to engage this institutionalization of theory as a cloistered, reified neo-scholasticism in the light of the uses and abuses of the discourse of an over-elaborate scholasticism. Indeed, much of the "resistance to theory" or the rejection of theory is not only a willful anti-intellectualism (which it often is) but it is also a resistance to, or rejection of this neo-scholasticism. This kind of reactive response however ignores crucial aspects of this institutionalization of theory as hermetic academicism; most in particular, it ignores the fact that it is primarily a Euro-American phenomenon, an aspect of the intellectual division of labor of the metropolitan centers of the world system of late capitalism. I believe that one ignores these crucial aspects of the determinations on "theory" in literary and cultural studies at the present time only at the cost of perpetuating dangerous, obfuscatory myths about global literary and intellectual relations. Regrettably, the discourses and counter-discourses in the debate on "decolonized theory" are, even at their most perspicacious and sophisticated, enshrouded by these myths. Let me give a brief instantiation of this point.

LITERARY THEORY AND THEORIES OF DECOLONIZATION

3.1

Two related but distinct tropes or elaborated *topoi* represent vectors around which positions in the debate on "decolonized theory" coalesce: *travel* and *quest*. The topos of *quest* figures powerfully in what has been designated the nationalist or *nativist* counter-discourses in this debate. This involves a search for theories outside the Western exclusivity posited by the powerful inscriptions and practices of contemporary theory as described above, theories "native" or indigenous to non-Western literary traditions. The fundamental premise here is that each literary culture generates the theories most appropriate to its own historical experience and socio-cultural specificities. And since for non-canonical, non-Western literatures their histories and specific traditions were disavowed and delegitimized by the ethnocentric universalism of Western theories, it becomes a daunting task to excavate the theories embedded in these traditions. The topos of quest or search is thus an *archaeological* one and it traces alternate genealogies for criteria and rubrics of critical discourse. Houston Baker in *Blues, Ideology and Afro-American Literature*, Alice Walker in *In Search of Our Mother's Gardens* and H.L. Gates in *The Signifying Monkey* are perhaps the outstanding exemplifications of this (alter)-*native* theorizing. More recently we have the examples of *After Europe*, edited by Stephen Slemon and Helen Tiffin, and *The Empire Writes Back* of Bill Ashcroft and others as wide-ranging explorations of expressions of "decolonized theory" in Africa, parts of Asia, the Caribbean and Australasia. Gates' programmatic justification of *The Signifying Monkey* stands as good as any enunciation of this topos of the quest in the debate on the decolonization of theory: "The book attempts to identify a theory of criticism that is inscribed within the black vernacular tradition and that in turn informs the shape of the Afro-American literary tradition. My desire has been to allow the black tradition to speak for itself about its nature and various functions, rather than to read it, or analyze it, in terms of literary theories borrowed from other traditions, appropriated from without."

3.2

In the "travel" topos we encounter a fundamentally different force field in the discourses on "decolonized theory." The underlying premise here is that the proof or worth of a theory is demonstrated by how well, or conversely how badly, it fares outside its place of origin or cultural provenance. In this perspective theory is deemed fundamentally homeless and rootless, it constantly undergoes revision, differentiation and transformation as it encounters new and divergent contexts and milieux in its constitutive peregrinations. If this is the case, the so-called nativist project in the decolonization of theory seems delusional. Anthony Appiah in a recent essay in *The Yale Journal of Criticism* titled "Out of Africa: Topologies of Nativism" while not directly deploying or invoking this journey motif nevertheless draws on its basic arguments to stage a heady, withering assault on what he calls "nativism in theory." Consider the following quote from the essay: "There is, at all events, a fundamental reason why nativism in theory is unlikely to lead us away from where we already are. Time and again, cultural nationalism has followed the route of alternate genealogizing. We end up always in the same place; the achievement is to have invented a different past for it. In the fervor of cultural reassertion, as Immanuel Wallerstein has observed, 'the antecedents of scientificity were rediscovered under many different names'; today certain African intellectuals are doing the same for literary theory. If we start with a conception of hermeneutics borrowed from the Western academy, we may well succeed in producing an 'elegant variation' inserting the odd metaphor from indigenous oracle-interpretation, say. But the whole exercise puts me in mind of a certain disreputable trading concern I once visited in Harare -- a product of the frankly desultory attempts at sanctions against the Republic of South Africa. Their specialty was stamping "Made in Zimbabwe" onto merchandise imported, more or less legally, from the South. Perhaps a few are really fooled; but the overall effect of the procedure is only to provide a thin stain of legitimacy to stretch over existing practices."

It should be pointed out that though Appiah's strongest criticisms in this essay are reserved for "nativism" and "nativists," he is also highly critical of Eurocentric claims and premises in contemporary literary theory. But one would have to go elsewhere for a more balanced and historically aware deployment of the journey motif in the debate on the decolonization of theory. Such a book is *Travelling Theory and Travelling Theorists*, edited by James Clifford and Vivek Dhareshwar.

4.1

The seeming opposition between the topos of travel and that of quest is precisely that, merely *seeming*, more apparent than real, more discursively produced than a definitive fracture in theory as epistemic behavior and institutional practice. Theories and theorists travel, sometimes in complex and often dimly perceptible ways, as Jonathan Arac has shown by revealing the unacknowledged influence of Anglo-American currents on as *French* and "continental" a theoretical discourse as Lyotard's *The Postmodern Condition*, an influence which runs counter to the more generally assumed itinerant trajectory in the other direction -- from French, German and continental currents to enclaves within the mainstreams of intellectual life in Britain and America. All the same, theorists often quest after new, unaccustomed connections and syntheses. Whatever the results of the excavation might have been, this, it seems to me, was the impulse behind Harold Bloom's forays in his book *Kabbalah and Criticism* into Talmudic texts, into the Kabbalah, for paradigms of hermeneutic strategies.

4.2

It is thus necessary to recognize that these two topoi -- travel and quest -- express not necessarily contradictory, but rather distinct aspects of the project of "decolonized theory" which are no doubt in tension but are not mutually exclusive or structurally antagonistic. Indeed I would urge that one ought to read a book like *Travelling Theory and Travelling Theorists* as locked into a productive tension with *The Empire Writes Back* which adumbrates the quest for indigenous African, Indian, Caribbean theories of literature and criticism. The important point, I believe, is to recognize that the problems of the decolonization of theory are elsewhere, that the bodies are buried in other groves, that is to say in precisely the double reification and misrecognition of theory as theoreticism, and as an intellectual institution of an exclusively Western, high-canonical provenance.

4.3

Thus, as productive as the travel motif is in the project of decolonizing theory, it does involve its own rather massive reinscriptions of colonialist, hegemonizing and Eurocentric predilections of much of contemporary Western intellectual currents. For if in "travelling" and thus raising questions about their general applicability beyond their originating locations, milieux and traditions, theories and theorists implicitly carry the seeds of their own transmutations and thus seem to be in agreement with the project of decolonization, it remains true that the notion of decolonization involved here is too vague, too ambiguously positioned in relation to the theories of decolonization, theories which have shaped historic decolonization as one of this century's greatest epochal events *and which are compositely figured as a major aspect of the century's intellectual legacy.*

It is thus a great gap in the discourses of the travel and quest motifs in "decolonized theory" that with the possible exception of Frantz Fanon, there is a great silence on the thought and ideas of this century's great theorists of decolonization like C.L.R. James, Amilcar Cabral, Jose Mariategui, Samir Amin, and Andre Gunder Frank and the dependency school of "world system" analysis. This gap, this lacuna, is indeed portentous of the prospective "decolonization" involved in discourses of the travel motif, given the fact the many of these theorists of decolonization also wrote extensively on literature in particular and cultural politics more generally. For the rest of this essay I shall address some ramifications of this lacuna in the spirit and with the central ideas of these theorists of decolonization.

5.1

The discussion so far might seem to indicate that what is at stake here is that we recognize that "theory" is produced in both Western and non-Western, central and peripheral formations of the capitalist world system. The issues however go far beyond, and far deeper, than a plea for liberal pluralist, relativist perspectives, no matter how justified and well-motivated such a plea might be. Crucial processes and issues are obscured by such neo-liberal perspectives.

Among other things, the neo-liberal discourse conflates two sets of distinctions which it is important to identify and register in their separate connotations. There is, first, a *culturalist* distinction between the Western and the non-Western and, secondly, there is a *systemic*, socioeconomic distinction between center and periphery. On the face of it, the conflation does seem indeed justified by actual historical realities since most of the Western societies constitute the central social formations of the world system and the bulk of the non-Western societies make up the peripheral social formations. It therefore seems *natural* that one should conflate the two sets of distinctions. It is, however, important to *denaturalize* this conflation for reasons which exceed the framework and perspectives of neo-liberal pluralism and relativism.

5.2

Only if we bear these issues in mind can we crasp how, by the implicit operation of a discursive synecdoche in which the part stands for the whole, developments in culture and critical thought in the center are "naturally" thought to be developments in human culture and thought in general. Leading ideas and developments in the central social formations of the world system metonymically stand for leading ideas and developments everywhere, in the whole world in effect. All those innumerable books, anthologies, readers and journals on "Twentieth Century Theory" or "Contemporary Theory" without a single non-Western entry operate by the implicit registration of this discursive metonymy which converts systemic processes into a powerful *culturalist* ideology: Western singularity and exceptionalism. It is this culturalist construction that Samir Amin in *Eurocentrism* has brilliantly uncovered as an overarching, all-pervasive ideology of Western capitalist hegemony.

To understand the force of contemporary non-Western or Third World *nativist* positions on critical theory, one must fully engage this culturalist metonymy by deconstructively reading the syllogism which is inscribed in it.

1. Only the theories produced in the central social formations of the world system matter and qualify as "Contemporary Theory" or "Twentieth Century Theory";

2. Western societies are located at the central social formations of the world system: theories produced in these central social formations *are* in effect Western theories;

3. Only Western theories matter or qualify as "Contemporary Theory" or "Twentieth Century Theory."

The nativist positions on contemporary critical theory are polemical counter-discourses to this implicit syllogism. Two distinct, but often interlocking composite "nativisms" are involved in this polemic: an extreme, or "strong" nativism, and a moderate, or "soft" nativism. "Strong" nativism implicitly or unwittingly accepts that "theory" *is* indeed Western and it therefore completely rejects "theory" in toto. The nativist polemic is often couched in the form of the binarism of "their" theory and "our" literature and speaks of its project as one of total "decolonization." Moderate or "soft" nativism calls for flexibility and vigilance in applying "their" theory to "our" literature and furthermore, it additionally calls for generating "our" own theory from "our" own literatures and cultural traditions, a theory which would be more "authentic" and more "relevant."

It would be counter-productive to ignore certain crucial aspects of these nativist positions: the tremendous emotional charge, the ideological uses, limited as these may be, as counter-discourses of Eurocentrism in critical theory, and the cases of genuine theoretical reflection that have emerged from so-called nativist views. (It is all the more necessary to make these points since it has now become fashionable with certain theorists of "postcolonial hybridity" to trash nativism without however engaging the Eurocentric culturalist misrecognition and reification of theory which produces nativist purism in theory and fuels its polemical extremism.) Nevertheless it must be added that, like Eurocentrism, nativism also entails a *culturalist* obscuring of the *systemic* features of the center-periphery contradition of the world capitalist system. A critique of nativism must thus foreground these very systemic features which, like the Eurocentric culturalism it opposes, it tries to repress. As a fundamental dimension of the debate on the decolonization of theory, it might indeed be useful to present some of these repressed systemic features as working theses toward the critique of both Eurocentric *and* nativist culturalisms.

6.1

THESIS ONE

The center-periphery contradition produces vast concentrations of cultural capital in the central social formations of the world system; at the same time it depletes and distorts the cultural resources of the peripheral social formations. For this reason, most of the major advances in thought and culture, within, and only within the historical and structural limits of the world system, take place in the central social formations. It is thus not a question of whether theories produced by, and in, the central social formations should be applied in the periphery; they *are* in fact aplied and *will* be applied, no permission sought. This is illustrated by the fact that in this century at least, every new wave or paradigm of critical theory in particular and philosophy and thought in general that has emerged in the central social formations has been "applied" to the periphery and has found its disciples and pundits there: Leavisism, New Criticism, Freudian Psychoanalysis, Surrealism, Gestalt Psychology, Cambridge Anthropology, Structuralism, Phenomenology, Deconstruction, Analytic Philosophy, Althusserian Marxism, Feminist Critical Theory, etc., etc. Given these complexly determined and determinate processes of cultural and intellectual history generated by the center-periphery contradiction, it is vital to avoid exclusively *culturalist* explanations (as elaborated above) of this lopsided and asymmetrical relationship.

Thesis Two

The center-periphery contradition also provides the tendency, even the necessity, for intellectual and cultural movements of the peripheral social formations, especially those of the elites and the intelligentsia, to be extraverted, to look to developments and currents in the central social formations for cues, for inspiration, for authentication. This is a matter of both structural, systemic dependency as well as purposive choices about issues of adaptability and survival: developments at the central social formations literally put peripheral social formations to the sword, so to speak: adapt in the light of borrowed or grafted ideas and models or perish! (This quite apart from the aggressive cultural imperialism and racism which as Fanon has brilliantly shown, set about the wholesale distortion and inferiorization of "native" cultures.)

Thesis Three

The cultural and intellectual extraversion of the peripheral social formations notwithstanding, ideas and cultural and political currents which potentially exceed the historical and structural limits of the world system are in the main (though not exclusively) generated in the peripheral social formations: the periphery is the weakest link in the chain of global accumulation and concentration of economic, technological and cultural capital in the centre, in the West. These currents of critical reflection and creativity in the periphery which challenge this global pattern may be inchoate, millenarian and chiliastic, like the rash of Islamic fundamentalisms around the Third World, or they may be disciplined, purposive and resilient, like the theories and practices of the "Theatre for Development" movement in the Third World, or the theories and practices in Latin America and Africa of a "Third Cinema," or the traditions of theories of revolutionary "national culture" and "cultural revolution" which seek to transcend the historic splits in the central social formations between high culture and popular culture, between the legacy of bourgeois humanism and workers' "proletarian" culture.

Thesis Four

These diverse points and observations indicate that theories of literature and cultural production at the central and peripheral social formations respectively follow different trajectories, and engage different agendas. This also applies to oppositional, counter-hegemonic theories generated both in the centre and in the periphery. And this principle, which involves a dialectical materialist view of cultural and intellectual production, also holds true even when there is a demonstrable intersection between theoretical movements at the center and the periphery, as in movements like Marxism and feminism. It is a daunting, if necessary task to map these divergent trajectories in fine, in their detailed articulations in the center and in the periphery. To give only one brief illustration, *Leavisism*, perhaps the most influential critical methodology of English literary studies in this century, has operated in decisively divergent ways in the central and peripheral literary cultures of the English-speaking world. In the English-speaking peripheral social formations, principally in Africa, India and the Caribbean, the very fact that Leavisism never had the secure social base in an empire-building bourgeoisie that it had in Britain made it even more desperately elitist, more absurdly cut off from the social and historical currents of these societies. Thus at Delhi, Ibadan, Legon, Makerere and the University of the West Indies, Leavisism did not survive as a credible, effective critical and pedagogical paradigm beyond the first decade of the post-Independence era. It is impossible to grasp the force of the historic document produced by Ngugi and others in Nairobi in the early Seventies calling for the abolition of the English Department without taking into account the fate of Leavisism in the peripheral ex-colonies of the oldest and most dominant of the "classical" European imperial orders. This pattern is further complicated by the fact that Leavisism had markedly different trajectories in India, Africa and the Caribbean. Indeed, recent archival scholarship in the colonial culture of the British Raj in India suggests that Leavisism may have had its origins in India.

Thesis Five

In the main, the trajectories of theories of literature in the central social formations in this century have generally followed a shift from theories stressing the historical, diachronic and extrinsic features of literature and its medium, language, to theories emphasizing structural, synchronic and intrinsic features. While responding fitfully to this shift, theories of literature in the peripheral social formations have continued to emphasize precisely the historical, diachronic and extrinsic features.

According to Eagleton, the movement of literary theory in the central social formations this century has generally taken the following pattern: from an emphasis on the *author*, to a shift of emphasis to the *reader* and finally and currently to an obsessive focus on the *text*. (Actually this is an extrapolation from Eagleton who, in making this point, simply stated that this is the movement of twentieth century literary theory, thereby following the culturalist metonymy which takes developments in the central social formations to be "world developments.") This merely states the external outline of what is nothing short of an epochal shift in the central social formations in critical methodology and in ways of perceiving and talking about literature, no less. For the *text* here is not simply and only the text of the literary work. It is *textuality* itself, the microdynamics of the play of language, and the rhetoricity or metaphoricity of *all* discourse, including the discourses of "objective," impersonal, positivist or empiricist science. A fundamentally radical view of the politics of how "textuality" inscribes history is involved here, a *micropolitics* of history which holds suspect all grand, abstracting, totalizing ideologies, knowledges and narratives. *Textuality* in this sense also involves a microtextual politics of reading which emphasizes ruptures, lacunae, silences, gaps, the surfaces of language without the *depths* of referentiality, permanently deferred meaning, and crises of representation which, ultimately in deconstruction, issue into dogmas of the undecidability or unrepresentability of meaning and the "real." By very sharp contrast, this epochal paradigmatic shift has not taken place in the peripheral social formation and, what is more, it is very vigorously resisted and contested by major writers, critics and teachers of the developing world. [Important, even decisive centres of the critical establishment of the West, of the central social formations, also remain resistant to this shift]. The theories of the peripheral social formations are thus deeply embedded in discourses and constructions of collective destinies, of national cultures and identity, of the reclamation of devalued "mother tongues," and of language itself all conceived as unifying forces for the common destinies of embattled peoples. To ignore these sharp cleavages, or worse, to be unaware of them (as is evidently the case in curricular courses on "theory" in the Euro-American academies) entails enormous epistemological and political consequences.

WORKS CITED

Amin, Samir. *Eurocentrism*. New York: Monthly Review Press, 1989.

Ashcroft, Bill et al. (editors). *The Empire Writes Back*. Routledge, 1989.

Baker, Houston. *Blues, Ideology and Afro-American Literature*. Chicago University Press, 1984.

Bloom, Harold. *Kabbalah and Criticism*. New York: Seabury Press, 1975.

Clifford, James, and Vivek Dhareshwar. *Travelling Theories, Travelling Theorists*. Santa Cruz, Center for Cultural Studies, 1989.

Lyotard, Jean Francois. *The Postmodern Condition*. U of Minnesota P, 1984.

Gates, Henry Louis, Jr. *The Signifying Monkey: A Theory of Afro-American Literary Criticism*. New York: Oxford University Press, 1988.

Said, Edward. "Travelling Theory" in *The World, the Text and the Critic*. Harvard University Press, 1983.

Slemon, Stephen, and Helen Tiffin. *After Europe*. Dangaroo Press, 1989.

Weiss, Peter. *Marat-Sade*. New York: Atheneum, 1984.

Walker, Alice. *In Search of Our Mothers' Gardens*. San Diego: Harcourt Brace Jovanovich, 1983.

LITERARY THEORY AND AFRICAN LITERATURE
edited by J. Gugler, H.-J. Lüsebrink, J. Martini
Münster/Hamburg 1993, pp. 31-41

THEORY AND MORAL COMMITMENT IN THE STUDY OF AFRICAN LITERATURE

RICHARD BJORNSON

Despite an explosion of theoretical activity in the various literary disciplines since the mid-1960s, consensus has hardly been reached with regard to defining the sort of relationship that should obtain between what literary scholars do in their role as scholars and what they do in their day-to-day lives. Some literary theorists maintain that there is no necessary relationship between these two realms of activity because the practice of literary scholarship takes place in a self-contained (scientific or aesthetic) universe of discourse. Others contend that the credibility of literary scholarship depends upon the contribution that it makes to the attainment of some extra-literary goal: the liberation of oppressed peoples, the dissemination of enlightened opinion, the mobilization of support for social justice, economic development, or some other worthy cause. Defining an appropriate relationship between literary scholarship and moral commitment represents an especially urgent task for scholars who are involved in the study of African literature, for they cannot easily overlook the social, political, and economic crisis that haunts contemporary Africa.

African writers themselves have espoused a variety of different attitudes toward the question of moral or social commitment. Ngugi wa Thiong'o, Mongo Beti, and Sembène Ousmane have all, at one time or another, defended the idea that the act of writing is a political act for which the writer must assume responsibility. Chinua Achebe, Ahmadou Kourouma, and Wole Soyinka have all expressed their faith in a literary vocation that transcends partisan politics without renouncing its claim to moral efficacy. Henri Lopes has argued that it is more important for literary works to be "engaging" than to be "engaged"; thus he concludes that, even though writers might be personally committed to social justice, their works should not be judged according to ideological content or the extent to which their are comprehensible to mass audiences. In contrast, Nurrudin Farah claims that all his works are infused with a desire to expose the oppressiveness of traditional and modern social structures in Africa.

Confronted with such disparate attitudes toward moral and social commitment among African writers, it is not surprising that critics of African literature have generated an equally diverse set of approaches to literary texts from the continent. Under such circumstances, the recent preoccupation with literary theory has been salutary for a number of reasons. For example, it has produced a greater clarity, if not a consensus, about what it is we do when we engage in the act of criticizing, analyzing, or interpreting literary texts. It has also obliged us to develop more rigorously articulated explanations about the outcomes of such activities.

In reflecting upon the ways in which the contemporary impulse toward literary theory intersects with the dominant concerns of African literature and with the need for moral commitment in the face of a crisis situation, we might do well to keep in mind a certain number of provisos about the nature of theory-building, especially when it is applied to cultural and verbal artifacts such as literary texts. On the most general level, we all theorize. We cannot avoid doing so, because we need to construct mental models of an object world in which we are obliged to live. These mental models enable us to map our surroundings in such a way that we can devise plans for achieving the goals that we set for ourselves. However, these models can never be directly compared with the object world; they can only be judged in terms of their adequacy in facilitating the fulfillment of our goals.

These "theories" or overall images of the world are flexible and can be modified as the result of experience. Conversely, experience comes to be regarded as meaningful insofar as it can be related to existing mental models. Thus, we are all involved in an ongoing dialectic of theory-building and interpretation. Because people in the same cultural environment tend to have similar experiences and to exchange their perceptions of the world with each other, there can be a considerable amount of inter-subjective agreement about the way in which they understand the world. This does not mean that their shared image of the world is objectively true; it merely signifies that a theoretical construct, a framework of knowledge, constitutes a common point of reference for them. Obviously much theory-building on this level remains unconscious. The contemporary emphasis on theory has obliged us to explicitate the assumptions behind our habitual (and often unconscious) ways of theorizing about the world and our capacity to understand it. Those who object to this enterprise are not really objecting to theory; they are euphemistically expressing their dislike or disapproval of a theory that does not happen to agree with their own.

If we necessarily orient ourselves in the world by constructing mental models of it, we soon realize that no event, object, person, or text can be understood in isolation from the other events, objects, persons, or texts in relation to which it exists. In *Steps to an Ecology of Mind*, Gregory Bateson argues that the smallest possible unit that can be successfully studied is not an organism by itself, but an organism plus its environment. The by now commonplace image of a green-blue sphere floating in space communicates a sense of the systems connectivity that links together everything that exists in our world, reminding us that, if we hope to preserve our capacity to reach the goals we set for ourselves, me must respect the interconnectivity of the system to which we belong. Within the domain of literary theory, this ecological model suggests that no text can ever be adequately understood when it is divorced from its various contexts -- literary, linguistic, cultural, social, psychological, political, economic, etc.

We invariably bring the same mental models or "theories" to the understanding of literature as we bring to the understanding of the world. It is of course possible to separate one's interpretation of literary texts from one's interpretation of the world, just as it is possible for a scientist to believe that he is understanding an organism when he isolates it from its surroundings and places it under a microscope. In fact, a good deal can be learned by adopting such procedures, but they will always produce partial insights that distort our comprehension of texts and organisms until these partial insights are integrated into a more holistic vision that embraces the larger context to which they belong. Moreover, the attempt to sustain incompatible values or criteria of evaluation in different spheres of activity can only lead to a schizophrenic disharmony within the individual who seeks to do so.

Yet if we reflect upon where we have obtained the various elements that comprise our theories or images of the world, it soon becomes apparent that we are all eclecticians. In other words, we take whatever is available to us, and insofar as it is relevant to our goals and interests, we incorporate it into the system of mental models that we employ to situate ourselves in the world. Existing theories tend to be coherent and internally consistent; as a consequence, people often appropriate them in their entirety. This tendency contributes to inter-subjective agreement on a number of issues in any given culture, but traces of idiosyncracy remain in every individual's understanding of a theory because he or she will have reconstructed it on the basis of experiences that are not identical with those of others who hold the same theory.

In any case, theory is largely the systematization of existing observations, and literary theory is the codification of existing practice. Thus, Aristotle's *Poetics* is the reduction of Athenian dramaturgical practice to a system of rules, and T. S. Eliot's critical writings are justifications for the sort of poetry that he himself had been composing. In seeking to articulate a viable theory of African literature, one might thus expect to find the principal elements of it in the existing corpus of African literary works.

The acceptance of any particular theory or image of the world has tangible consequences, for it predisposes those who accept it to engage in certain types of behavior and to avoid other types of behavior. For example, the products of literary theory are the institutions (e.g., canons, school and university reading lists, journals, prizes, publishing houses, associations) that influence what texts shall be read, what texts shall not be read, and how the favored texts shall, in general, be understood.

Construed in the broadest possible sense, theory has always been applied to African literature. For those involved in the study of this literature, the recent explosion in theoretical speculation is an invitation to articulate the underlying assumptions behind these theories and behind their own approaches to African literary texts, because theory itself is essentially no more than an awareness of method, situatedness, and purpose. In the present climate of theoretical discussion, however, two tendencies threaten to obscure the potential usefulness of literary theory within the African context. First, as practiced in Europe and North America, literary theory has tended to evolve into competing schools, each of which cultivates an esoteric vocabulary that impedes rather than fosters dialogue with others. If the creation and reception of literary texts depends upon the same images of the world that we ourselves draw upon in our daily lives, it seems implausible to suppose that we actually need to acquire a new vocabulary every few years in order to speak authoritatively about these texts. Second, the social, economic, political, and environmental crises facing the world in general and Africa in particular are so serious that new patterns of thinking must be elaborated if we hope to preserve the possibility of a decent future for the human race. The tendency of contemporary literary theory to dismiss the relevance of this problem to its area of specialized knowledge strikes me as morally irresponsible and ultimately schizophrenic in its consequences.

The gravity of the present crisis in Africa can hardly be exaggerated. In many countries, mushrooming debt, deteriorating terms of trade, corruption, explosive population growth, and environmental degradation have combined to produce societies in which the living standards of the majority have declined precipitously while the wealth of a small privileged elite has grown out of all proportion to any real contribution that its members make to the well-being of the society as a whole. Contemporary African literature exists within the context of this crisis. Directly or indirectly, it bears witness to the impact of this crisis upon the images of the world that are embedded in the texts of all African writers -- of writers as diverse as Chinua Achebe, Nadine Gordimer, Abdelkabir Khatibi, and Ibrahim Hussein. Under such circumstances, it behooves scholars of African literature to articulate a theoretical position that would enable them to situate African literary texts in this context of crisis while at the same time reflecting their own concern with the possibility of addressing these problems in a constructive way. In other words, it seems to me that scholars of African literature cannot afford to ignore the moral dimension of their theoretical activity.

Understood in the terms outlined above, this theoretical activity is part of our enterprise, whether or not we acknowledge it. The real challenge for scholars of African literature is to define the assumptions behind this enterprise and to accpet moral responsibility for them. If theory-building is inherently eclectic, such a process might profitably draw upon insights that have been articulated during the recent explosion of theoretical activity in Europe and North America. This activity has been extremely useful in the sense that it has demonstrated the arbitrariness of the assumptions behind many commonly accepted interpretive practices in the West; it has also cast new light on the way in which texts function within linguistic and cultural systems.

But as Terry Eagleton and others have shown, many of the theoretical positions that have crystallized during the past forty years are profoundly conservative in terms of their practical consequences. In surveying these various positions, therefore, scholars of African literature should examine them with a sceptical critical eye, retaining what is relevant to their project and discarding the rest. Ultimately, however, whatever stimulus they receive from non-African theoretical writings must be translated into terms that could have been derived from African literary texts in the first place. In other words, non-African literary theory can only serve a maieutic function, facilitating the birth of an understanding with which African literature itself was already pregnant.

Keeping this stricture in mind, we can look at some of the currently fashionable modes of literary theory and ask ourselves what they can contribute to a heightened understanding of African literature and the various contexts in which it participates. Schools of literary theory can accommodate a relatively broad spectrum of opinion, and internecine squabbling is frequently more intense than conflicts between opposing schools of thought, but there is usually a set of core principles or beliefs that justify the inclusion of diverse theoretical positions under the same rubric.

For example, deconstructionist critics tend to agree that texts constitute an endless play of signifiers and can therefore never contain the meaning that their authors intended to inscribe in them. Because every element of a text bears traces of extraneous elements, they contend, all texts are inherently slippery and ambivalent -- all contain a series of unresolved contradictions. Those who seek self-consistent meanings in texts are regarded as being engaged in a futile attempt to suppress such contradictions by elevating certain arbitrarily selected ideas to the level of "centers" or "origins" of meaning. For the deconstructionist, the appropriate role of the writer or critic is thus to become a willing participant in the "free play of signifiers," thereby acknowledging the illusory nature of any univocal meanings that are habitually associated with words. What this means in practical terms is that ideas often accepted as givens (e.g., the foundational assumptions of the Euro-American humanist tradition, the notion of the autonomous self, the supposed universality of human nature, the concept of objective truth) can no longer be employed with any assurance that their meanings are unequivocal.

The deconstructionist school has made us much more aware of the intertextual matrix in which all literary texts are embedded. It also offers us an instrument for revealing the arbitrariness of political or religious systems that demand allegiance to a single set of principles that are presented as constituting the "truth." Nevertheless, there are serious weaknesses in the deconstructionist approach to literature. When its own "universal solvent" is applied to the implicit claim that it has described the "true" state of affairs, it actually deconstructs itself by destroying any possible rationale for accepting its underlying view of the world. Furthermore, deconstruction is a negative method that is far more successful at pointing out contradictions and fallacies than it is in suggesting how positive action can be envisaged in the present. For this reason, Jacques Derrida, the most well-known proponent of deconstruction, has been incapable of justifying his personal opposition to apartheid in terms that are compatible with his theoretical position. His dilemma illustrates the incompleteness of the deconstructionist position, its inability to cope with social and historical situatedness, its basic amorality. The fact that we can never know the truth with certainty does not exempt us from the need to act in the world.

Deconstruction thus leads eventually to an impasse. By drawing on post-structuralist theory (especially the work of Michel Foucault) and on anthropological thick description (as exemplified in the writings of Clifford Geertz), the New Historicists have sought to overcome the shortcomings of deconstructionist theory. Foucault offered the New Historicists a way of identifying mental models behind texts as well as behind historical events. Ironically, Geertz had initially found inspiration for his sort of anthropological analysis in the hermeneutics of literary interpretation at a time when anthropologists in general were seeking a way out of the crisis into which their entire field had been precipitated by the collapse of the colonialist system in Africa and elsewhere. What he offered the New Historicists was the notion that culture could be read like a literary text in order to uncover the homologous patterns that underlie them both. For example, when he subjected the Balinese cockfight to meticulous scrutiny, he interpreted it as a re-enactment of the fears and fantasies that comprise male identity concepts in Balinese society -- concepts that are also manifested in other forms of cultural activity.

By acknowledging the historical situatedness of texts and the textual qualities of history, New Historicists such as Louis Montrose and Stephen Greenblatt bridged the gap that the deconstructionists had excavated between text and society. According to them, insights into representations of the self in literature, for example, could also constitute insight into the way such constructs function in society. The New Historicists tended to regard relations of power and struggle as the master trope both in literary texts and in history construed as a text. For them, both sorts of texts comprise fields of force in which dissenting voices subvert dominant ideologies while established power seeks to coopt such voices by channeling them into politically harmless cultural forms.

New Historicism has generated a number of provocative insights that might well serve scholars of African literature as points of departure in their own attempts to achieve greater clarity with regard to method, situatedness, and purpose in the study of African texts, but there are also pitfalls in the New Historicist approach. It is instructive to regard culture and history as texts, but they are only texts in a limited metaphorical sense. To confuse a metaphor with real-world situations is to diminish the likelihood of undertaking constructive action in those situations; in fact, New Historicists have consistently avoided questions about the moral dimensions of critical theory, and they have retreated from the need to develop an adequate concept of historical causation.

Neither of these criticisms can be levelled at an emergent form of literary theory that deals specifically with minority literature or "literature at the margins." A good example of such theorizing can be found in the work of African-American scholars such as Henry Louis Gates, jr. and Houston Baker. They too have drawn on post-structuralist theory, but they also attempt to define that which differentiates the object of their study (in this case African-American literature) from the dominant literary discourse to which it had previously been subordinated. Both draw attention to the black vernacular component of African-American literature, Gates by placing primary emphasis on the practice of signifyin(g), which involves echoing, revising, and responding to an existing universe of black discourse, and Baker by highlighting the role of the blues matrix as a repository for articulations of black identity.

The "theories" of Baker and Gates were formulated at least partially in response to the dominant white culture's assumption that African-Americans were incapable of high culture. What these two scholars make clear is that African-American writers often appropriated literary forms and conventions from the dominant white culture, emptied them of their ideological content, and then used them as vehicles for the communication of an ideological content quite different from the one that was originally associated with them. A similar phenomenon occurred in the Europhone literature of Africa and even in many written African-language literatures. The approaches of Gates, Baker, and other scholars of minority or "marginalized" literature offer provocative suggestions for achieving a better understanding of such phenomena, but as Gates himself warns, theory is always text-specific, and its appropriateness to its subject matter derives from its having evolved in a never-ending dialogue with it.

Frederic Jameson's notion of the "political unconscious" represents another sort of effort to bridge the gap between the radical undecidability of textual meaning (as defined by the deconstructionists) and the need (most forcefully articulated by Marxists) to justify moral and political engagement in the present. According to him, history is not a text, but it is only accessible to us in textual form as a narrative in the "political unconscious." He interprets this text by reading it as the Marxian master trope of "the collective struggle to wrest a realm of Freedom from a realm of Necessity." To comprehend the dialectic between Necessity and utopian human aspirations as it has been represented in literary texts and in history, he concludes, one must radically historicize the mental operations according to which contradictions (such as those pointed out by the deconstructionists) are interpreted.

Within the terms of his own theoretical position, Jameson experiences some difficulty in crafting a philosophical justification for his account of historical causation or in establishing a credible rationale for his belief in extra-textual reality; in fact, he circumvents these difficulties by positing the existence of an inexorable framework of events -- what the Greeks called "Ananke" or the necessary order of things. An acceptance of this framework ultimately requires a leap of faith, but perhaps a leap of faith is precisely what is needed to overcome the unbridgeable separation between subjective and objective reality, between the world of words and the world of the things or events that these words are supposed to represent. According to Zeno's paradox, an arrow can never reach its target because it must always travel halfway to the target before reaching it, and if any finite distance from the target can always be divided in half, the arrival of the arrow will be constantly deferred by the logic of infinite regression. Yet we all know that arrows actually do reach their targets. As Jameson recognizes, we are obliged to act even when our linguistic practices are inadequate to represent the world in which we are living and to gauge the impact of our own actions upon it.

The utopian impulse discussed by Jameson suggests one of the most common ways in which literature can be linked with real-world problems; in fact, it is already present in many, if not most, theorizations of African literature. In *The Theory of African Literature*, for example, Chidi Amuta expresses the belief that Africans should produce writing that testifies to the historical conditions obtaining in contemporary Africa, while remaining committed to "the struggle to banish those conditions which dehumanize humankind and threaten the nobility of art itself." In *Decolonizing the African Mind*, Chinweizu and his fellow "bolekaja" critics argue that African literature and criticism should reaffirm an authentic African identity that can be adapted to the industrial mode of production and that is capable of promoting an heroic act of will by Africans intent upon assuming control over their own destiny.

According to Chinweizu, this reaffirmation of an authentic identity presupposes the need to purge the African mentality of all the "complexes and disorientations" that have been imposed upon it by centuries of colonial and neocolonial domination. From a deconstructionist or New Historicist perspective, Chinweizu's authenticity concept is obviously a constructed image, but if we are obliged by the "necessary order of things" to govern our lives according to constructed images, perhaps we can only justify any engagement in real-world problems on the basis of a "leap of faith" in the adequacy of constructed images or theories.

But even though theoretical positions are always to some degree arbitrary, the acceptance of a particular theory does have practical consequences. For this reason, it seems to me morally imperative that we take into consideration the consequences of applying to real-world situations the theoretical principles that we consciously or unconsciously bring to the study of African literary texts. In doing so, we do not have to "reinvent the wheel"; many of the ideas that might help us to achieve a better understanding of African literature are readily accessible in the vast theoretical literature that has emerged in recent years. There is no shame attached to building one's theories with the materials at hand. Everyone has always done so, even if they do not always acknowledge their indebtedness.

Those who are engaged in the study of African literature can indeed learn from the deconstructionists about the limits of linguistic expression, from the New Historicists about homologous patterns in literature and society, or from Jameson about the dialectic of Necessity and utopian aspiration in the "political unconscious." Yet if we invariably appropriate elements of our theories from wherever we happen to find them, we must also, as Gates and Baker demonstrate, seek to make them our own. We need to set them into an ongoing dialogic relationship with the object of our study.

In this process, we cannot avoid assigning arbitrary meanings to ambiguous phenomena, or taking stances on linguistically undecidable issues, or having recourse to imperfect tools of analysis. Such choices are prerequisites for action in the world, and whether we admit it or not, we are obliged to act in the world. In light of the present crisis in Africa, a judicious and morally responsible approach to literary theory would seem to demand that we recognize the interrelatedness of all things, our own dependency on fragile ecological systems, and the long-term folly of perpetuating socially unjust ways of distributing wealth.

The point is not that literary theory must explicitly address all the real-world problems that confront us today or even that it can contribute significantly to the solution of these problems. Nevertheless, if those who theorize about African literature are to escape the amorality that results from a failure to contextualize both the object of their study and the perspective from which they themselves are studying it, they must consciously elaborate a thoretical position -- a view of the world -- that is capable of integrating the interpretation of cultural productions such as literary texts with an understanding of real-world problems and the utopian quest to find solutions for them. We delude ourselves if we imagine that we can divorce our theories about literature from our activities as human beings. In studying a particular text or literary development, we might, for the purpose of analysis, restrict the number of contextual factors that we take into consideration, but such thought experiments remain embedded in real-world situations; they have practical consequences, and we must be willing to accept responsibility for those consequences.

WORKS CITED

Amuta, Chidi. *The Theory of African Literature*. London: Zed Books, 1989.

Baker, Houston. *Blues, Ideology, and Afro-American Literature: A Vernacular Theory*. Chicago: University of Chicago Press, 1984.

Bateson, Gregory. *Steps to an Ecology of Mind: Collected Essays in Anthropology, Psychiatry, and Epistemology*. New York: Ballantine, 1972.

Bjornson, Richard. "Cognitive Mapping and the Understanding of Literature." *SubStance* 30 (1981): 51-62.

Chinweizu, Onwuchekwa Jemie, and Ihechukwu Madubuike. *Toward the Decolonization of African Literature*. Enugu: Fourth Dimension, 1980.

Derrida, Jacques. *Writing and Difference*. Trans. A. Bates. Chicago: University of Chicago Press, 1978.

Eagleton, Terry. *Literary Theory: An Introduction*. Minneapolis: University of Minnesota Press, 1983.

Foucault, Michel. *The Archaeology of Knowledge*. Trans. A. Sheridan. New York: Pantheon, 1972.

―――. *The Order of Things: An Archaeology of the Human Sciences*. Trans. A. Sheridan. New York: Vintage, 1973.

Gates, Henry Louis, Jr. *Figures in Black: Words, Signs, and the "Racial" Self*. Oxford: Oxford University Press, 1987.

―――. *The Signifying Monkey: A Theory of African-American Literary Criticism*. Oxford: Oxford University Press, 1988.

Geertz, Clifford. *The Interpretation of Cultures*. New York: Basic Books, 1973.

Greenblatt, Stephen. *Shakespearean Negotiations: The Circulation of Social Energy in Renaissance England*. Berkeley: University of California Press, 1988.

Jameson, Frederic. *The Political Unconscious: Narrative as a Socially Symbolic Act*. Ithaca: Cornell University Press, 1981.

Montrose, Louis. "Renaissance Literary Studies and the Subject of History." *English Literary Renaissance* 16 (1986): 5-12.

―――. "Professing the Renaissance: The Poetics and Politics of Culture." *The New Historicism*. Ed. H. Aram Veeser. New York: Routledge, 1989.

LITERARY THEORY AND AFRICAN LITERATURE
edited by J. Gugler, H.-J. Lüsebrink, J. Martini
Münster/Hamburg 1993, pp. 43-62

PRESUPPOSES THEORIQUES ET METHODOLOGIQUES A UNE THEORIE DE LA LITTERATURE AFRICAINE

GEORGES NGAL

Qui tente une approche théorique de la littérature africaine se heurte d'emblée à des préalables incontournables. S'agit-il d'une théorie régionale, propre à la littérature africaine, qui se demande à la fois comment elle se pense et comment elle peut se confronter à d'autres territoires du savoir (philosophie analytique, histoire, anthropologie, herméneutique contemporaine, linguistique, psychanalyse, etc.) ou s'agit-il de l'application particulière d'une théorie générale à ladite littérature (p.ex. confronter les théories du récit aux expériences littéraires africaines)? Mais cette question suppose elle-même cette autre non résolue, à savoir celle de l'unité des littératures africaines qui permet de dire "la littérature africaine" au lieu des "littératures africaines" au pluriel. En d'autres termes, s'agit-il d'inviter la littérature africaine à son autoréflexion au moyen d'une entreprise de description théorique - l'acte critique rencontrant l'acte créateur de l'écrivain - : interrogations théoriques, théories, modèles interprétatifs, problématique d'évaluation, présuppositions théoriques et méthodologiques, outillage intellectuel développés au sein des systèmes ou du système culturel africains? Accepter tout ce questionnement, c'est s'inscrire dans une tradition qui accepte des échanges interdisciplinaires, car comme l'écrit T. Todorov, "un véritable théoricien de la littérature doit nécessairement réfléchir à autre chose que la littérature" (Todorov: 1981, 7).

Je vois l'histoire littéraire et l'histoire de la littérature africaines présentes dominées par deux préoccupations . La première considère la théorie littéraire de la littérature africaine comme une simple application (illustration) de la théorie littéraire générale ou des théories de la littérature nées dans des contextes socioculturels et géographico-culturels occidentaux. Le Père E. Mveng a bien perçu le problème lorsque, en 1973, au Colloque de Yaoundé sur *Le critique africain et son peuple comme produc-*

teur de civilisation, il intitulait sa communication: *Introduction à l'herméneutique négro-africaine.* Mais c'est pour aussitôt, après avoir défini l'herméneutique comme "la science de l'interprétation" (Mveng: 1977, 122), prendre ses distances à l'égard de l'herméneutique générale: "S'agissant des oeuvres de civilisations négro-africaines, le premier écueil à éviter sera de forger ou d'emprunter une méthode a priori de déchiffrement ou d'analyse, et de tenter de soumettre ces oeuvres à cette methode au risque de les violer. Pour nous il faut partir des oeuvres de civilisation négro-africaines, telles qu'elles ont existé dans le passé et telles quelles existent aujourd'hui. Il faut les interroger pour qu'elles expriment, à travers leurs structures et leur cohérence, leur propre intelligibilité (Mveng: 1977, 122). L'herméneutique négro-africaine n'est autre chose que l'expression des lois de cette intelligilité". Ce faisant, Mveng se situe résolument dans la deuxième tendance qui demande à l'univers de référnces socio-culturelles africaines les lois de son 'intelligibilité' (*déchiffrer, pénétrer, identifier et comprendre,* selon les termes de Mveng). Il doute qu'unc déduction a priori des règles universelles présidant à la production d'oeuvres d'art soit possible. Cette radicalisation est largement partagée, sans pour autant tourner le dos à l'éclairage des apports des théories élaborées à l'extérieur.

SUIVONS CES DEUX TENDANCES AVANT DE DEVELOPPER NOTRE PROPRE POSITION

Le reve universaliste

Une théorie littéraire voit le jour quelque part, dans un univers socioculturel qui la fonde, la justifie, aussitôt la tentation d'en faire un modèle d'analyse universel se profile à l'horizon. L'exemple le plus clair est constitué par les nouvelles "écoles de poétique": celle de Roman Jakobson, le structuralisme depuis 1960, le formalisme russe. Vladimir Propp cerne-t-il "les lois qui régissent la structure" du conte populaire russe, aussitôt les applications qu'on en fait tendent à dépasser l'univers d'enracinement de la théorie. Pour nous en tenir à la littérature africaine, Denise Paulme tire de la succession des phases (virtualité, passage à l'acte, achèvement) des propositions originales afin de jeter les bases d'une typologie des contes africains, qui doit la conduire à une théorie générale des formes du récit (Paulme: 1976). Il en est de même de tous les modèles d'analyse du récit inspirés par Propp: *La logique du récit* (1973) de Cl. Bremond qui se caractérise par la triade (*éventualité, passage à l'acte, achèvement, assortis du jeu d'alternatives, non-passage à l'acte et non-achèvement*) appelée "séquence", la théorie des actants de A.J. Greimas et d'Etienne Souriau etc. visent à la même prétention à l'universalité. Pour leur part, R. Richard et J. Sevry, s'essayant à la "sociocritique et littératures africaines", se "proposent, en toute modestie, d'essayer de déterminer dans quelle mesure la critique marxiste (représenté par G. Lukacs, L. Goldmann, H. Lefèbvre, par exemple) peut s'appliquer à la littérature africaine" (Sevry et Richard: 1959). C'est à Goldmann également que la *Sociologie du roman africain* d'Anozie Sunday demande le modèle d'analyse. Seul B. Mouralis, en 1969 se fondant sur l'idée qu "'en Afrique, le roman est un genre transplanté et la société bourgeoise de type européen n'a jamais existé" (Mouralis: 1969, 150), se refuse à appliquer, dans *Individu et collectivité dans le roman négro-africain d'expression française*, le schéma goldmannien au roman africain. En 1983, en dépit de la remarque de Mouralis, Marcien Towa n'hésite pas à imposer à la *Poésie de la négritude* l'approche structuraliste (Towa: 1983) inspirée librement de l'auteur de *Le Dieu caché*.

L'impression d'ensemble qui se dégage de la plupart des applications de ces théories est un certain totalitarisme méthodologique. Claude Bremond avoue: "Sous le nom de logique, j'avais en projet l'élucidation, par une déduction presque a priori, des règles universelles et nécessaires du raconté" (Bremond: 1990), mieux du racontable. Si raconter revient, synthétiquement parlant, comme le dit Paul Ricoeur, à "fabriquer une intrigue, c'est-à-dire un schème qui permet de composer ensemble des circonstances, des intentions, des motifs, des conséquences non voulues, des rencontres, des adversités, des secours, la réussite, l'échec, le bonheur, l'infortune ... . Bref, c'est un agencement d'incidents en un système" (Ricoeur: l984). Ceci admis, on peut douter qu'une "déduction à priori des règles universelles et nécessaires" soit possible. La limitation des possibilités de combinaisons que réprésente ce "laboratoire imaginaire"(Ricoeur) appelé récit paraît utopique. Il y a là un réductionnisme qui me paraît insoutenable. L'enjeu paraît être le langage ou le discours. Aussi bien dans le structuralisme que dans le formalisme russe et les écoles apparentées, le langage est réduit à un simple problème soit de thématique, soit de techniques linguistiques pour rendre compte de l'oeuvre. Le discours se trouve ainsi mutilé dans ses composantes fondamentales qui se résument dans son caractère dialogique et référentiel comme vont le revendiquer bon nombre de critiques africains aujourd'hui: à savoir une conscience parlante à quelqu'un ou suivant les termes habituels, un locuteur interpellant un interlocuteur, une référence et ce au sujet de quoi l'on parle. De ces éléments, ce sont la référence et l'aspect dialogique qui se trouvent mutilés. Comment éviter la mutilation? C'est en prenant en compte le contexte socio-historique.

Telle est la démarche suivie, en gros, par le premier courant. Comme on l'aura soupçonné, ce qui est présupposé dans le premier courant, c'est une théorie générale de l'oeuvre d'art (du sens) et du texte. Qu'est-ce qu'une oeuvre d'art? Qu'est-ce qu'une oeuvre belle? Que signifie-t-elle? Les seuls constituants verbaux ne suffisent-ils pas à la compréhension de l'oeuvre littéraire? Ne faut-il prendre en compte que les éléments immanents? Il est évident que l'horizon d'attente des lecteurs critiques africains, si l'on se place dans la terminologie de H.R. Jauss, semble s'inscrire en faux contre une position qui se réfugierait dans la seule immanence. Mais leur position n'est compréhensible que replacée dans le contexte des annees 70, qui coïncident avec la fin de la première décennie des indépendances africaines. Années du constat de leur faillite qui appelèrent une réévaluation des voies et des concepts de la création et de la définition de nouveaux outils du discours africain. Période d'une intense activité intellectuelle de l'élite qui s'est traduite en symposiums, colloques, congrès, créations de sociétés savantes. Le mot de passe à l'époque, je m'en souviens bien, était l'élaboration de l'intérieur d'un nouveau discours scientifique africain, par opposition à celui élaboré par ceux du dehors. Ce fut la période de récusation radicale du discours ethnologique et anthropologique, du procès de la négritude (*Négritude et négrologues* de St. Adotévi, 1972, *Le manifeste de l'homme primitif*, 1972, de Diawara). On demandait aux sciences humaines de réviser leurs concepts dans l'approche des sociétés africaines. C'est dans ce contexte qu'il faut situer la lettre circulaire de la Société Africaine de Culture (SAC) en son Bulletin intérieur du deuxième et troisième trimestre 1970, qui préparait la grande rencontre de Yaoundé, en 1972, sur *le Critique africain et son peuple comme producteur de civilisation*. Citons les passages essentiels de la lettre.

Chaque société a ses normes d'appréciation. Celles-ci sont partie intégrante de l'ethique de la vie. Les courants extérieurs, si généreux soient-ils, ne sauraient remplacer l'effort personnel de recherche et de confrontation qui seul, permet d'éclairer le jugement à travers le contexte d'une civilisation spécifique.

Les oeuvres artistiques et littéraires de l'Afrique sont présentées au peuple africain, son destinataire légitime, par la critique occidentale. Celle-ci apprécie, consacre ou désavoue la démarche de nos créateurs. Elle s'arroge le droit de tracer les lignes directrices, d'intégrer dans des catégories élaborées par elle, une part importante de notre patrimoine culturel. L'on est grand écrivain, grand peintre, grand sculpteur, par la volonté des tenants de telle ou telle école de Paris ou de Londres, de Bruxelles ou de New York. Et, très souvent, si ces marques extérieures de considération flattent le peuple africain, celui-ci ne se sent pas profondément concerné. C'est que le peuple africain, d'où sont issus les écrivains et les artistes en question, n'a pas les moyens d'apprécier le talent de ceux-ci.

Question de langues et de méthodes - le support des oeuvres est emprunté à l'extérieur.

Question de vision du monde aussi, qui implique une information large et constante, non seulement sur les problèmes nationaux, mais aussi, sur tout ce qui se passe à l'extérieur des frontières de nos pays.

(...) Qui pourrait mieux que celui-ci apprécier cette condition, ou indiquer aux écrivains la voie à suivre, les écueils à éviter? Il s'agit d'intégrer le créateur africain dans la vie de sa civilisation et de libérer de l'emprise excessive de l'Occident. Il s'agit d'intégrer le peuple tout entier, avec ses artistes, aux responsabilités que la vie moderne impose, à chaque nation, et à chaque civilisation".

Arrêtons-nous un instant sur cette prise de position. Elle est faite deux ans avant la rencontre importante de Yaoundé, en avril 1972, regroupant des enseignants universitaires anglophones et francophones. Sa visée principale est d'orienter les travaux de cette rencontre. Pour une bonne part, elle reflète les idées contenues dans un article de Thomas Melone sur *La critique et les problèmes du langage en Afrique*, paru dans *Présence Africaine* en 1970.

La prise de position de la SAC comporte un certain nombre de postulats. Elle pose l'existence d'un patrimoine artistique et littéraire africain. Elle ne définit pas ce que ce qu'est une oeuvre "artistique et littéraire". Encore moins ce qu'on appelle aujourd'hui la "littérarité" . Elle n'est pas, en tout cas, posée en termes linguistiques. L'intelligibilité du patrimoine artistique et littéraire africain passe par ses propres ressources symboliques, c'est-à-dire des catégories, des normes, des règles, internes à l'Afrique qui lui "fournissent les règles de signification en fonction desquelles telle conduite peut être interprétée ou tout simplement identifiée" (Ricoeur: 1983, 93). Il faut entendre interprétation au sens fort du terme: "interpréter c'est considérer quelque chose comme étant ceci ou cela, donc conférer une déterminité, et aussi mettre au jour, déchiffrer, expliciter un sens ou une cohérence qui n'apparaît pas clairement. Cette attribution peut revêtir plusieurs modalités différentes" (Quéré: 1987, 210). L'attribution se fait "par un acte, et non par une assertion, la manière dont nous avons déterminé, identifié ce dont il s'agissait ou la valeur que nous avons conférée à une occurrence, c'est-à-dire ce comme quoi nous l'avons considérée" (Ibidem). On en devine les conséquences. L'intelligibilité des oeuvres ne se livre que par argument herméneutique. Par argument herméneutique, on peut entendre avec L. Quéré "la proposition qui affirme que la réalité sociale ne se livre que dans et par l'interprétation" (Quéré:

1987, 211). Si l'on se réfère à la définition globale de l'herméneutique comme science de l'interprétation des textes ou art d'interpréter les textes, force est de reconnaître les présupposés suivants. Si un texte, en effet, écrit C. Bouchindhomme, demande à être interprété, c'est que d'une façon ou d'une autre son sens ne s'impose pas ou ne s'impose plus, soit que les mots utilisés n'ont plus cours, soit que leur sens littéral est (ou peut être) énigmatique; l'interpréter consiste alors à retrouver un sens manifeste qui restitue le sens premier dans sa vérité. Simple dans son principe, cette opération fait jouer dans son effectuation (...) des dimensions complexes telles que le sens et la vérité (à travers des notions comme celles d'adéquation, de littéralité, etc.)" (Bouchindhomme: 1990, 166). Mais la question qui vient à l'esprit est de savoir sur quoi le Bulletin fonde-t-il l'interprétation? Il semble que c'est l'usage des langues étrangères en tant que support d'emprunt des oeuvres africaines. Celui-ci est source de non-transparence, d'infidélité au sens premier. En d'autres termes, la langue étrangère ne traduirait pas avec fidélité le sens premier, authentique. D'où le recours à des interprètes. L'interprétation serait exigée parce que non seulement la langue étrangère est inconnue du peuple mais aussi parce qu'elle est frappée d'inaptitude à la traduction du sens authentique. L'interprétation apparaît comme un moment nécessaire.

Mais sommes-nous pour autant débarrassés de tout soupçon? L'interprétation ne serait-elle pas liée à une culture, notamment grecque, judéo-chrétienne? Elle évoque les oracles, les augures, le vol des oiseaux, et autres présages perçus comme des signes adressés aux hommes soit pour les prévénir d'un danger, soit pour les ouvrir à une révélation surnaturelle. Mais comme ces signes sont obscurs, ils nécessitent une interprétation. La Bible des Juifs et des chrétiens abonde en récits obscurs. D'où également la nécessité d'une interprétation. Si l'on en croit la *Grammaire d'objets en tous genres* de Vincent Descombes (1983), le concept d'interprétation aurait ainsi été arraché à son espace naturel par des herméneutes de tous genres qui ont "indûment élargi le domaine de validité originairement spécifique de la situation herméneutique" (Descombes: 1983, 23): son espace naturel est oraculaire, exégétique de la divination et de la révélation. Il y aurait abus, déplacement indu par toutes les disciplines qui en font usage, notamment l'herméneutique philosophique (Heidegger, Gadamer, Ricoeur etc.). On aurait donc glissé hors de la sphère proprement herméneutique où la compréhension de la signification trouverait sa seule pertinence. V. Descombes appelle cet espace spécifique le temple. Aussi peut-il écrire: "Hors du temple, point d'herméneutique".

Les cultures africaines font largement usage de la pensée herméneutique. Quand le devin ndembu (Turner: 1972, 39s.) agite son panier divinatoire de manière que les figurines qu'il contient, en se déplaçant d'un bout à l'autre du panier, se rangent sur des positions fortuites, les unes restant en dessous, les autres au-dessus, il interprète l'"événement" ainsi produit. Le devin "lit" la situation décrite par chacune des figurines. La situation est jugée favorable ou défavorable, suivant la position des figurines. De même le cri nocturne des hibous est interprété généralement comme signe de malheur. Les systèmes divinatoires sont très développés dans l'ensemble des tribus africaines. Comme dans la civilisation grecque, civilisation à faibles connaissances technologiques, ici également la pensée interprétative intervient parce qu'on est en présence de signes ambigus. On distinguera deux niveaux. On dira que, dans le cas du cri des hibous, l'interprétation se situe à un niveau spontané, faible, une sorte de pré-interprétation par la société, tandis que chez les Ndembu on accède déjà a une certaine sophistication, qui reste malgré tout dans le champ de la pré-interprétation par la société pour le maintien de l'équilibre de l'ordre social.

Nous admettrons "qu'il y a interprétation chaque fois qu'un interprétant attribue un sens à quelque chose i.e. transforme un donné en signe (...). Si le donné se donne lui-même comme signe (texte, oeuvre, histoire narrativisée, comportement verbalisé, etc.), l'interprétation consiste à dégager sous le sens donné, manifeste et littéral, un sens second, latent, profond, anagogique; elle devient déchiffrement (exégèse, psychanalyse, philosophies de l'histoire, etc.)" (Petitot: 1987, 41).

Quant à la notion de texte, elle sera prise ici au sens de tout discours signifiant déjà constitué: écrit ou oral. Le Bulletin nous convie donc à nous éveiller à une conscience méthodologique, exempte de tout arbitraire subjectif dans la lecture: pratiquer une technique de retour au sens premier et pur, débarrassé des ajouts et altérations produits par le recours aux "courants extérieurs" et par la soumission des oeuvres africaines artistiques et littéraires aux "normes, catégories, théories extérieures".

La problématique ainsi dessinée est posée en termes de langage, du moins implicitement, c'est-à-dire impliquant les quatre composants du discours: un locuteur (ici créateur), un interlocuteur (le peuple africain), le sens, la signification (thème) et la référence. Le créateur africain ne crée que suivant certaines règles, dans un cadre dialogique au sens fort du terme. Il est ainsi rappelé qu'un créateur comme un énonciateur ne peut se définir sans se préoccuper de son destinataire. On rejoint ici Bakhtine (*Le marxisme et la philosophie du langage*) et aussi H.G. Gadamer *pour qui le langage n'est que pour autant qu'il est dialogue* (cf. la formule célèbre: "ce dialogue que nous sommes", *de Vérité et méthode*). L'idée féconde ici est que l'interprète tient un rôle dialogique dans la compréhension, Lorsque le

Bulletin affirme avec force la place du destinataire, il est en parfait accord avec Gadamer: l'acte de langage du créateur a comme éléments constitutifs la requête du créateur (locuteur) et la reconnaissance de la requête en tant que requête par le destinataire. C'est avec raison que Mihaly Szegedy-Maszak peut adopter l'acte de langage comme principe dans l'analyse de la structure des textes littéraires: "un acte de langage est une requête, non seulement à cause de l'intention du locuteur, mais aussi parce qu'il est reconnu en tant que requête par un destinataire" (Szegedy-Maszak: 1989). La situation d'énonciation globale doit être prise en compte - notamment la propre historicité du lecteur. La compréhension s'effectue par la médiation du langage dans sa dimension historique, c'est-à-dire dans le dialogue des textes littéraires qui font le réseau des intertextualités entre les interprétations successives du passé et du présent.

L'autre idée abordée par le Bulletin est celle du support des oeuvres, "emprunté" à l'extérieur: les langues. Le postulat avancé est le suivant: une oeuvre écrite en langue non africaine porterait atteinte au sens de l'oeuvre. Car au lieu de la transparence, le créateur poserait les conditions de l'incompréhension de l'oeuvre et condamnerait, dans la pire des hypothèses, à la traduction du sens de l'oeuvre. On devine ce que cela soulève comme problèmes. On le reprendra un peu plus loin avec l'évocation de certaines poétiques, notamment celle de J.-P. Makouta-Mboukou. Pour l'instant indiquons seulement qu'il s'agit d'un cadre de réflexion tracé par le Bulletin pour orienter et canaliser les recherches des critiques africains. On notera que dans la conception du Bulletin, il y a un privilège accordé implicitement au schéma de la communication. Les oeuvres sont vues du point de vue du destinataire: le peuple ou le public. Le code, la langue, fait problème. L'émetteur, le créateur, qui doit transmettre son expérience d'écrivain, le fait au moyen d'un code (langue étrangère) qui limite d'avance ses possibilités d'expression, mieux lui interdit d'exprimer le "sens pur" de son expérience singulière, on dirait de son expérience muette. La transmission du sens de son message est donc compromise: le code est inadéquat par rapport au message. Il y a inadéquation entre le signifiant et le signifié. Ce qui se passe, c'est que l'émetteur prend certaines initiatives pour sauvegarder "l'identité du sens" de son message. Le code subira des aménagements comme on le verra un peu plus loin avec Makouta-Mboukou.

C'est à l'intérieur de ce cadre que nous nous plaçons pour poser le problème de la théorie littéraire. Nous verrons d'abord comment certains l'ont posé et ensuite comment nous-même nous l'avons posé et le poserons.

C'est dans ce cadre ainsi tracé, avec ses présupposés que se situent les premières approches globales, systématiques et théoriques de la littérature africaine - esquissant une synthèse générale et cohérente des oeuvres africaines. On aurait pu réserver une place à Léopold Sédar Senghor et à d'autres penseurs. Mais cela nous aurait trop éloignés de l'essentiel que nous poursuivons. Par ailleurs, nous avons voulu, dans un premier temps, nous en tenir à un seul genre, le genre narratif.

Longtemps préparé, et organisé conjointement par l'Université de Yaoundé et la SAC, du 16-20 avril 1970, dans la capitale du Cameroun, regroupant les principales universités africaines anglophones et francophones, le colloque offre la première occasion de tester les orientations du Bulletin. Elles sont réaffirmées: l'enjeu des oeuvres comme langage, le privilège accordé au destinaire dans le schéma de la communication, l'importance de la langue du critique en tant que véhicule du sens vers le destinataire, les enjeux du contexte et de la référence, le procès de la lecture à partir de la demande du destinataire, garant et fondement des responsabilités du critique dans ses rôles scientifique, pédagogique, politique et esthétique (Atelier n°3). Il apparaît que le fait d'être attentif aux préoccupations et requêtes du destinataire (peuple) dans l'acte de lecture devient une compréhension humaine ou une herméneutique littéraire (Jauss).

L'HERMENEUTIQUE DE MVENG

Dans le lot des communications présentées celle du Père Mveng me paraît importante du point de vue de notre propos. L'intérêt vient de ce que l'auteur situe le débat immédiatement dans la problématique du langage et de l'herméneutique considérée comme voie d'accès aux oeuvres africaines. S'il choisit l'herméneutique, ce n'est pas pour opérer une lecture ou une relecture des oeuvres à partir d'une herméneutique générale appliquée à l'Afrique. Il admet une seule voie d'approche: celle d'une herméneutique régionale, c'est-à-dire une herméneutique qui "obéit a ses lois propres": "Pour nous", accorde le Père Mveng, "il faut partir des oeuvres négro-africaines, telles qu'elles ont existé dans le passé et telles qu'elles existent aujourd'hui. Il faut les interroger pour qu'elles expriment, à travers leurs structures et leur cohérence, leur propre intelligibilité. L'herméneutique négro-africaine n'est autre chose que l'expression des lois de cette intelligibilité". La tâche du critique n'est plus que celle d'un herméneute, c'est-à-dire savoir interpréter les signes au sens presque divinatoire: "qui disent ce que nous sommes et ce que nous avons à être" (Descombes: 1983, 17). Herméneutique est pris ici au sens primitif et heideggerien, c'est-à-dire "mettre au jour ce qui fait connaître un destin" (Descombes). Mais qu'est-ce que l'art négro-africain?

Pour Mveng, "toute oeuvre nègre exprime l'homme" (Mveng: 1977, 122). Cette expression est "langage", "globalisant et totalisant. Il embrasse tout l'homme, tous les aspects de sa vie, et donc toutes leurs expressions": la musique, la danse, la parole, le costume, l'architecture, les masques et les statues des ancêtres, les symboles sculptés, gravés ou peints, etc. Ils sont "écritures symboliques" et "signes" (signes graphiques Foulbé, les masques Dogon, le motifs Adinkra du Ghana, les poids Baoulé de Côte d'Ivoire, les reliefs d'Abomey, les masques Glédé de Kétou, les bronzes d'Ifé et de Bénin, les motifs Bamoun et Bamileké, les Abbia des Fang-Beti du Sud-Cameroun, l'art Tchokwe, le langage graphique des Bakouba du Kasaï, les dessins muraux de l'Uganda, etc.). "Toutes ces expressions sont les moments d'un seul et même langage, (...) forment la trame d'une immense liturgie où l'homme célèbre son *destin*, la lutte dramatique de la vie aux prises avec la mort, et le triomphe final de la vie sur la mort" (Mveng: 1977, 123).

Dans le cadre de cette herméneutique, l'auteur distingue cinq éléments structurels du langage négro-africain: le *rythme* qualifié d'"expression primordiale de la liberté créatrice de l'homme", "traduit le destin de l'homme déchiré entre la vie et la mort et le triomphe de la vie sur la mort" (Mveng: 1977, 124). Le *geste*, deuxième élément, apporte un "complément dramatique nécessaire là où il y a une oeuvre orale, plastique ou musicale en Afrique. Dans le style oral, la rythmisation se fait par le geste. Mais le moment le plus important d'après le Père Mveng du langage est la *parole*. Non pas l'opposition saussurienne langue/parole mais le discours, de caractère dialogique, qui met l'homme en communication avec l'autre, le monde, Dieu. En tant que discours la parole s'incarne dans le rythme dont il est consubstantiel," parce qu'il est consubstantiel au vivant et à toute activité" (Meschonnic: 1982, 121). C'est elle qui "donne leur consistance, leur vérité et leur originalité" (Mveng: 1977, 126). Dans les oeuvres d'art, le langage négro-africain est essentiellement *langue*, conclut Mveng. Si toute oeuvre de civilisation est langage, ce langage se traduit toujours dans une langue dont il faut connaître la structure fondamentale, c'est-à-dire les tons et le rythme: ce sont eux qui façonnent la vision de l'homme, du monde et de Dieu, les styles littéraires, plastiques musicaux et chorégraphiques. La langue constitue le trait d'union entre le rythme, le geste, le signe et la *signification*. Enfin, la *signification*, cinquième élément, est constituée essentiellement par le message que porte l'oeuvre d'art exprimé en rythme, geste, paroles et signes. Il est la grande célébration cosmique par l'homme de l'humanisation de la nature, c'est-à-dire l'intégration à son propre destin.

Quelle méthode utiliser? "L'étude scientifique de la littérature dite orale doit donc comporter désormais l'étude de sa version écrite dans l'art traditionnel. Aucune méthode, à l'heure actuelle", affirme Mveng, ne permet à ce langage d'avoir accès à nos écoles (Mveng: 1977, 133; et 1977, 124). "C'est la raison pour laquelle les programmes de littérature négro-africaine comportent l'étude de la littérature traditionnelle ancienne. Son herméneutique demande une immense érudition, et souvent, trop souvent encore, nous demeurons analphabètes en face de notre propre culture" (Mveng: 1977, 124).

Il est évident que le Père Mveng place l'herméneutique "dans le temple", c'est-à-dire dans la *"situation herméneutique élémentaire"* (Descombes: 1983, 17-27), propre au champ interprétatif du devin et de l'exégète telle que décrite par la *Grammaire d'objets en tous genres* de V. Descombes (1983). Les oeuvres d'art sont traitées, en effet, comme des signes destinés à nous, conformément à une intention de sens authentique". Les signes sont porteurs de *paroles qui nous disent ce que nous sommes et ce que nous voulons être*. Mais ceci suppose l'existence d'un sens authentique qui s'adresse à nous et s'exprime à notre intention; que ce sens nous délivre une "vérité" ou un message où il y va de notre destin, "où l'homme célèbre son destin" (Mveng: 1977, 124).

Voilà le critique devenu herméneute. Sa mission est d'aider à comprendre le sens. Mais comme note justement Descombes, "comprendre n'est jamais déchiffrer à l'aide d'un code - soit qu'on le possède d'avance, soit qu'on ait à le reconstituer - c'est toujours interpréter des signes deux fois singuliers, par leur manière de signifier en chaque circonstance et leur destinataire" (Descombes: 1983, 18). La question à poser est de savoir si tous les graphismes africains relèvent de la situation herméneutique comme semble le prétendre Mveng. Certains ne devraient-il pas être déchiffrés à l'aide d'un code connu d'avance? Les Abbia au Cameroun et au Gabon appartiennent, semble-t-il, à un système de divination. Lorsque le client choisit librement les motifs de ses pictogrammes, le devin consultant lui donne l'interprétation appropriée à partir d'eux. Faut-il y voir un déchiffrement de code ou une réelle interprétation? Les pagnes adingra imprimés, brodés ou tissés au Ghana et en Côte d'Ivoire comportent un nombre considérable de motifs graphiques représentant des proverbes et des symboles connus de la population. Ce sont des sortes de phrasogrammes évoquant des messages sous forme de proverbes ou dictons. Il y a là, sans doute, un langage codé. Dans bien des cas la frontière entre le signe herméneutique et le signe codé est difficile à tracer. Il serait abusif de voir dans tous les graphismes, et partant, dans tous les arts nègres des signes herméneutiques. Par ailleurs, il est difficile de donner un traitement interprétatif (herméneutique) identique à tous les champs artistiques africains. La littérature a son autonomie par rapport aux autres arts.

LA POETIQUE DE LA TRADUCTION DE MAKOUTA-MBOUKOU

La deuxième théorie choisie est celle du linguiste et critique littéraire congolais, Jean-Pierre Makouta-Mboukou. Comme le Camerounais Mveng, il s'inscrit lui aussi dans le courant récusateur des discours extérieurs au fait littéraire africain: "N'ayant pas de théorie analytique à proposer ici - peut-être n'en mettrai-je au point - j'appliquerai celle qui est à la portée de tous: analyser les textes de l'intérieur: la vérité apparaîtra d'elle-même (...). Je ne ferai pas appel ici aux grands courants de la critique occidentale. Y recourir serait contraire à la coutume négro-africaine (...). La littérature négro-africaine est une maison fermée. L'on ne peut inventorier ses richesses que de l'intérieur". (Makouta-Mboukou: 1980, 172-173). Fidèle à ce postulat, il procède à une double analyse du roman africain, enraciné, selon lui, dans l'espace géographique et humain, spirituel et religieux. Il explore ce quadriple contexte. Il constate que le "roman explique et parle réellement aux Nègres d'Afrique" (Makouta-Mboukou: 1980, 226). Ceci dit, l'auteur s'emploie à la description linguistique, dans le cadre des contextes géographique, socio-ethnologique, socio-historique et socio-linguistique. La thèse centrale est la suivante: la structure linguistique de tout texte négro-africain (francophone) est un "compromis entre la langue française et la langue maternelle de l'écrivain, qui apparaît dans l'oeuvre tantôt traduite, tantôt calquée, tantôt enfin insérée telle quelle dans le texte" (Makouta-Mboukou: 1970, 270). Développons ces trois cas de figure.

Dans le premier cas il nous invite: "il faut admettre qu'un roman négro-africain est écrit en deux langues au moins" (op. cit. 270), dont l'une est nécessairement la langue maternelle de l'auteur. C'est ainsi qu'il voit dans *Crépuscule des temps anciens* de Nazi Boni un double contexte linguistique français-bwamu; dans tous les romans de Ousmane Sembène et les poèmes de Senghor, un contexte français-wolof; dans les romans de Mongo Beti et de F.Oyono, un contexte français-éwondo (op.cit. 268). Pour lui, "l'écrivain négro-africain, dans la plupart des cas, pense en sa langue, et s'exprime en français" (p. 270). Aussi la langue de l'écrivain est-elle un compromis. La traduction se produit chaque fois que l'écrivain veut rendre le plus "fidèlement" possible l'expression en langue maternelle, notamment en ce qui concerne l'ordre des mots. Makouta-Mboukou appelle ce procédé le "calque". Il illustre la thèse par l'analyse de *La Palabre stérile* de son compatriote Guy Menga, et par celle de *La Légende de Mfoumou ma Mazono* de cet autre congénère Jean Malonga. On pourrait ajouter à cette liste *Les soleils des indépendances et Monnè, outrages et défis* d'Ahmadou Kourouma et les romans de Seydou Badian. Le double contexte linguistique de tout roman négro-africain n'est qu'un cas particulier des langues en situation de contact ou un cas de bilinguisme individuel. Si chaque romancier africain est "traducteur", "l'influence de la langue qu'il traduit peut être décelée par des interférences particulières, qui dans ce cas précis sont des erreurs ou fautes de traduction, ou bien des comportements linguistiques très marqués chez les traducteurs: le goût des néologismes étrangers, la tendance aux emprunts, aux calques, aux citations non traduites en langue étrangère, le maintien dans le texte une fois traduit de mots et de tours non traduits" (Mounin: 1976, 4). Ce texte concerne les traducteurs professionnels, mais appliqué au romancier négro-africain appelle quelques nuances. D'une part, il n'est toujours pas conscient des interférences et d'autre part, les néologismes, les emprunts, les citations peuvent être des effets esthétiques et/ou idéologiques recherchés par le créateur. Ainsi chez Ngandu Nkashama des fins idéologiques sont satisfaites par la juxtaposition de pans entiers de texte en sa langue maternelle. D'une manière générale, on dira avec Georges Mounin que "le problème linguistique fondamental qui se présente, eu égard au bilinguisme, est de savoir jusqu'à quel point deux structures en contact peuvent être maintenues intactes, et dans quelle mesure elles influeront l'une sur l'autre. Nous pouvons dire qu'en règle générale, il y a une certaine quantité d'influences réciproques, et que la séparation nette est l'exception" (Mounin: 1976, 5).

Le deuxième cas de figure est celui de la re-création ou de la traduction libre. Ce cas a lieu quand le calque s'avère impossible, par exemple le cas des formules figées telles que les proverbes, les dictons. L'écrivain estime le transfert de sens inadéquat. Il "recourt à la langue maternelle par re-création" ou transpose en français l'idée ou le sentiment contenu dans l'expression en langue maternelle. L'auteur pense que ce procédé "se manifeste dans l'oeuvre par le recours constant du romancier à des éléments de la littérature orale. Mais aucune fois, ils y apparaissent en langue maternelle. Ils sont toujours traduits très librement" (op.cit. 303). L'écrivain n'est plus soumis ici aux contraintes de fidélité envers les structures grammaticales de sa langue maternelle et du français qu'il peut recréer à son gré avec maîtrise par renouvellement d'images comme on le voit dans les romans de Ahmadou Kourouma.

Le troisième cas se produit quand l'écrivain transcrit en langue maternelle des expressions ou énoncés jugés difficilement traduisibles en français. Cette troisième possibilité se manifeste souvent dans le roman africain par des anthroponymes, des toponymes, noms d'objets, d'animaux ou d'arbres, et plus souvent par l'insertion d'expressions figées comme les proverbes, les dictons ou des chansons.

Consequences methodologiques

De ces analyses Makouta-Mboukou tire certaines conséquences pour le critique littéraire. Pour l'auteur, c'est la notion de signe qui est au centre du dispositif méthodologique, c'est-à-dire "toute unité de sens": monème, syntagme, énoncé plus long ou un texte de roman entier. Le sens est la propriété du texte (combinaison de signes dans une situation donnée de parole) tandis que la signification est propre au signe. Makouta-Mboukou retient donc que le langage d'un texte romanesque est formé par l'ensemble des signes qui forment le tissu d'un roman. Ce langage "peut être celui de toute une communauté culturelle ou particulier à un homme".

Le critique littéraire devra "montrer, par l'analyse du langage, si le signe, le système de signes a été judicieusement utilisé, s'il est apte, en d'autres termes, à porter et à révéler le message de l'auteur" (op.cit. 271). Il devra particulièrement être attentif au double système linguistique qui habite l'écrivain africain, notamment "constamment être attentif aux nombreux sous-entendus, aux idées inachevées, aux trahisons sémantiques commises par le traducteur infidèle, les auteurs eux-mêmes. C'est ce qui (...) fait apparaître la critique d'un roman négro-africain comme infiniment plus délicate et plus difficile que celle d'un roman d'auteur français" (op.cit. 280).

Telle est, dans ses traits essentiels, la position de Makoutou-Mboukou. Mais que conclure? La traduction doit tenir compte de la relation du sens, du texte et du contexte. Le contexte est tout l'environnement culturel supporté par le texte, la "vision du monde" propre à chaque langue, comme le disent W. v. Humboldt et G. Mounin.

Par ailleurs un texte est défini par des multiples interférences qui le tissent. La traduction est possible parce qu'il y a interférence entre deux langages. Elle n'est pas un échange de signes mais la compréhension d'un sens. Makouta-Mboukou semble avoir cerné le problème de la lecture du roman africain. Mais les exigences de connaissances anthropologiques encyclopédiques que sa position pose pour le lecteur paraissent exorbitantes.

Pour une lecture du langage intégral

Que ce soit chez Mveng ou chez Makouta-Mboukou, ce qui est central c'est le langage et, par ricochet, l'homme dialogal. L'homme africain, comme tout être humain, est par nature dialogal. Mais "dialogue" est à prendre dans un sens large, c'est-à-dire non pas seulement comme couple question/réponse mais comme interlocution générale: l'interaction linguistique en face à face; toutes les instances dialogales entre deux partenaires; les échanges de paroles à plus de deux partenaires (plurilogues) (Hagège: 1985); toute expression de réciprocité entre partenaires. Ainsi, sur le plan linguistique, les questions, injonctions, négations y tiennent des rôles manifestes et latents.

En élargissant le champ, il faut inclure tous les secteurs de la communication interculturelle qui s'opère dans un espace linguistique individuel (aspect subjectif). L'énonceur est psychosocial. Il réunit en lui comme le souligne Hagège tous les types des usages de la langue en fonction des situations. (...) "Il est à la fois, selon les circonstances, le locuteur qui prononce et l'énonciateur qui agit; tout comme il est à la fois, quand ce n'est pas lui qui parle, l'allocutaire, auquel sont adressés les mots, et le destinataire des actes de langage, ainsi que, si l'on se plaît à ces catégorisations, le narrataire à qui s'adresse un narrateur" (Hagège: 1985, 239). La communication interculturelle s'exerce dans les représentations de l'Autre, dans le mimétisme comportemental, dans toute la symbolique gestuelle. On entre ici dans une phénoménologie linguistique existentielle. Nous sommes là dans la "théâtralisation du corps parlant" (Ladmiral) dans laquelle les Africains sont passés maîtres (Ngal: 1972; Octave: 1981, 97-98).

Le théâtral comme structure et construction

Dans les civilisations africaines traditionnelles toute création littéraire s'accomplit dans la théâtralisation. Celle-ci constitue le fond permanent des cultures africaines et structure les oeuvres. La conceptualisation que j'en avais effectué notait, en 1972, les rapports suivants: le discours de l'artiste a un caractère dialogique et référé à la culture et à la communauté. La communauté et la culture n'interviennent pas de l'extérieur. Transposé en termes linguistiques habituels, ce discours comporte les composantes suivantes: un locuteur (producteur, énonciateur, narrateur), interlocuteur (communauté: auditeur, narrataire), une thématique porteuse de sens (relecture des traditions), héritage dont le contenu est doté de sens, et une référence, c'est-à-dire ce au sujet de quoi on parle à la communauté. La relation entre ces quatre éléments s'effectue théâtralement. La relecture de la tradition n'est rien d'autre que ce qu'on appelle aujourd'hui intertextualité ou dialogue avec les textes du passé, élargis aussi bien aux textes de la tradition orale africaine qu'à ceux de l'interculturel (d'autres traditions littéraires). Ce qui a pu faire dire à Todorov: "l'interculturel est constitutif du culturel". Les sens (manifestes et cachés) n'émergent qu'à partir de cette intertextualité. L'homme théâtral institue un auditeur et un locuteur. C'est ce schéma communicationnel, inspiré du conteur, que je privilégie dans la lecture des oeuvres littéraires africaines. Ces éléments de la théorie littéraire se trouvent épars et romancés dans mes trois textes essentiels: "L'artiste africain: tradition, critique et liberté créatrice" (1972); *Giambatista Viko ou le viol du Discours Africain (1975) et L'Errance (1979).*

LE SCHEMA IDEAL DU CONTEUR ET LE ROMAN

Il est bien des romans africains très proches du style de communication du conteur. Dussoutour-Hammer le caractérise de la manière suivante. Le narrateur s'adresse directement à son public: "par la parole, l'intonation, le geste, la mimique, la danse, le chant, le silence, agit sur les gens qui l'écoutent, le regardent. Les réactions de ceux-ci se répercutent sur lui. Entre le conteur et l'auditoire se créent des liens, des échanges. Selon son talent personnel et le climat du lien, les deux se renforçant l'un l'autre, il pourra allonger le récit, ajouter une explication, faire une réflexion, poser une question, répondre à une intervention, un rire, un défi, mimer une scène, danser une danse. Ses jongleries de langage, sa virtuosité, son ingéniosité à dénouement sont connus. Passionnante sera alors l'attente ainsi prolongée de l'attendu" (Dussoutour-Hammer: 1976, 27). Style formel éminemment érigé en héritage porteur de sens parce qu'il est langage, formulable en propositions. Style corporel que l'écriture récupère.

Ce schéma se trouve plus ou moins réalisé dans maints romans africains. On serait tenté de dire qu'on a affaire à un héritage culturel de la tradition. Le récit du *Débrouillard* (1964), à la première personne, commence le texte non par "l'acte de naissance de l'auteur", mais par l'acte de naissance du discours. Le "je" qui implique le "tu", le "vous", mime la communication directe avec un interlocuteur imaginaire. La relation unissant le "je" à "vous" semble du type "défi à relever": "croyez-moi que"; "vous verrez que ...", "vous saurez comment on traitait les enfants africains", etc. Le style est du type dialogal. Le narrateur garde le contact permanent avec le narrataire. Celui-ci participe activement, du moins dans *Giambatista Viko* et dans l'*Errance*, au processus d'élaboration et de lecture du texte. On retrouve le même schéma d'interlocution dans *Le roi Albert d'Effidi* (1976). Dans les romans de Seydou Badian, on rencontre la même structure. Mme Nora-Alexandra Kazi-Tani montre que certains procédés, qui peuvent causer une "certaine irritation au lecteur occidental", "manifestent sur le plan de l'énonciation (...) (l'intention) de cet auteur malien de maintenir le 'contact' avec son narrataire d'une manière particulièrement tendue" (Kazi-Tani: 1985: 413). Ce "narrataire apparaît comme capable de "lire" tous les éléments culturellement connotés, notamment ceux de la tradition orale" (ibidem). Les romans se déroulent dans une "teinte émotionnelle". L'auteur arrive même à dresser les portraits du narrataire et du narrateur. Le narrataire postulé par Seydou Badian n'est autre que la communauté des jeunes du village d'abord, ensuite ceux de la nation malienne invitée à assumer l'idéologie antimoderne. La conclusion de Kazi-Tani paraît pertinente: "Le choix du narrataire, la subversion de certaines normes du roman réaliste "classique" par des procédés caractéristiques de la littérature orale (comme le recours aux procédés du théâtre populaire, le "dialogue" explicite avec le public, les énigmes qu'on "pose" à un moment donné du récit et que l'on "résout" par la suite, les jeux de mots, l'usage des proverbes destinés à stimuler le travail de réflexion, etc. ...), traduisent chez le narrateur une préoccupation d'ordre didactique ..." (Ibidem). Il n'est donc pas exagéré de dire que le narrateur chez Seydou est théâtral ou dialogal. Chez A. Kourouma, les procédés de prise de contact entre le narrateur et le public sont plus variés. Celui-ci est tantôt pris à témoin ("vous les connaissez bien", p.46), tantôt observé dans son rôle de participant au récit. Ses moindres réactions sont relevées: "vous paraissez sceptiques!" (p. 17). Le narrateur, par contre, s'autocorrige souvent: "Donc c'est possible, d'ailleurs sûr, que ... (p. 5)". Il renforce sa position de meneur de jeu par des interpellations destinées au public. L'oeuvre tient son sens et son existence comme oeuvre de l'autre, par la médiation de l'autre. Celle-ci est constitutive de son sens. On pourrait multiplier les exemples. En rapprochant ces analyses de la théorie de Michel Charles (*Rhétorique de la lecture*, 1977), on dira qu'on a affaire à une rhétorique orientée vers le destinataire ou à une poétique qui, selon Roman Jakobson, ne met plus l'accent sur l'orientation du message vers lui-même dès lors que, comme le rapporte Ricoeur, "le message qui est à lui-même sa propre finalité *se questionne*" (Charles: 1977, 78; Ricoeur: 1985, 240).

Que devient alors la dichotomie des couples écriture/oralité, écriture/lecture, auteur pluriel/auteur singulier, auteur/lecteur, producteur/consommateur de texte, narrateur/ narrataire, identité/distinction des genres? Tout est saisi ici dans la dynamique de l'"identification" et de la "distinction" par le jeu de la théâtralisation. S'il faut poser, avec Paul

Ricoeur (*Temps et récit III*) la question de savoir où réside l'"identité narrative" (l'identité personnelle narrative du personnage et l'identité propre à l'intrigue sans laquelle celle du personnage n'existerait pas) dans la littérature africaine, la réponse est à chercher dans l'interaction et "relativisation des dimensions écrite et orale" (Octave: 1981: 97) et à cette instance de la création artistique.

Je voudrais terminer ces propos par une confirmation cherchée chez les psychanalystes. Ceux-ci parlent, en effet, de "la reprise du corps dans l'écriture", de "récupérer le corps dans le style", de "traces du corps dans l'écriture" (Anzieu: 1981). Un récit est "non pas raconter un événement, mais rendre le rythme, la vitesse, la lenteur, les méandres, les coupures, les éclatements avec lesquels un événement (extérieur ou intérieur) a été vécu, ou est revécu, par une ou par plusieurs consciences" (Anzieu: 1981, 180). Le style africain est une reprise du corps théâtral de l'homme africain. Ainsi Thomas Melone peut-il écrire au sujet de l'oeuvre de Mongo Beti: "L'art personnel, le style, grâce à la contribution de tout l'arsenal de moyens de communication qu'il peut inventer - paroles parlées, gestes, rythmes, mélodies, danses, silence, etc. - sert alors d'outil fondamental pour rehausser l'éclat, souligner l'atmosphère dramatique du déploiement de l'oeuvre" (Melone: 1971, 252).

OUVRAGES CITES ET CONSULTES

Ablegmagnon, N. *Sociologie des sociétés orales d'Afrique noire*. Paris: Mouton, 1969.

Adotevi, S. *Négritude et négrologues*. Paris: 10/18, 1972.

Afrique Littéraire et Artistique, *Critique et réception des littératures africaines*, n° 50, Paris, 1979.

Angenot, M. et al. *Théorie littéraire*. Paris: PUF, 1989.

Anozie, S. *Sociologie du roman africain: réalisme, structure et détermination dans le roman moderne ouest-africain*. Paris: Aubier-Montaigne, 1970.

Anzieu, D. et al. *Psychanalyse et langage*. Paris: Dunod, 1981.

Austin, J.L. *Quand dire, c'est faire*. Intr. et traduction de G. Lane. Paris: Seuil, 1970.

Bal, M. *Narratologie. Les instances du récit*. Paris: Klincksieck, 1977.

Bakhtine, M. *Esthétique et théorie du roman*. Traduction de Daria Olivier. Paris: Gallimard, 1978.

Bouchindhomme Ch. et al. *Temps et Récit de P. Ricoeur en débat*. Cerf, 1990.

Bremond Cl. *La logique du récit*. Paris: Seuil, 1973.

Charles, M. *Rhétorique de la lecture*. Paris: Seuil, 1977.

CNRS (Collectif). *La narrativité*. Paris: CNRS, 1980.

CONFRONTATION (Cahiers), *L'interprétation*. n° 17, Paris, 1987.

Coquery-Vidrovitch, C. *Afrique noire. Permanences et ruptures*. Paris: Payot, 1985.

CRITIQUE (revue). *Confrontations philosophiques*. n° 464-465, janvier-février, Paris, 1986.

Descombes, V. *Grammaire d'objets en tous genres*. Paris: Éd. de Minuit, 1983.

Diawara, F. *Le manifeste de l'homme primitif*. Paris: Grasset, 1972.

Dussutour-Hammer, M. *Amos Tutuola: Tradition orale et écriture du conte*. Paris: Présence Africaine, 1975.

Finnegan, R. *Oral Poetry: Its nature, significance and social context*. Cambridge: Cambridge University Press, 1977.

Hagège, Cl. *L'homme de paroles*. Paris: Fayard, 1985.

Gadamer, H.G. *Vérité et méthode: les grandes lignes d'une herméneutique philosophique*. Paris: Seuil, 1973.

Greimas, A.J. *Du sens*. Paris: Seuil, 1970.

──────. *Sémiotique: dictionnaire raisonné de la théorie du langage*. Paris: Hachette, 1979.

Grondin, J. "Rationalité et agir communicationnel chez Habermas." *Critique*, n° 464-465, janvier-février, 1986, 40-60.

Irele, A. *The African Experience in Literature and Ideology*. Londres: Heinemann, 1986.

Jahn, J. *Muntu: L'homme africain et la néo-africaine*. Paris: Seuil, 1961.

Jauss, H.R. *Pour une esthétique de la réception*, trad. fr. de C. Maillard, préface de J. Starobinski, Gallimard, 1978. "La jouissance esthétique. Les expériences fondamentales de la poièsis, de l'aisthèsis et de la catharsis", in Poétique n° 39, Paris: Seuil, 1979, 261-274.

──────. *Pour une herméneutique littéraire*. Paris: Gallimard, 1985.

Kazi-Tani, Nora-A. *La signification du recours au mythe dans l'oeuvre romanesque de Seydou Badian* (mémoire de magister, Université d'Alger, 1985) inédit.

Kristeva, J. *Le texte du roman*. Paris: Mouton, 1970.

Krysinski, Wl. *Carrefours de signes: essais sur le roman moderne*. Paris: Mouton, 1981.

Ladmiral, J. R., et Lipiansky, E. M. *La communication interculturelle*. Paris: Armand Colin, 1989.

Locha, M. *La littérature africaine et sa critique*. Paris: Karthala, 1986.

Makouta-Mboukou, Jean-Pierre. Introduction à la littérature noire. Yaoundé: 1970.

──────. Introduction à l'étude du roman négro-africain de langue française. Dakar u.a.: Les Nouvelles Editions Africaines, 1980.

Melone, Thomas. *Mongo Beti, l'homme et le destin*. Paris: Présence Africaine, 1971.

Meschonnic, H. *Pour la poétique I*. Paris: Gallimard, 1976.

──────. *Critique du rythme*. Paris: Verdier, 1982.

Mounin, G. *Les problèmes théoriques de la traduction*. Paris: Gallimard, 1963.

Mouralis, B. *Individu et collectivité dans le roman négro-africain d'expression française*. Abidjan: Annales de Université, 1969.

──────. *Littérature et développement*. Paris: Silex, 1984.

Mveng, E. "Introduction à l'herméneutique négro-africaine" in *Le critique africain et son peuple comme producteur de civilisation*. Colloque de Yaounde, 16-20 avril 1973, Paris: Présence Africaine, 1977.

Ngal (M.a M.), *Giambatista Viko ou le viol du Discours africain*: récit. Paris: Hatier, 1984.

Octave (Collectif). *Demain l'Afrique*. Paris: PUF, 1981.

Paulme, D. *La mère dévorante*. Paris: Gallimard, 1976.

Petitot, J. "Schématisme et interprétation ou la logique transcendantale comme ontologie herméneutique." *Cahiers Confrontation* 17, 1987.

Présence Africaine. *Le critique africain et son peuple comme producteur de civilisation* (colloque). Paris: Présence Africaine, 1977.

Quéré, L. "L'interprétation en sociologie." *Cahiers Confrontation* 17, 1987.

Rastier, F. *Sémantique interprétative*. Paris: PUF, 1987.

Revue des Sciences Humaines, 158, *Problèmes de la traduction*, 1975.

Ricoeur, P. *Temps et Récit I, 1983; II, 1984 et III, 1985*. Paris: Seuil.

──────. *Du texte à l'action. Essais d'herméneutique, II*. Paris: Seuil, 1986.

──────. *Soi-même comme un autre*. Paris: Seuil, 1990.

Senghor, L.S. *Liberté I*, 1964; *II*, 1971; *III*, 1977 et *IV*, 1983. Paris: Seuil.

Soyinka, W. Myth and Literature and the African Word. Cambridge University Press, 1976.

Szegedy-Maszak, M. "Le texte comme structure et construction." Ed. Angenot, Marc et al. *Théorie littéraire*. Paris: PUF, 1989, 183-219.

Todorov, T. *Mikhaïl Bakhtine. Le principe dialogique*. Paris: Seuil, 1981. *Symbolisme et interprétation*. Paris: Seuil, 1977. *Les genres du discours*. Seuil. *Théorie de la littérature*. Paris: Seuil/Poétique.

Turner, V.W. *Les tambours d'affliction: analyse des rituels chez les Ndembu de Zambie*. Traduction de Marie-Claire Giraud. Paris: Gallimard, 1972.

Vernier, F. *Une science du littéraire est-elle possible?* Paris: Nouvelle Critique, 1972.

Wellek, R., et A. Warren. *La théorie littéraire*. Paris: Seuil/Poétique, 1971.

LITERARY THEORY AND AFRICAN LITERATURE
edited by J. Gugler, H.-J. Lüsebrink, J. Martini
Münster/Hamburg 1993, pp. 63-73

LA LITTERATURE NEGRO-AFRICAINE DE LANGUE FRANÇAISE: PRISE DE PAROLE ET SITUATION DE COMMUNICATION

BERNARD MOURALIS

Dès ses premières manifestations - *Batouala* (1921), *Légitime Défense* (1932), *Pigments* (1937), *Cahier d'un retour au pays natal* (1939), etc. -, la littérature négro-africaine peut apparaître comme une *prise de parole*, comme une parole qui vient des Africains et qui se substitue désormais au discours que l'Europe tient traditionnellement sur l'Afrique et dans lequel les Africains ne se faisaient entendre que dans la mesure où on voulait bien leur *prêter la parole*, en les faisant parler (dans les fictions mettant en scène des Africains ou des Antillais) ou en recueillant les propos d'individus réels, comme le fit Westermann dans ses *Autobiographies d'Africains* (1943).

Dès lors, l'historiographie et la critique qui s'intéressent à la littérature africaine sont tentées d'envisager la naissance de celle-ci et son fonctionnement comme une illustration caractéristique de ce que Jakobson (1963) appelle la "fonction (...) expressive ou émotive, centrée sur le destinateur" et qui "vise à une expression directe de l'attitude du sujet à l'égard de ce dont il parle" (p. 214). Perspective qui conduit ainsi à opposer, d'un côté, une parole nouvelle, brute, "primitive" - "intempestive", en somme -, et, de l'autre, un cadre institutionnel, marqué notamment par les contraintes inhérentes au système colonial (ou impérialiste) et contre lequel ou à travers les interstices duquel se développerait cette parole neuve.

On le voit en particulier dans l'intérêt que la recherche ou la critique ont fréquemment manifesté pour la question des *origines* de la littérature africaine et qui se traduit, comme j'ai eu l'occasion de le souligner dans *Littérature et développement* (1984), par la mise en place de deux conceptions concernant la naissance de cette littérature: "la maturation progressive", plus ou moins dialectique, et "la mutation brusque" (p. 229).

Cette façon de procéder, en dépit des schémas réducteurs auxquels elle a pu conduire, par exemple chez Fanon, dans *Les Damnés de la terre*

(1961), a sans aucun doute le mérite de bien souligner l'enjeu qu'a représenté, à travers ses premiers textes, la littérature négro-africaine.

Celle-ci a été une opération visant à substituer au discours européen considéré jusqu'alors comme le seul que l'on pouvait légitimement tenir sur l'Afrique et le monde noir une parole proprement africaine autochtone. Processus d'émergence d'un sujet africain qui ne fut pendant longtemps qu'un objet, qu'un référent du discours européen. D'où l'importance qu'il convient d'accorder à l'irruption dans le champ littéraire d'un locuteur qui s'exprime à la première personne. *Je* romanesque, "réel" chez Camara Laye (1953): "J'étais enfant et je jouais près de la case de mon père" (p. 9) ou fictif chez Mongo Beti (1956): "Catherine s'est approchée de moi; elle m'a saisi par les épaules comme faisait ma mère et elle a enlevé mon caleçon. J'étais stupéfait mais je l'ai laissée faire. Elle m'a lavé en me frottant longuement entre mes cuisses" (p. 122). *Je* poétique chez David Diop (1961):

> Alors mère je pense à toi
> A tes belles paupières brûlées par les années
> A ton sourire sur mes nuits d'hôpital
> Ton sourire qui disait les vieilles misères vaincues
> O mère mienne et qui est celle de tous
> Du nègre qu'on aveugla et qui revoit les fleurs (p. 9).

Ces quelques énoncés qui peuvent sembler aller de soi constituent pourtant, si l'on y réfléchit bien, un véritable bouleversement par rapport à toute une tradition: Caliban parle.

Une telle perspective présente cependant en même temps l'inconvénient de reprendre le schéma en définitive peu opératoire opposant une parole "nue", "primordiale", et une parole instituée et institutionnelle que l'Europe tenterait d'imposer à l'Afrique. Cette façon de voir n'est pas sans rappeler la conception qui a été développée, à partir de la fin du XVIIIe siècle et tout au long de l'époque romantique, à propos de la littérature "populaire", considérée comme l'expression d'une parole naïve, spontanée.

En fait, les choses sont plus complexes. Cette parole africaine a beau se donner à entendre comme "cri" qui viendrait se substituer à la parole européenne, elle n'en demeure pas moins insérée dans tout un ensemble de contextes institutionnels qui renvoient à la fois à l'Afrique et à l'Europe. Ignorer la façon dont un texte, à telle ou telle époque ou dans telle ou telle région du monde noir, s'inscrit dans un tissu institutionnel revient à penser que seul l'énoncé doit être pris en compte par la critique ou la recherche. Or, comme on le verra, l'énonciation est un facteur tout aussi essentiel dans la production du sens: "Le procès de communication participe à la délivrance des significations et, plus encore, des valeurs" (p. 99), nous rappelle fort justement Michel Hausser, dans *Pour une poétique de la négritude* (1988).

I.

Une première illustration de ce problème apparaît dans la relation que les écrivains africains entretiennent avec la "tradition" et dans l'usage qu'ils font de celle-ci dans leurs textes. Une analyse des textes montre ainsi que les écrivains qui entendent se référer à la littérature orale et à l'oralité (deux notions qu'il convient de distinguer et qui correspondent mieux à la réalité que l'expression souvent employée de "littérature traditionnelle") usent de trois modalités principales. Ils peuvent en premier lieu introduire dans la trame narrative d'un récit un texte oral qui apparaît ainsi sous la forme d'une *citation*: le narrateur suspend le fil du récit et donne la parole à un personnage qui va dire un conte, un proverbe, une chanson. Ils peuvent également recueillir des textes oraux, les transcrire, les traduire et produire un livre qui sera un *recueil de contes*. Ils peuvent enfin tenter d'introduire dans leurs oeuvres les caractéristiques de la *communication littéraire orale* en substituant à la relation auteur/lecteur la relation interprète/auditoire. C'est ce que l'on observe par exemple dans *Les Soleils des indépendances* (1968) où le narrateur s'efforce d'apparaître tout au long du roman comme un griot.

Ceci dit, reste à savoir quelles sont les modalités de la relation que l'écrivain établit avec la littérature orale et l'oralité. Celles-ci sont de deux sortes. Il y a d'abord le contact personnel que l'écrivain entretient avec cet univers culturel et qui pourra apparaître dans son parcours biographique. Sur ce plan, un des témoignages les plus riches est celui que nous donne Birago Diop, dans l'"Introduction" des *Contes d'Amadou Koumba* (1947), texte a la fois autobiographique et anthropologique qui retrace les différentes formes prises par cette relation, de l'enfance à l'âge adulte, de l'Afrique à l'Europe et de l'Europe à l'Afrique, à travers une dialectique subtile de la mémoire et de la culture.

Mais, en règle générale, et Birago Diop lui-même n'y échappe pas complètement, cette relation de l'écrivain africain avec "sa" culture ne se situe pas dans un cadre totalement autochtone. L'Afrique est inscrite dans une Histoire où l'Europe joue un rôle déterminant, sur le plan politique et économique comme sur le plan culturel. Et, à cet égard, il faut se souvenir que, dès les débuts de son entreprise, le colonisateur met en place un savoir sur l'Afrique et des institutions spécifiques (organismes de recherche, revues, enquêtes, etc.) dont la finalité est à la fois politique (mieux administrer) et scientifique (mieux connaître) auxquels vont être confrontés les Africains et notamment les écrivains. Pour ne retenir qu'un seul exemple, songeons au rôle qu'a pu jouer ce monument qu'a été pour l'Afrique de l'ouest *Haut Sénégal-Niger* (1912) de Maurice Delafosse.

Ce savoir va jouer un rôle de médiation entre l'écrivain et la culture africaine. Il est une clef qui lui est offerte pour tracer l'inventaire de celle-ci et y entrer plus avant, pour passer du vivre au connaître. Mais, en même temps, comme toute médiation, il peut être un obstacle qui s'interpose entre le sujet et l'objet.

Ce caractère d'obstacle tient d'abord au fait que le savoir élaboré par le colonisateur repose sur un certain nombre de choix qui ne sont pas nécessairement les plus vrais mais qui sont dictés par des impératifs plus politiques qu'anthropologiques. Jean Bazin (1985) et Jean-Loup Amselle (1990) ont, sur ce plan, bien montré comment la doctrine française de "politique des races" (formulée notamment par Gallieni) s'inscrit dans le cadre général d'une historiographie européenne qui a privilégié comme modèle explicatif "le principe de la lutte des races" (Amselle, 1990, p. 72) et engendre à propos de l'Afrique une vision qui rend compte "des différents *types* de sociétés présents sur le continent, ainsi que des *stades* auxquels ils sont parvenus" (*ibid.*). Types et stades permettent notamment de repérer des groupes conquis et des groupes conquérants. Une telle démarche postule des discontinuités qui n'existaient pas nécessairement à l'époque pré-coloniale et ouvre la voie à un discours identitaire que le nationalisme africain recevra des mains du colonisateur sans s'interroger outre mesure sur sa validité. Ainsi, on accréditera l'idée d'une culture mandingue ou on s'efforcera de montrer, comme le fait Jacques Fame Ndongo (1985), que l'oeuvre de Mongo Beti est l' expression de la culture pahouine.

Par ailleurs, le chercheur ou l'écrivain qui veut rendre compte de tel ou tel aspect de la culture africaine est rarement un individu qui travaille seul. Son activité s'exerce dans le cadre d'une institution qui, à l'IFAN hier comme à l'université aujourd'hui, lui apporte une aide dans son travail et surtout vient légitimer son discours. C'est dire les contraintes qui peuvent peser sur lui et qui ont été analysées en particulier par V. Y. Mudimbe dans *L'Odeur du Père* (1982) et, également, dans son roman *L'Ecart* (1979). D'où l'intérêt que présentent les tentatives visant à échapper à ces contraintes. Par exemple, la démarche "hérétique" de C. A. Diop, arrachant sur le terrain universitaire le monopole détenu par l'Europe en matière d'histoire africaine, avec sa thèse *Nations nègres et culture* (1954).

Ou encore, celle d'Amadou Hampaté Ba dont l'oeuvre peut être considérée comme un travail très concerté pour sortir du cercle de l'africanisme dont il semble avoir vu très tôt et l'intérêt et les limites. Pour cela, il a fait porter ses efforts dans deux directions. Il est d'abord passé du stade de collaborateur (voire de simple informateur) ou de collecteur de traditions au stade d'*auteur* (ainsi, il est le seul signataire de la deuxième édition de *Vie et enseignement de Tierno Bokar*, 1980). Ensuite, il s'est attaché avec une malice tout à fait digne de Wangrin à brouiller quelques points de repères chers à l'africanisme. Ainsi, il joue de sa double "identité" peul et bambara et invite son lecteur à se dire que tout cela n'est peut-être pas très important. Parallèlement on est en droit de se demander si un récit comme *Kaydara* (1968 et 1978) n'est pas en définitive une sorte de "recherche-fiction" que n'aurait pas désavouée Borges. Enfin, sur un plan plus général, on sera sensible chez lui à cette attitude qui le conduit à mettre l'accent sur *la recherche de la vérité*, beaucoup plus que sur la *vérité*, et qui est à l'opposé de la conception naïve, fort répandue pourtant chez les savants et consistant à penser que le savoir est déjà là, déjà constitué, et qu'il suffit de creuser pour y accéder et en bénéficier.

II.

Des remarques analogues pourraient être faites à propos de la littérature de la négritude. Envisagée sous l'angle de ses contenus thématiques, celle-ci peut apparaître à juste titre comme une production littéraire qui se propose tout à la fois de protester contre la situation faite à l'homme noir, dans le régime esclavagiste comme dans le système colonial, et de montrer l'éminente dignité de la culture négro-africaine, traditionnellement niée ou bafouée par l'Europe. Ce que résument bien les vers célèbres de Jacques Roumain dans son poème *Bois d'ébène* (1939):

> Afrique j'ai gardé ta mémoire Afrique
> tu es en moi
> comme l'écharde dans la blessure
> comme un fétiche tutélaire au centre du village (p. 232).

Mais, en dépit de l'indéniable nouveauté du ton qui caractérise ce texte ou tant d'autres, ce double mouvement n'est pas totalement autochtone. Ainsi, le souci de défense et illustration de la culture négro-africaine s'opère dans la littérature de la négritude écrite entre 1930 et 1950 selon deux modalités principales. Dans un premier cas, les écrivains vont chercher à s'opposer à la conception souvent développée à propos de l'Afrique et qui fait de celle-ci une "table rase" et mettront en avant les réalisations que les peuples africains ont accomplies au cours de leur histoire sur le plan esthétique, intellectuel, littéraire ou politique. Mais, comme on le sait depuis longtemps, l'information utilisée par les écrivains est largement tributaire de l'anthropologie occidentale qui joue de nouveau un rôle de médiation (ambivalente) entre ces derniers et l'Afrique. D'où la mise en place d'une image de l'Afrique qui a pu apparaître comme la forme subtile d'une aliénation, ainsi que le relève un personnage de *L'Isolé Soleil* (1981) de Daniel Maximin : "Tu cherches au plus profond notre essence noire, et c'est chez un ethnologue blanc ! Et nous appelons à l'appui la psychanalyse, l'ethnographie, le marxisme et le surréalisme. Aurons-nous donc toujours besoin d'*eux* et de leurs raisons? A quoi sert de rejeter leur raison si c'est pour adopter leur science ?" (p. 192).

Dans un deuxième cas, la valorisation de la culture négro-africaine va consister à mettre l'accent, non plus sur des *réalisations*, mais sur tout ce qui la sépare de la civilisation occidentale. Celle-ci, dans son projet prométhéen, veut connaître et dominer le monde. Le négro-africain, au contraire, comme l'écrit Césaire dans le *Cahier*, est "poreux à tous les souffles du monde", "insoucieux de dompter, mais jouant le jeu du monde" (p. 72), il se fond dans le cosmos, il se glorifie de n'avoir "jamais su dompter la vapeur ni l'électricité" (p. 68) et ne peut éprouver que de la "pitié" pour ses "vainqueurs omniscients et naïfs" (p. 73).

Mais, là encore, l'écrivain de la négritude emprunte largement à tout un courant de la pensée occidentale qui depuis le XVIe siècle, avec la découverte de l'Amérique, valorise le "sauvage" et discrédite le "civilisé". Et, de ce point de vue, la notion de "mentalité primitive" développée par Lévy-Bruhl n'est qu'un nouvel avatar du thème. Le rapport que l'homme noir entretient avec le monde, tel que le définit Senghor dans ses essais, puis Sartre dans *Orphée noir* (1948), reprend un des éléments essentiels de la "mentalité primitive": la fusion du sujet et de l'objet et l'incapacité où se trouve le sujet de se percevoir distinct de l'objet. Le thème permet aussi de définir la colonisation, non comme un conflit entre deux civilisations, mais comme l'irruption violente de la "civilisation" dans un espace jusqu'alors harmonieux et heureux parce que soumis à la loi naturelle. Schéma déjà envisagé par Montaigne et Diderot dans le *Supplément au voyage de Bougainville* (1778-1779).

En revanche, si l'on tient compte de la situation de communication que les écrivains de cette époque tentent d'instaurer, la littérature de la négritude risque de nous apparaître dans une dimension sensiblement différente. A cet égard, on notera tout d'abord que la protestation contre l'ordre colonial est fréquemment l'occasion d'affirmer une solidarité avec d'autres catégories d'opprimés, victimes eux aussi d'une discrimination sociale et/ou raciale: le prolétariat et les Juifs. Le climat menaçant des années 30, marqué notamment par le fascisme et le nazisme, est largement présent chez Senghor, Damas ou Césaire pour lesquels la défense de l'homme noir doit se situer par rapport à des valeurs universelles susceptibles de mobiliser tous les hommes épris de justice.

Parallèlement, sur le plan de ce qu'on pourrait appeler la stratégie littéraire, il faut être sensible à la façon dont les écrivains de la négritude tentent de s'insérer dans le réseau de la production européenne ou mondiale en conférant tout simplement à des oeuvres comme *Pigments* ou le *Cahier* le statut *d'oeuvre littéraire*, au même titre que *Capitale de la douleur* ou *Nadja*. Georges Hardy préface *Doguicimi* mais ce sera Desnos qui présentera, dans sa première édition, *Pigments*: il y a là plus qu'une nuance.

Le rôle de Paris comme lieu de production et d'édition d'une part importante de la littérature de la négritude risque de prendre du coup une autre signification. Paris, lieu d'exil sans doute, mais aussi espace prestigieux où s'opère la légitimation des textes littéraires. *Présence Africaine* peut ainsi apparaître au lendemain de la guerre comme une revue comparable par le travail dont elle est le théâtre à *Esprit* ou aux *Temps modernes* - ces publications ayant d'ailleurs des collaborateurs communs.

On voit ainsi se dessiner ce qu'a pu être l'un des enjeux essentiels de la littérature de la négritude: il s'est agi pour les écrivains qui en furent les promoteurs d'échapper à une folklorisation où on voulait les enfermer et de produire une parole dotée d'un statut proprement littéraire, et non plus régional ou périphérique. Ceux-ci ont voulu apparaître avant tout comme des *écrivains* et cette revendication marque en particulier de façon pathétique, puisqu'elle va jusqu'au suicide, l'itinéraire exemplaire à cet égard de Rabéarivelo qui voit dans la conquête de ce statut le seul moyen de sortir de sa condition de colonisé.

III.

La critique et la recherche font preuve depuis une dizaine d'années environ d'un intérêt marqué pour ce que l'on peut appeler la question des littératures nationales en Afrique. Cette orientation dont témoignent nombre de colloques et de publications répond à un souci légitime de rendre compte de la diversité de la production littéraire en Afrique noire. Et, dans cette perspective, il est intéressant de se demander si la production littéraire ne prend pas des formes spécifiques selon les pays ou, tout au moins, les régions. Les réponses apportées à cette question montrent à l'évidence qu'il existe des particularités qui autorisent à parler de "littérature sénégalaise", de "littérature ivoirienne", de "littérature zaïroise", de "littérature congolaise" ou de "littérature camerounaise".

Les particularités relevées pour procéder à ces regroupements par pays ou par région sont de deux sortes. Les unes renvoient aux référents présents dans les textes de tel ou tel pays. Ainsi, pour ne retenir qu'un exemple, l'existence de l'Islam au Sénégal, d'une part, et le développement en Afrique centrale (Congo, Zaïre) des mouvements politico-religieux (Kibanguisme, Matsouanisme), d'autre part, déterminent des univers littéraires sensiblement différents.

Les autres renvoient à des aspects institutionnels. En dépit d'une histoire coloniale commune (qui elle-même est diversifiée), l'évolution des différents pays africains depuis leur accession à l'indépendance ne s'est pas déroulée de façon uniforme. En particulier, les options idéologiques prises par tel ou tel régime, les conceptions qui en découlent dans l'exercice du pouvoir, la présence ou l'absence (avec tous les intermédiaires possibles entre les deux) d'espaces de liberté ont une incidence directe sur la forme que peut prendre la production littéraire. Ainsi, il existe des pays où, sans que la situation soit toujours facile pour eux, les écrivains peuvent travailler et ont leur place: Congo, Côte d'Ivoire, Sénégal. D'autres au contraire où l'écrivain ne peut que choisir l'exil: Zaïre, Guinée du temps de Sékou Touré.

Le cas du Cameroun est à cet égard intéressant. L'une de ses figures les plus marquantes, Mongo Beti, vit en France. L'autre, F. Oyono, paraît être entré depuis longtemps dans un silence définitif. Mais, pour le reste, le Cameroun peut apparaître comme un pays dont la production littéraire est importante, active, diversifiée et qui bénéficie de l'existence d'une presse qui accorde de l'intérêt à la littérature ainsi que d'un réseau éditorial (CLE, SOPECAM).

On a souvent insisté sur le caractère régionaliste de la littérature camerounaise volontiers présentée comme une littérature du "terroir", bon enfant et peu attirée par la spéculation ou les recherches formelles. *L'Homme-Dieu de Bisso* (1974) d'Etienne Yanou pouvant sur ce plan être considéré comme un prototype.

Mais, si l'on entre plus avant dans la connaissance de l'institution littéraire camerounaise, on découvrira une réalité quelque peu différente.

C'est ce qu'a fait en particulier Ambroise Kom dans deux articles: "La tentation de l'institué: *Une vie à l'envers* de Patrice Etoundi Mballa" (1988) et "Littératures nationales et instances de légitimation: le cas du Cameroun" (1990). Sans entrer dans le détail de cette enquête minutieuse, je me contenterai de rappeler les deux faits essentiels que met en lumière l'auteur de ces articles.

Kom montre d'abord qu'à la différence de ce qui se passe dans nombre d'Etats africains où ils sont marginalisés, les intellectuels au Cameroun sont très présents dans l'appareil d'Etat et tentent de fonder leur légitimité sur leurs titres universitaires. Ainsi, Hubert Mono Ndjana, auteur de *L'Idée sociale chez Paul Biya* (1985), est titulaire d'un doctorat en philosophie et enseigne à l'université de Yaoundé (qui a d'ailleurs édité cet ouvrage).

Parallèlement, l'appareil d'Etat intervient de façon très concertée dans la vie littéraire en faisant interférer trois instances essentielles: les responsables proches du pouvoir, la presse, l'édition contrôlée par l'Etat (SOPECAM). Si bien qu'on en arrive à une vraie manipulation: on écrit un livre, on l'édite, on organise sa promotion grace à la presse et/ou en le consacrant meilleur livre de l'année. Ce *on* étant totalement absorbé dans le pouvoir. De la sorte, l'écrivain se voit en somme dépossédé de ses prérogatives, il cesse d'être le moteur premier de la vie littéraire.

Quant à l'objectif visé par une telle stratégie, il consiste essentiellement à contrôler le contenu des écrits en montrant qu'un "bon" livre doit véhiculer une certaine idéologie. Les intellectuels au service de cette cause n'hésiteront pas au besoin à condamner les oeuvres les plus marquantes de la littérature négro-africaine. C'est ce que fait, par exemple, Jacques Famé Ndongo, écrivant dans *Le Prince et le scribe* (1988): "Car, au fait, il ne manque guère d'esprits doués et caustiques pour présenter la contrepartie des romans comme *Le Devoir de violence*, *Les Soleils des indépendances*, *Le Cercle des tropiques*, etc. Les universités africaines et les divers instituts de recherche, (...) regorgent de "cerveaux" pouvant tenir la dragée haute à la "classe contestante" en produisant (...) des romans soulignant les vertus de l'unité nationale et du progrès économique dans la paix en exhortant tous les Africains à s'unir pour bâtir un continent fort et prospère" (p. 316). Précisons que l'auteur de ces lignes a une solide formation universitaire et qu'il est chargé de mission à la Présidence de la République.

IV.

L'examen de ces différentes situations permettra de définir quelques uns des problèmes que pose l'analyse des textes littéraires négro-africains. L'étude des motifs thématiques et des procédés d'écriture reste bien entendu un préalable nécessaire. Mais une approche de ce type n'épuise pas le sens des textes.

Celui-ci apparaît aussi à travers la situation de communication dans laquelle se place ou que tente d'instaurer l'écrivain africain ou antillais. Et, comme on l'a vu, les exemples donnés précédemment montrent de quelle façon la prise en compte de cette situation de communication renouvelle, voire contredit, l'idée que l'on pouvait avoir d'un même texte.

Cette dialectique entre une approche purement textuelle et un examen de la situation de discours me paraît être une voie intéressante pour la critique ou la recherche. Ceci dit, il ne faudrait pas la réduire à quelque chose de schématique qui opposerait le dedans et le dehors du texte, une approche interne et approche externe de type sociologique. En effet, la situation de communication n'apparaît pas seulement dans le fonctionnement de l'institution littéraire. Elle est lisible aussi, à travers toute une série d'indices, dans les textes eux-mêmes, et la tâche du critique ou du chercheur est de les repérer en se demandant pourquoi, par exemple, J. Fame Ndongo s'attache avec tant d'insistance à montrer que l'oeuvre de Mongo Beti ne peut se comprendre que par référence à l'esthétique pahouine dont elle serait une expression exemplaire.

OUVRAGES CITES

Amselle, Jean-Loup. *Logiques métisses: anthropologie de l'identité en Afrique et ailleurs.* Paris: Payot, 1990.

Bâ, Amadou Hampaté. *Kaïdara: conte initiatique peul.* Abidjan: NEA, 1978.

―――――. *Vie et enseignement de Tierno Bokar: le sage de Bandiagara.* Paris: Seuil, 1980.

――――― et Marcel Cardaire. *Tierno Bokar: le sage de Bandiagara.* Paris: Présence Africaine, 1957.

――――― et Lilyan Kesteloot. *Kaïdara: récit initiatique peul.* Paris: Julliard, 1969.

Bazin, Jean. "A chacun son Bambara." *Au Coeur de l'ethnie: ethnies, tribalisme et etat en Afrique.* Ed. Jean-Loup Amselle et Elikia M'bokolo. Paris: La Découverte, 1985.

Césaire, Aimé. *Cahier d'un retour au pays natal.* Paris: Présence Africaine, 1960.

Damas, Léon-Goutran. *Pigments.* Paris: Présence Africaine, 1972.

Delafosse, Maurice. *Haut-Sénégal-Niger.* Paris: Maisonneuve et Larose, 1972.

Diop, Birago. *Les Contes d'Amadou Koumba.* Paris: Présence Africaine, 1961.

Diop, Cheikh Anta. *Nations nègres et culture.* Paris: Présence Africaine, 1965.

Diop, David. *Coups de pilon.* Paris: Présence Africaine, 1973.

Fame Ndongo, Jacques. *L'Esthétique romanesque de Mongo Beti: essai sur les sources traditionnelles de l'écriture moderne en Afrique.* Paris: ABC/Présence Africaine, 1985.

———. *Le Prince et le scribe: lecture politique et esthétique du roman négro-africain post-colonial*. Paris: Berger-Levrault, 1988.

Fanon, Frantz. *Les Damnés de la terre*. Paris: Maspero, 1961.

Hausser, Michel. *Pour une poétique de la négritude*. Paris: Silex, 1988.

Hazoumé, Paul. *Doguicimi*. Préface de G. Hardy. Paris: Larose, 1938.

Jakobson, Roman. *Essais de linguistique générale*. Paris: Minuit, 1963.

Kom, Ambroise, "La tentation de l'institué: *une Vie à l'envers* de Patrice Etoundi Mballa". *Peuples Noirs, Peuples Africains* 59-62 (1987-88): 229-39.

———. "Littératures nationales et instances de légitimation: le cas du Cameroun". *Etudes Françaises*, sous presse.

Kourouma, Ahmadou. *Les Soleils des indépendances*. Paris: Seuil, 1970.

Laye, Camara. *L'Enfant noir*. Paris: Presses Pocket, 1976.

Léro, Etienne, éd. *Légitime défense*. Paris: 1932.

Maran, René. *Batouala: véritable roman nègre*. Paris: Albin Michel, 1921.

Maximin, Daniel. *L'Isolé soleil*. Paris: Seuil, 1981.

Etoundi Mballa, Patrice. *Une Vie à l'envers*. Yaoundé: Sopecam, 1967.

Mongo Beti. *Le Pauvre Christ de Bomba*. Paris: Présence Africaine, 1976.

Mono Ndjana, Hubert. *L'Idée sociale chez Paul Biya*. Yaoundé: Editions de l'Université, 1965.

Mouralis, Bernard. *Littérature et développement: essai sur le statut, la fonction et la représentation de la littérature négro-africaine d'expression francaise*. Paris: Silex, 1984.

Mudimbe, Valentin-Yves. *L'Ecart*. Paris: Présence Africaine, 1979.

———. *L'Odeur du Père*. Paris: Présence Africaine, 1982.

Roumain, Jacques. "Bois d'ébène". *La Montagne ensorcelée*. Paris: Editeurs Français Réunis, 1972.

Sartre, Jean-Paul. "Orphée noir". Préface à Léopold Sedar Senghor. *Anthologie de la nouvelle poésie nègre et malgache de langue française*. Paris: PUF, 1948.

Westermann, D. *Autobiographies d'Africains*. Traduction F. de L. Homburger. Paris: Payot, 1943.

Yanou, Etienne. *L'Homme-Dieu de Bisso*. Yaoundé: CLE, 1974.

LITERARY THEORY AND AFRICAN LITERATURE
edited by J. Gugler, H.-J. Lüsebrink, J. Martini
Münster/Hamburg 1993, pp. 75-88

OF COLONIAL AND CANONICAL ENCOUNTERS:
A RECIPROCAL READING OF
L'IMMORALISTE AND *UNE VIE DE BOY*

EILEEN JULIEN

My understanding of and interest in literary theory have shifted considerably from graduate school days when I thought that performing a structuralist analysis of an African oral tale was quite a feat -- one to which every graduate student surely aspired. Today there is, of course, much that remains muddled in debates on theory, but of one thing, at least, I am sure: theory is not the equivalent of so much computer software into which (African) variables must be plugged -- either to display one's virtuosity or to valorize marginalized texts so as to raise them to the status of Literature.

The study and teaching of African literature has thus made me what Patricia Hill Collins calls the "outsider within." It has changed me in ways that the study and teaching of European and French literature could not. Or, to be more precise, it is the encounter of these two disciplines that has been extremely instructive.

The works of Ronsard, Molière and Flaubert, for example, seemed to me for many years quintessentially literary (in the traditional sense of the word). That is to say, they were taught to me and I, in turn, read and taught them through the narrowest attention to metaphor and aesthetic detail: "style," point of view, temporal markers, and so on. I began to notice that I taught African texts less "aesthetically." Part of the explanation lay, of course, in the age of the work in question and whether or not its author had been dead for more than a few decades. But this was not the entire explanation. I also taught African texts in English or English translation less aesthetically than I did African works in French. Indeed I realized that by some standards I was being wayward: colleagues in French might spend an entire semester on "le détail réaliste au dix-neuvième siècle," often without reference to the socio-political work of literature in nineteenth century

Europe.

I infer that my training taught me to think of *literary* as narrowly textual, *opposed* to extra-textual, and since my first training was in French literature, it was particularly with regard to French language texts that I felt I might be doing a disservice, to my students and the texts, if other aspects of literary production encroached on our time for pure "textual analysis."

African texts thus have expanded the meaning of "literary" for me and taught me to re-see the literariness of European writers as also bearing contextuality. The actuality of the African texts we read, their embeddedness in volatile political and social currents and debate reveal literature as less sacred, therefore, and correct that peculiar intellectual distortion in which aesthetics, cloistered from the socio-historical, can become fetishized. A case in point is the reciprocal reading of André Gide's *L'Immoraliste* (1902) and Ferdinand Oyono's *Une vie de boy* (1956). A non-normative comparative reading of these texts extends rich possibilities to each of them, as I hope to demonstrate.

Commentators of *L'Immoraliste* have paid scant attention -- if any -- to the place of this narrative in colonising discourse. On the basis of some visceral hunch about its appropriateness, I decided to include it in my course on "Colonialism and Literature." Moreover, for the first time, I would read and teach -- which is, for me, the most advanced stage of reading -- "francophone" and metropolitan texts in the *same* course, as voices in a single discourse. I felt there was something to be learned in such a juxtaposition. Having read *L'Immoraliste* as a graduate student some years ago, I remembered that it occupied an important place in twentieth century French literature. The fact that it had existed for at least twenty years in the Macmillan and Prentice Hall series, complete with preface, introduction, footnotes, and glossary, meant at the very least that teachers all over America were using it and that consequently, it had been become part of the infamous canon. On re-opening it the summer preceding the course, I found that I had indeed correctly remembered its stature, as described by the editors Elaine Marks and Richard Tedeschi. As one might expect, the introduction, published in 1963, struck me, reading in 1990, as alternately hyperbolic and incomprehensible, and at all moments self satisfied and ethnocentric, embarrassingly naive about matters of class, gender, and race. It is worth revisiting that introduction.

> *L'Immoraliste* is the first important fictional work of the twentieth century. Like all literary masterpieces, it is infinitely expansible. Most of the dominant themes of contemporary literature are contained in Michel's *récit*: the theme of the stranger, the trial, death and resurrection, the quest for identity, the discontinuity of the human personality in time. Michel himself recalls many of the major figures in Western myth and literature: Adam, Job, Narcissus, Faust, Don Juan.

> He foreshadows Proust's narrator, Camus' Caligula, Meursault and Jean-Baptiste Clamence, Sartre's Mathieu. For Michel, as for Nietzsche, whom Gide discovered while he was writing *L'Immoraliste*, "God is dead." For Michel, as for the poet Rimbaud, "L'amour est à réinventer."
>
> When Gide, in his preface to *L'Immoraliste* refers to such illustrious personages as Alceste and Philinte, Hamlet and Ophelia, Faust and Marguerite, Adam and Jehovah, he is encouraging us to place Michel and Marceline in this distinguished company of great fictional creations. Gide might perhaps have been more modest had he not wanted to impress upon us, before we begin to read the *récit*, the fact that despite the first-person narrator, his protagonists exist only in the world and work of art ...
>
> The *récit*, with variations on the Gidian form, thus far appears to be the dominant fictional genre of our century. It is eminently well adapted to the moral-aesthetic bias or the purely aesthetic bias of many contemporary writers. A sophisticated form, the *récit* posits insoluble human problems which can be resolved only within the context of the work itself. The function of literature as Gide saw it, and as is illustrated by the Gidian *récit*, is to instruct through the presentation of moral disorder and to please through aesthetic equilibrium. (11-13)

This introduction says something about Gide as a writer and still more about the values on the basis of which a place has been accorded him in the *American* French canon. Let us note that the editors have signaled some of the criteria -- specific themes and "infinite expansibility," for example -- by which literary "masterpieces" are determined. Moreover, the editors indicate the potency and primacy of the work of art as distinct from and outside material and historical reality and apart from the act of reading when they refer to "insoluble human problems which can be resolved only within the context of the work itself."

In 1956, a half century after Gide published *L'Immoraliste* and seven years before Elaine Marks and Richard Tedeschi composed their introduction, Ferdinand Oyono, the Cameroonian writer, published *Une vie de boy*. Written as colonialism (in its pure form) was breathing its last gasps, *Une vie de boy* deflates colonialist pretensions in its unflattering portrait of the French. But given the satiric mode of the novel, what I felt to be its rather narrow objectives had struck me for many years as ultimately somewhat shallow. Mohamadou Kane also faults the novel for flawed characterization and for the passivity of the protagonist, Toundi, "[qui] subi[t] le monde nouveau plus qu'il n'agi[t] sur lui" (217).

We usually think of an earlier novel or poem making possible or comprehensible a later one. Yet my experiment in "Colonialism and Literature" reminds me of Borges' essay, "Kafka and His Precursors" in which Borges tells us that Kafka made possible a new reading of Aristotle, Han Yu, Kierkegaard, Browning, Léon Bloy and Lord Dunsany:

> In each of these texts we find Kafka's idiosyncrasy to a greater or lesser degree, but if Kafka had never written a line, we would not perceive this quality; in other

> words, it would not exist. The poem "Fears and Scruples" by Browning foretells Kafka's work, but our reading of Kafka perceptibly sharpens and deflects our reading of the poem. Browning did not read it as we do now. In the critics' vocabulary, the word "precursor" is indispensable, but it should be cleansed of all connotation of polemics or rivalry. The fact is that every writer *creates* his own precursors. His work modifies our conception of the past, as it will modify the future. (201)

It seems to me now that I have never read (or taught) *L'Immoraliste* with greater success than I did in light of Oyono's *Une vie de boy,* just as Oyono's novel has become, in the bargain, a more interesting piece of writing. In this pairing and mutual interrogation, both protagonists' passivity, their acts of observing and writing, the sexual dramas which are at the heart of each narrative -- all can at last be seen as preeminent signs of colonial encounter.

Both narratives are, first of all, first person accounts, mediated by a third party. In Michel's case, the story is written down by one of his friends, who has come to hear Michel's story in Tunisia and who writes to another friend back in France. Michel knows his story's outcome as he begins his narration, whereas the narratee does not; this cognitive gap allows Michel to manipulate his listeners and future readers, and, indeed, Michel constructs the story in such a way as to exonerate himself. Moreover, he dissimulates outright at least once by omission: knowing at the moment he recounts the scene of the mirror that Moktir saw him, Michel tells the scene to his listeners and the readers as though he did not know it. In *L'Immoraliste* Michel's manifest confusion, the temporal gap between the events and their telling, the additional narrative voice of the friend, and the silence of still other voices -- all cast doubts on the reliability of narration and suggests the complicity of listener/reader with the speaker/writer. This modernist récit highlights the issue of its own textuality and Michel's self willed misinterpretation.

In Toundi's case, as he lies dying, he passes his journal on to a stranger who, we are told, translates it from Ewondo to French. Toundi's journal is thus kept day to day and is meant only for himself. Presumably, we are to infer its lack of artifice and consequently its sincerity. Moreover, the greater knowledge of the narratee, who is conscious of Toundi's fate, allows for a more informed, ironic reading of the text while Toundi himself reads the experiences of his life naively, at least for a time. Oyono seems to mishandle the complexity of this narration -- or does he? -- for Toundi occasionally seems too perceptive, his words too critical for the naive young boy he is supposed to be, as in the scenes at the church and at the party which the Commandant throws to celebrate the arrival of his wife.

In both narratives, the choice of the experiential, subjective voice has particular significance in the colonial and pre-colonial contexts. One cannot but situate such texts in the tradition of anthropological writing, travelogues and travel literature (Pierre Loti, Ernest Psichari, Blaise Cendrars, Louis Ferdinand Céline, Joseph Conrad, Michel Leiris, Raymond Roussel) in which the voice describes both external phenomena (flora and fauna, including human beings) and internal reflection and transformation through contact with this strange new world. Gide's famous *Voyage au Congo/Retour du Tchad* (1927) are two such travel journals, written with great self-consciousness about colonialism and its injustices. So much so that they deal a severe blow to French colonial prestige, despite the fact that they, too, are heir to all sorts of colonialist or Africanist thinking.

The travelogue is thus a first person account whose seemingly photographic testimony to sights, sounds and experiences is paradoxically reliable -- experience confers authority -- although admittedly subjective. In this regard, the travelogue is Montaignesque, for the *je*, a groping humanist subjectivity, reflects, when in contact with the provocative stimuli of foreign places and curious customs -- precisely the experience of travel that Montaigne himself advocated. The travelogue thus presents a vacillation or hesitation between description and reflection, between a certain realism and the search for meaning that is incited by the objects perceived. The journal thus presupposes or "pre-constructs" the hollowness of those objects, their waiting for the plenitude or meaning provided by the observer -- a symbolism of sorts. To the extent that the "traveled to" place or its inhabitants remain veiled, they are subsumed, consumed by the thinking subject. They find realization only in the subject and in the writing. They are emptied of their contextual sense or self-definition and become the vehicle by which the subject grows and affirms itself. The world is thus a vast classroom to enhance the thinking subject's powers.

Une vie de boy is an inversion of the techniques and issues present in *L'Immoraliste*, as in other such accounts of travel in Africa. In Oyono's novel, the journal that has inscribed Africans as the European other becomes for Toundi a means of liberation. The journal simultaneously partakes of the tradition I have just described and yet provides for Toundi the meager means of learning, coming slowly -- too slowly, of course -- to self-affirmation.

But there is a strange irony operative in *Une vie de boy*, from the very moment Toundi picks up his pen. For that world outside his journal commands Toundi in such a way that his attempt to control it as the thinking subject cannot silence it and make it what he wills it to be as can Michel's writing. Toundi's cruel death, communicated to the narratee by Toundi's translator, makes this clear. The meaning of the world outside prevails and imposes itself, despite the thinking subject's appropriation of the journal form. The world has force, it is not an empty signifier waiting for Toundi's gratuitous vision, unlike Michel's "Tunis," which evokes not a real place but the mythologized one as in Du Bellay's exquisite sonnet, "Nouveau venu, qui cherches Rome en Rome/Et rien de Rome en Rome n'aperçois" (47). Michel's account orders the world; Toundi's -- even as it provides a means of personal growth -- can merely "record" it.

Within this convention of the journal, then, *L'Immoraliste* and *Une vie de boy* engage similar issues, motifs and themes. We shall consider three of these: the gaze, the body, and, related to both of these, sexuality. To a greater or lesser degree, these are indeed the stuff of colonial encounters and writings.

In *L'Immoraliste*, the question of the gaze is highlighted in these remarks of Marceline, who says to Michel: "Vous, vous n'êtes content ... que quand vous leur avez fait montrer quelque vice. Ne comprenez-vous pas que notre regard développe, exagère en chacun le point sur lequel il s'attache, et que nous le faisons devenir ce que nous prétendons qu'il est?" (141). The theme runs throughout Gide's work and reaches its fullest expression, perhaps, in *Les Faux Monnayeurs*. Here it takes on special meaning in light of the African setting of Michel's adventure, where power differentials are significant in the matter of representation. Marceline is in effect describing that process of the journal in which the "other" is an empty signifier awaiting the "meaning" provided by the subject who writes or, as Marceline says, looks.

Nowhere is this process more obvious than in the pivotal scene in which Michel, looking into the mirror, observes Moktir's stealing Marceline's scissors (55-56). Moktir is, in fact, observing Michel. Who, then, is the author of this act? As becomes immediately obvious when Michel admits experiencing "de l'amusement, de la joie" at Moktir's theft, Moktir acts out Michel's very own desire for rupture with Marceline and the well ordered life he has led until now. Gide's use of the mirror is thus not gratuitous. In looking at Moktir, Michel constructs a surrogate, sees his own reflection, looks into his own soul. The narration of this episode, of course, as of many others, tends to exonerate Michel, for Moktir "acts," Michel is "led" into vice.

In *Une vie de boy* the motif of the gaze is appropriated. Toundi becomes a Moktir of sorts, watching the degradation of his colonial masters, who, unlike Michel, must maintain the illusion of the "mission civilisatrice" and, consequently, of racial, cultural and moral superiority. Toundi thus becomes a reminder, a sign of this fall from grace. His presence becomes intolerable, for in his eyes his colonial masters read -- not the flattering portrait that would justify them and their presence in Africa -- but that of their weakness and failure to live up to this all important self image:

> J'avais bêtement tressailli quand je l'avais vue regarder imperceptiblement l'ingénieur. Mes yeux avaient rencontré ceux de Madame par-dessus la tête de l'amant de Sophie. Cela ne dura que le temps d'un éclair. Elle détourna les siens. Je me sentis envahi de gêne, comme le jour où mon regard s'arrêta sur le sexe incirconcis du commandant. (76-77)

Or when Toundi has brought in the Commandant's suitcase, we read:

> Je baissai les yeux. Dans l'espace d'un éclair je les relevai. Ils rencontrèrent ceux de Madame. Je les vis devenir tout petits. Puis ils s'agrandirent comme si elle avait assisté à une scène d'épouvante. Instinctivement, je regardai à mes pieds pour voir si je n'étais pas à la portée de quelque reptile venimeux. J'entendis Monsieur demander à Madame s'il y avait quelque chose qui n'allait pas.
> — Mais tu es toute verte, Suzy!
> — Oh! ce n'est rien, répondit-elle.
> Le patron me tournait toujours le dos. Madame ne me quittait pas des yeux. Le commandant desserra son étreinte. Ils entrèrent au salon. (104)

Kalisia thus warns Toundi, "puisque tu connais toutes leurs affaires, ils ne pourront jamais oublier tout à fait tant que tu seras là. Et ça, ils ne te le pardonneront pas. Comment pourraient-ils encore faire le gros dos et parler, la cigarette à la bouche, devant toi qui sais! Pour eux, c'est toi qui as tout raconté, et malgré eux ils se sentent jugés par toi ..." (152-153).

Unlike Michel, the Commandant and his wife have only disdain for Toundi and other Africans, but like Michel, they project their own weaknesses and passions onto them: "il arriva que les yeux de Madame errèrent du côté du réfrigérateur, à proximité duquel j'attendais les ordres. Elle devint tout rouge et détourna aussitôt la conversation sur les nègres" (109). A similar displacement takes places earlier on at the party which the Commandant organizes to celebrate his wife's arrival in the colony.

> — Alors tu dors? me dit le Blanc qui désinfecte Dangan, en me montrant son verre vide ...
> Je débouchai à tout hasard une bouteille de whisky. J'en versai dans le verre du Blanc. Je ne m'arrêtai qu'après qu'il eut crié "Stop, top, top! Stop! Bonne mère de bonne mère!", à plusieurs reprises. Cela avait déchaîné une hilarité générale.
> Mon z'ami, dit Gosier-d'Oiseau en imitant faussement le petit nègre, nous pas buveurs indigènes!
> Les Blancs éclatèrent encore de rire.
> — Vous savez, dit encore Gosier d'Oiseau en tournant son long cou vers Madame et en levant le bras dans ma direction, ces gens-là boivent au-delà de toute imagination ...
> Tous les Blancs se tournèrent pour le regarder. Il balbutia, lissa sa chevelure et reprit:
> — Un jour ... un jour ... en tournée ...
> Il se gratta le pavillon de l'oreille et devint tout rouge. Un jour, j'avais demandé à un chef ce qu'il souhaitait pour la nouvelle année. "Que toutes les rivières se transforment en rivières de cognac!" me répondit-il le plus sérieusement du

> monde!
> Le docteur fit glisser ses galons sur ses épaules, vida son verre et commença:
> — L'hôpital manquera toujours d'alcool, c'est effarant! Les infirmiers tournent toutes les mesures que je prends pour empêcher le marché noir (les Blancs pouffèrent de rire à ces mots) de l'alcool à 90%. (77-78)

The satire of the passage resides, of course, in Toundi's representing the whites as the very drunkards they claim the natives to be. Two aspects of colonial representation become clear. On the *cognitive* level, the African representee is a "blank darkness," in Joseph Conrad's terminology via Christopher Miller, while the representer's *affective* attitude may vary from disdain to desire. It becomes obvious, then, that *desire* ("going native," by the representer's definition) is not therefore a more enlightened response. Michel's desire, for example, does not indicate an informed apprehending of the dark skinned boys and men to whom he is drawn. I submit, moreover, that Michel's desire does not free him from a still arrogant sense of superiority to those whose supposed licentious freedom he so covets.

Let us consider now the narrative focus on the body, as it operates in these two tests. In *L'Immoraliste*, Michel's gaze on the body is expressive once again of hedonistic desire. The body in question is, of course, silent, an empty signifier which will stand for Michel's yearnings:

> je vois entrer derrière [Marceline] un petit Arabe au teint brun. Il s'appelle Bachir, a de grands yeux silencieux qui me regardent. Je suis plutôt un peu gêné, et cette gêne déjà me fatigue; je ne dis rien, parais fâché. L'enfant, devant la froideur de mon accueil, se déconcerte, se retourne vers Marceline, et, avec un mouvement de grâce animale et câline, se blottit contre elle, lui prend la main, l'embrasse avec un geste qui découvre ses bras nus. Je remarque qu'il est tout nu sous sa mince gandourah blanche et sous son bournous rapiécé ...
>
> Au bout d'un peu de temps, je ne suis plus gêné par sa présence. Je le regarde; il semble avoir oublié qu'il est là. Ses pieds sont nus; ses chevilles sont charmantes, et les attaches de ses poignets. Il manie son mauvais couteau avec une amusante adresse. Vraiment, vais-je m'intéresser à cela? Ses cheveux sont rasés à la manière arabe; il porte une pauvre chéchia qui n'a qu'un trou à la place du gland. La gandourah, un peu tombée, découvre sa mignonne épaule. J'ai besoin de la toucher. Je me penche; il se retourne et me sourit. Je fais signe qu'il doit me passer son sifflet, le prends et feins de l'admirer beaucoup. (40-41)

Bachir and the other dark skinned boys can be known by Michel's listeners and narratee only as Michel has constructed them. Note that Michel's attention here, as elsewhere, is riveted on a child, who is less articulate and less assured than an adult might be: Moreover, Bachir is exotic *fauna* ("grâce animale et caline"), and his body is fetishized and aestheticized ("ses chevilles sont charmantes," we see "sa mignonne épaule"). The contact with him sets off for Michel the process of self realization and transformation ("J'ai besoin de la toucher.")

In Oyono, although Toundi's fate reveals his white masters' ongoing power, Toundi's description of white bodies and their gestures is not unlike that of Michel and other colonialist scribes. Toundi describes those bodies in minimalist terms with no attempt to contextualize them, to imagine the voice with which they might articulate their own positions. The result here is that they are stripped of depth and humanity, demonstrating fictionally Césaire's theoretical assertion that "la colonisation travaille à *déciviliser* le colonisateur, à *l'abrutir* au sens propre du mot" (11).

> Tous les Blancs qui ont l'habitude de s'amuser au Cercle européen semblaient s'être donné rendez-vous à ce quartier de Dieu ... . Mme Salvain avait caché *ses mollets de coq* dans un pantalon de toile qui faisait encore plus ressortir *son gros derrière*. Elle vint encore au commandant, *les bras tendus*, et *sursauta à la scène des baisers* sur les poignets ... . On put voir ensuite les arrivées du docteur -- toujours très fier de ses galons de capitaine -- et de sa femme, du Blanc qui désinfecte Dangan au D.T.T., des demoiselles Dubois, *deux filles énormes avec des nattes et des chapeaux de cow-boy*, et enfin de Mme Moreau, la femme du régisseur de prison, accompagnée de quelques Grecques *venues exhiber leurs robes de soie* ... .
>
> Dans l'église Saint-Pierre de Dangan, les Blancs ont leurs places dans le transept, à côté de l'autel. C'est là qu'ils suivent la messe, confortablement assis dans des fauteuils de rotin recouverts de coussins de velours. Hommes et femmes se coudoient. Mme Salvain était assise à côté du commandant tandis qu'au deuxième rang *Gosier-d'Oiseau* et l'ingénieur agricole *se penchaient avec un ensemble parfait vers les deux grosses filles*. Derrière eux, le docteur *remontait de temps en temps ses galons dorés* qui descendaient le long de ses épaulettes trop longues. Sa femme, bien qu'*elle fît semblant d'oublier ciel et terre* dans la lecture de son missel, *suivait du coin de l'oeil* les manigances de Gosier-d'Oiseau et de l'ingénieur avec les demoiselles Dubois. Elle relevait parfois la tête pour voir où en étaient le commandant et Mme Salvain. Le docteur, quand il ne remontait pas ses galons, s'évertuait, par gestes excédés, à attraper une mouche qui tournoyait autour de ses oreilles écarlates. (52-54, emphasis added)

These "colons" are so many marionnettes whose corporeality, gestures and crude emotions -- vanity, jealousy, carnality -- are exposed. Like the worst of anthropological writing or ethnographic photographs, Toundi's journal documents "strange native (here, colonialist) customs" but does not embed them or embeds them minimally. They present an unelaborated image, without its contextualizing and attenuating circumstances.

This emptiness is further manifested in the party which the Commandant organizes to fete his wife's arrival. The vacuity of colonial pretensions and lives is revealed in a string of verbs au *passé simple*. The colons go from one action to the next, in a frantic attempt to disguise a certain malaise:

> [Madame] *regarda* tendrement son mari qui lui *caressa* le bras. La femme du docteur *revint* à la charge. Elle *cita* un journal qui disait beaucoup de bien des ballets japonais. Quand elle *n'eut* plus rien à dire, l'une des demoiselles Dubois la *relaya*. Elle *cita* plusieurs noms de Blancs qui devaient être des musiciens ou quelque chose dans la musique. Elle *regretta* de n'avoir pas eu la chance qu'avait

> eue Madame d'être à Paris au début de la semaine. Elle se *plaignit* que le court de tennis fût en poto-poto sous les premières pluies ... qu'elle ne trouvât pas de bon joueur de tennis à Dangan. Mme Salvain *parla* de chevaux. Elle maudissait la zone de la forêt où la mouche tsé-tsé empêchait les nègres d'élever des chevaux. L'ingénieur *suggéra* qu'on pourrait toujours tenter quelque chose ... . M. Janopoulos *discuta* les cours du cacao avec le commandant. Le docteur *formula* le voeu d'avoir une sage-femme européenne. L'instituteur *parla* avec autorité. Il *tint* à expliquer à tout le monde le comportement des nègres. Chacun, pour le contredire, *raconta* sa petite histoire personelle avec un indigène pour conclure que le nègre n'est qu'un enfant ou un couillon ... (81, emphasis added)

Like Ionesco's *Cantatrice chauve*, this passage reveals an empty formality and empty lives. Once again, theorizing "the African" (the school teacher "tint à expliquer à tout le monde le comportement des nègres") is a significant pastime that, for want of anything better, saves the day. It is worth noting that for Oyono, even the "kinder" theoretician's stance -- the belief that one could account for the blacks' behavior -- is reductive since it, too, sees race as sole and sufficient origin of behavior.

We have seen thus far variations on the motifs of the gaze and the body. Let us now turn to the issue that ties all these pieces together. Edward Said points out in *Orientalism* that Europeans of the nineteenth century especially traveled away from Europe for sexual freedom:

> for nineteenth century Europe, with its increasing *embourgeoisement*, sex had been institutionalized to a very considerable degree. On the one hand, there was no such thing as "free" sex, and on the other, sex in society entailed a web of legal, moral, even political and economic obligations of a detailed and certainly encumbering sort. Just as the various colonial possessions -- quite apart from the economic benefit to metropolitan Europe -- were useful as places to send wayward sons, superfluous populations of delinquents, poor people, and other undesirables, so the Orient was a place where one could look for sexual experience unobtainable in Europe. Virtually no European writer who wrote on or traveled to the Orient in the period after 1800 exempted himself or herself from this quest: Flaubert, Nerval, "Dirty Dick" Burton, and Lane are only the most notable. In the twentieth century one thinks of Gide, Conrad, Maugham, and dozens of others. What they looked for often -- correctly, I think -- was a different type of sexuality, perhaps more libertine and less guilt-ridden ... In time "Oriental sex" was as standard a commodity as any other available in the mass culture, with the result that readers and writers could have it if they wished without necessarily going to the Orient. (190)

The discourse Said describes is not limited to the "Orient." While French literary traditions from late nineteenth century through the 1930s, at least, would have the European male be an aggressive builder of empire in Africa, he is also a passive, helpless prey to the wily animal-like African or mulatto female and, by analogy, to Africa itself. Interracial sex, French writers of this period purport, leads to the degeneracy of the European male and, presumably, of European civilization itself. Note that Michel's discovery of homosexual desire in *L'Immoraliste* is but another avatar of this equation. The possibility of this discovery has as much to do with an "alien" racial contact as with an "alien" sexuality.

The most decisive blow to colonialist pretentions, then, is effected in Oyono's treatment of white sexuality, possibly the most important site of ideological struggle in literature of the colonial period. In *Une vie de boy* sexuality becomes the vulnerable pillar of the edifice through which Oyono attacks the self proclaimed superiority of European civilisation. It is not the sexual practices of European men nor interracial sexual relations -- the engineer's liaison with Sophie is taken for granted -- which come under particular scrutiny. It is -- misogynistically, it could be argued -- the sexuality of the white female. It is in the white woman's infidelity to her husband that excessive claims for white masculinity and the pretense of a superior European civilization are debunked.

As we have seen, Oyono mocks through Toundi's irreverential and comic vision of European bodies ("Gosier d'Oiseau," "ses mollets de coq," "son gros derrière"). As Madame's extra-marital liaison becomes ever more consuming, the joyous lyricism of Toundi's first response to Madame degenerates into a grotesque emphasis, à la Bakhtin, on bodily functions. Toundi discovers the "petits sacs en caoutchouc" and "les serviettes hygièniques." This grotesqueness attains a new high (or low) when Toundi goes to call Madame on behalf of a visitor and observes her asleep on her bed:

> Je courus à la chambre de Madame. Elle n'avait pas fermé la porte. Elle dormait la bouche ouverte, un bras pendant hors du lit et les jambes croisées. Une mouche, semblable à un grain de beauté, suçait sa pommette. Elle était en pantalon et avait déboutonné son corsage ajouré, laissant voir sa poitrine drue sous son soutien-gorge rose. (125)

The craving, sexual body is here exposed, in a vulgar disposition as the ironic fly takes the place of a "grain de beauté." On awakening, Madame realizes that she can no longer claim moral superiority and command Toundi's admiration: "Elle poussa un soupir, ouvrit les yeux et bondit de son lit en se couvrant la poitrine ... . Elle boutonnait son corsage tout en me regardant avec une colère méprisante contenue ... . -- Tu ne te donnes plus la peine de frapper à la porte maintenant? -- La porte était ouverte, Madame, répondis-je, et j'ai frappé quand même ..." (125). This scene is a microcosm of the conflict. The door is open and Toundi does see.

How could *Une vie de boy* be read without a sense of its response to and appropriation of the techniques and issues in colonialist writing? How could *L'Immoraliste* come to be enshrined with no reference to -- much less examination of -- the issues which *Une vie de boy* makes us perceive in it? Moreover, to what extent are these very motifs -- the subject *je*, traveling, describing, gazing, gazing anthropologically or libidinously at cultures and bodies that do not speak -- the unacknowledged source of its currency in 1902? To what extent is Gide's *aestheticizing*, that is, his camouflage of these acts the grounds on which *L'Immoraliste* could become *the* récit of the twentieth century? Ironically, it is precisely these obfuscated and unexamined gestures that make it for me that archetype of a certain twentieth century discourse.

Moreover, one is led to wonder whether colonialism would have occurred so brashly without a certain pre-existing mythology of masculine and feminine. And whether the impoverished definitions of mmasculine and feminine which the West has long taken for granted might not be different if there had not been colonialism. That, of course, is a topic for another day.

This encounter of Gide and Oyono brings us to the larger issue of how to read metropolitan and "francophone" texts comparatively. Shall we celebrate diversity or engage in meaningful dialogue concerning difference? How do we construct a healthy comparativism?

As my discussion of Gide and Oyono makes clear, I believe it is not enough to tack *L'Enfant noir* onto the end of one's syllabus and to read it complacently -- with attention to initiation and metaphor. We suffer today in the United States, at least, from a facile multiculturalism, a misunderstanding of cultural difference. For it is not enough to sample the Greek, Mexican, Italian, Chinese, and "soul food" dishes one can buy in the local shopping mall. Nor is it enough to appreciate so-called ethnic music, festivals and books. It is not a matter of integrating just one more element into what is otherwise a perfectly functioning system, because our systems have been forged and define themselves on the basis of an exclusion.

Claude Lévi-Strauss, like Walter Rodney, offers a crucial insight into this matter. In his essay "Cultural Discontinuity, Economic and Social Development," he writes:

> those societies which today we call "underdeveloped" are not such through their own doing, and one would be wrong to conceive of them as exterior to Western development or indifferent to it. In truth, they are the very societies whose direct or indirect destruction between the sixteenth and the nineteenth centuries have made possible the development of the Western world. Between them there is a complementary relationship. The same development and its greedy requirements have made these societies such as they are today. Thus we are not dealing with the contact between two processes each pursued in isolation. The relationship of estrangement between the so-called underdeveloped societies and the mechanized civilization consists mainly in the fact that this mechanized civilization finds in them its own creation; or, more precisely, the counterpart of those destructions it committed upon them in order to found its own reality. (315)

Lévi-Strauss' comments on metropolitan and peripheral societies -- African agency notwithstanding -- suggest why the two discourses emanating from those localities must be read together. Our history -- literary or otherwise -- premised on the notion of two parallel processes in isolation is not merely imcomplete, it is false. Satya P. Mohanty, in a recent article on the pitfalls of cultural relativism, makes the point explicitly:

> the call for respect for alternative canons can be made on the basis of a purely liberal respect for other literatures and experiences, but that will not necessarily comprise a challenge to the dominant order to the very extent that alternative canons are seen simply as coexisting peacefully in a pluralistic academy ... . For in the study of modern literatures, the most crucial political question that arises concerns a history "we" all share, a history whose very terms and definitions are now being openly contested and formulated. When pluralist arguments are used to support the proliferation of various minority canons and discourses, the question of historical imbrication, indeed the question of this unequal history itself, is obscured ... . The study of minority literatures, for instance, can be defended on the ground that an adequate definition of Literature must include all of "its" variant forms and all the various human experiences they represent. The difficulty with this formulation is that its *vagueness* leaves it open to all kinds of ironic recuperation ... . To read -- and teach -- [a colonial or postcolonial Francophone writer's] works as evidence of the universality of the French language, or even of the rich diversity of the human experience, is precisely to erase the specificity of the ... writer, ambivalently situated in the belly of the imperial beast. Ignoring the history of colonialism by merely celebrating God's literary plenty, the pluralist critic would be ... containing the potential significance of any otherness. (24-25)

I share Mohanty's view of this question. It is not a *natural* diversity that is at issue, for those diverse voices, emanating from shared and yet distinct historical experiences, present a challenge. They ask not that they be "added" to existing course materials. Part of their potential lies precisely in their capacity to examine or reorganize the premises of "literature," of "Western" or "French" literature. I am not suggesting that this is the sole appropriate location for Oyono's or any African text -- reminiscent of the Sartrean transcending of the moment of négritude in aspiration for the "universal." But to the extent that paradigms come to us from Gide (et al) make possible or impossible readings of Oyono (et al), this project seems to me justifiable and necessary.

This is not a matter of altruism, as I hope my discussion of *L'Immoraliste* and *Une vie de boy* has demonstrated. It may seem altogether plausible that *Une vie de boy* can be well read only *after L'Immoraliste*. The greater truth, however, is that Gide *needs* to encounter Oyono, and so do we.

WORKS CITED

Borges, Jorge-Luis. *Labyrinths*. Trans. James E. Irby. New York: New Directions, 1964.

Césaire, Aimé. *Discours sur le colonialisme*. Paris: Présence Africaine, 1955.

Du Bellay, Joachim. "Nouveau venu, qui cherches Rome en Rome." *Les Antiquités de Rome. French Poetry of the Renaissance*. Ed. Bernard Weinberg. Carbondale: Southern Illinois University Press, 1954.

Gide, André. *L'Immoraliste*. 1902. Toronto: Macmillan, 1963.

———. *Voyage au Congo/Le Retour du Tchad*. Paris: Gallimard, 1927 and 1928.

Hill-Collins, Patricia. "Learning from the Outsider Within: The Sociological Significance of Black Feminist Thought." *Social Problems* 33.6 (1986): 14-32.

Kane, Mohamadou. *Roman africain et tradition*. Dakar: Nouvelles Editions Africaines, 1982.

Lévi-Strauss, Claude. *Structural Anthropology*. Trans. Monique Layton. Vol. 2. Chicago: University of Chicago Press, 1976.

Mohanty, Satya P. "Us and Them: On the Philosophical Bases of Political Criticism." *Yale Journal of Criticism* 2 (1989): 1-31.

Oyono, Ferdinand. *Une vie de boy*. Paris: Julliard, 1956.

Said, Edward. *Orientalism*. New York: Random House, 1978.

LITERARY THEORY AND AFRICAN LITERATURE
edited by J. Gugler, H.-J. Lüsebrink, J. Martini
Münster/Hamburg1993, pp. 89-112

INHABITABLE WORDS:
TEXT, METATEXT AND CRITICISM IN YORÙBÁ ORAL PRAISE POETRY*

KARIN BARBER

In Africa, oral literature is still the discourse of the majority, the domain in which popular creativity originates. The oral mode of realisation is also the dominant one in the profusion of new, hybrid popular forms that have sprung up in the borderland between orality and writing: poetry written to be performed, popular theatre which has one foot in a literate universe without ever having been written down. Literature written in African languages arises out of the oral domain and often represents, in Abiọla Irele's words, 'a direct outgrowth' from it - even though 'already dissociated, as a result of writing, from the kind of immediate insertion into collective life that orality entails' (Irele 1990a).

African literature written in French and English, by contrast, appears to be decisively cut off from this productive engagement with orality. In Nigeria, Rọpo Sekoni points out, the impact of oral literature on the development of modern Anglophone written literature 'has been on the whole peripheral, erratic and sectional' (Sekoni 1988: 46), involving only 'partial and occasional borrowings ... from strategies of communication in orality' (1988: 47).

Most critics, however, have taken it for granted that elite Francophone and Anglophone African writers have 'oral roots', that their work has somehow 'grown out of' traditional literary forms, or that any divergence from a (highly over-schematised) European norm is the result of

---

* Pages 101-107 of this paper are a revised and abridged version of sections of Chapter 7 of my book, *I could speak until tomorrow: Oríkì, Women and the Past in a Yoruba Town*.

'oral influence' pushing up from underneath.[1] This kind of analysis has been assisted by a general vagueness, on the part of the critics of written literature, about what these 'oral traditions' actually consist of. This is partly though not entirely the result of lack of information. Fundamental questions about the relationships between different oral genres, the underlying principles of their constitution, and the mode of their reception and interpretation, have only just begun to be broached. It is as if the massive metropolitan bias installed by colonialism and perpetuated in the post-colonial state had reversed the objective order of things. Literature in English and French is more conspicuous and more prestigious than literature in African languages; and any written literature carries more weight than any oral text. The overdetermination of Euro-American cultural influence in African studies, forcefully outlined in a recent discussion by Biodun Jeyifo (1990), seems to have had the effect of impeding the emergence of an appropriate oral poetics.

Ọlabiyi Yai has argued that an indigenous criticism exists within the oral context of literary production and reception. Critical activity that takes place in the process of oral production, before, during and after the actual performance, is unlike the criticism of written literature in being a 'collective production'; in being indivisible from the poetry and thus 'self-productive'; in being 'generative' in the sense that it 'aims at arousing creative impulses in the audience'; in being 'expansive' in the sense of helping to augment the literary corpus, 'metamimetic and ameliorative', and 'participatory' (Yai 1989: 65). Yorùbá oríkì - 'praise poetry' - bear out Yai's diagnosis. The texts themselves are shot through with metatextual comments - on the performer's activity, on her procedures and purposes, and on the general moral and artistic character of her practice. Oríkì themselves, that is, suggest to the attentive listener how they should be interpreted.

The idea of the text[2] that emerges from this metatextual commentary,

---

[1] See Eileen Julien (1992) for a masterly and radical critical assessment of the roles assigned to 'orality' by critics of written Francophone African literature.

[2] I use the word 'text' deliberately, discounting the obvious connotations of fixity and closure which derive from the written critical tradition, and especially from scriptural exegesis. The emergent character of oríkì, their realisation only in and through performance, their effectuality as *utterance*, their lack of boundaries and closure, should become apparent even in the brief description to be given in this paper; for fuller and more detailed analysis, see Barber (1984, 1991). However, these characteristics are not in my view incompatible with a notion of text in its original signification as 'that which is woven, web, texture' (O.E.D.). Indeed, the people who create, perform, and listen to oríkì describe their activities as revolving around the constitution of text in precisely this sense. In a welcome reappraisal of the notion of oral text, Irele contends that 'it is just as

and the idea of how the text exists in society, is very much at odds with the 'common-sense' orthodox European view of literature which still dominates Africanist written literary criticism. 'Literature' is a constructed cultural category, not a universal, and its definition and content even within the European tradition have changed radically over time (Bennett 1979, Eagleton 1981). When critics treat their own locally and historically grounded notions of literature as universals, they block the possibility both of apprehending other literatures, and of gaining a vantage point from which to view the specificity of their own current critical assumptions. Yorùbá oral poetics, in fact, bears a resemblance in certain respects to medieval European views of the text, reminding us that the definition and evaluation of literature that we accept as 'natural' today is a specifically post-Renaissance phenomenon. Certain theoretical and practical possibilities that were open to us in the Middle Ages have been closed off since.

The central characteristic of modern critical orthodoxy is the conjunction, made at a fundamental level, between the idea of a 'literary' use of language and the notion of a fictitious, imaginative or imitative domain inhabited or created by texts. Literature is identified, first, by its special use of language, with the addition of supra-grammatical rules (metre, rhyme, or more diffuse stylistic qualities) and its selective abrogation of the grammatical rules that govern 'ordinary language'. Second, the texts exhibiting these stylistic features are felt to belong together in a domain which is segregated from 'real life'. Sir Philip Sidney's famous claim that the poet 'nothing affirms, and therefore never lieth' has reappeared in many forms since the sixteenth century. It is seen even in the work of a speech act theorist like Richard Ohmann, who argues that literary texts can be seen as strings of speech acts without illocutionary force: that is, as imitation utterance that does not *do* things as other utterance does. The conjunction of these two notions was decisively formulated by Jakobson, whose notion of the 'poetic function' represented literature as a special use of language distinguished by its self-orientation. Poetic language attracts attention to itself; the words themselves, rather than the addresser, addressee, context, 'code' or 'contact', are foregrounded. The text is thus immobilised and as it were quarantined, turning back on itself to inhabit a distinctive ontological domain. The notion of segregation is developed in the concept of poetic closure -- the demarcation of a poem from the 'flux of ordinary discourse' as well as from other poems.

---

relevant to orality as it is to literacy', and reminds us that 'in African orality, the imagination finds its proper manifestation as *organised text*, and even, in many societies, as a body of *consecrated texts*' (Irele 1990a).

This view, representing literature in a definitively separate domain from other discourse, is still dominant. However, there is plenty of evidence to undermine it. It is not just that it is a historically and culturally restricted view, inapplicable to most literatures in most places, but also that even with reference to its own period and culture it does not adequately describe our experience of literature. The notion of the complete conjuncture of fictionality and poetic language can be broken down from both sides. On the one hand, it has been shown that there is no such thing as a homogeneous domain of 'ordinary language' governed only by grammatical rules, against which the separate domain of 'poetic language' can be defined: rather, there is a multiplicity of speech registers (or 'speech genres' as Vološinov (1973) and Bakhtin (1986) called them) each governed by its own extra-grammatical conventions. Between them, these registers, as M.L.Pratt has shown, exhibit all the features claimed as exclusively 'literary': attention to form, imaginative and creative use of language, use of figures of speech, and so on (Pratt 1977). On the other hand, it is clear that there are genres of highly developed verbal art which are not 'fictitious'. Pratt shows that elaborate rhetorical devices found in fiction are also used to structure 'factual' biographical travel narratives (Pratt 1988). J.A. Burrow shows that in the Middle Ages, the concept of verbal art - 'eloquence' - was not necessarily tied to a notion of fictionality. Language use in texts was determined not by the fact/fiction distinction, which was relatively unimportant, but by the status of the person the text was intended for (Burrow 1982: 14-15). More generally, and for many centuries, the rhetorical tradition articulated a view of the text as a form of utterance, that is a species of social action, which by definition has real consequences in the world. Terry Eagleton has called for a return to this tradition, which asks, precisely, how texts act in the world, and by what linguistic means (Eagleton 1981, 1983). Yorùbá oral poetics may be regarded as reinforcing and contributing to this position from a cross-cultural vantage point.

It is only when *oríkì* texts are understood from the perspective of the poetics they themselves encapsulate that their remarkable capabilities become fully apparent: most strikingly, a polyvocal and plural textuality; the suspension of any resolution; and an ironical, ambivalent preservation of the possibility of alternatives, which though it is not critical in the strict sense, nevertheless subtly calls into question the inevitability of the way things are.

Oríkì

Oríkì are appellations or attributions, addressed to a named subject and believed to evoke that subject's powers and inner qualities. Every entity known to the Yorùbá world, whether animate or inanimate, human, animal or spiritual, abstract or concrete, is said to have its own *oríkì*; but the subjects for whom they are most extensive and most elaborated are individual human subjects who have made their mark in some way (*oríkì bòròkínní*), social groups claiming common origins in an ancient town or area (*oríkì orílè*) and the *oríkì* of the gods (*oríkì òrìṣà*). These celebrate and encapsulate in laconic or elaborated formulations whatever is felt to make the subject distinctive. *Oríkì bòròkínní* may allude to qualities of personality possessed by the subject; to his or her habits, appearance, and sayings; or to incidents in his or her life, whether public achievements or private oddities. *Oríkì orílè*, the *oríkì* by which membership of the principal constituent social units in the town is affirmed, revolve around the distinctive features of the ancient town of origin and its population, making reference to natural and geographical features, customs, taboos, historical events, and other characteristics which are believed to make those people different from groups originating elsewhere.

The *oríkì* belonging to individuals and 'lineages' (a shorthand term[3]) are accumulated over time. Fresh ones are composed or borrowed as the subject's characteristics become apparent: over a lifetime in the case of an individual, over a much longer period in the case of a lineage. Each epithet in a corpus of *oríkì*, then, may have been composed at a different time; by a different person; and with reference to a different characteristic or event. Many of them are formulated in such a way as to be condensed, obscure, and incomplete: each points away from the text in which it is performed to its own exegetical hinterland. The explanations of *oríkì* are carried in a tradition of narrative which partly converges with the *oríkì* tradition but is

---

[3] In Northern and Central Yorùbá towns, the principal socio-political institutions are *ilé*, usually translated by Yorùbá speakers as 'compound'. In Òkukù, the town in which this study was based (see note 4 below), *ilé* is a term with variable and negotiable references. Each *ilé* is made up of a core patrilineage onto which are usually attached a number of 'stranger' segments of different origins, often related through a daughter or wife. These segments occupy a wide range of positions in relationship to the core lineage, from virtual incorporation to a long-standing semi-autonomy. Each segment has its own *oríkì orílè*, marking its separate origin and linking it to the wider, scattered class of people who share that origin. That is, *oríkì orílè* tend to identify lineage segments -- both core and attached -- rather than the compound as a whole. However, the *ilé* is usually heavily dominated, both numerically and in terms of power, by the core lineage, and outsiders will identify the whole *ilé* by the core lineage's *oríkì orílè*.

partly independent. In Òkukù, where the research for this paper was done,[4] *oríkì* were performed mainly by women but *itàn* (narratives) were told mainly by old men.

In performance, the singer addresses herself intensively to the subject in question. Often this is a living individual, usually a man, physically present before her. In this case she locks eyes with him, and concentrates her utterance exclusively on him for as long as he is the subject of her address. In other cases, the subject may be absent. The dead are called in *oríkì*, and *òrìṣà* (gods) are invoked. When *oríkì orílẹ̀* are performed, they are addressed to a representative, or a group of representatives, of the lineage - whether living or dead. The characteristics shared by the lineage are concentrated upon and embodied in the person or persons receiving the utterance.

Oríkì can be recited in a normal speaking voice, or they can be chanted in a variety of modes. Personal and lineage *oríkì* are usually combined within one performance. The performer may also shift frequently from one subject to another, especially if the occasion is a festive one and large numbers of notables are gathered. On other occasions, such as solemn family ceremonials held during funerals, weddings and the propitiation of spiritual beings, the delivery may be concentrated exclusively on one or a few subjects. In all cases, however, the utterance is vocative. The performer speaks to the subject. Her utterance, in all cases, is assembled from a repertoire of materials available to her: formulas, epithets, and even extensive coherent passages. These chunks of material are diverse and heterogeneous. What they have in common, however, is that each chunk is in a sense autonomous. Its meaning does not arise from its relations with the other textual materials within the performance, but from its own independent referential context. This means that there are no fixed or inevitable connections between the items combined in a performance. The text is inherently fluid. Items can be added on and repeated at will. They can be performed in a different order each time, without affecting the meaning of the text. Different items are included in different performances. No two performers know exactly the same repertoire and no single performer gives two performances that are exactly alike. Indeed, innovative combinations, surprising twists and accretions to well-known material are positively valued (Ọlatunji 1979).

---

[4] Òkukù is a town in the Odò-Ọ̀tìn District of Ọ̀yọ́ State, Nigeria. It is fairly small by Yorùbá standards (population 20-30,000) but has a highly developed 'traditional' culture revolving around royal, religious and life-cycle celebrations, in which the performance of *oríkì* is central.

To a critic brought up within the written European-American literary tradition, texts like *oríkì* (and they exist in a less extreme form all over Africa: Hausa *kiraari*, Asante praise poetry, Zulu *izibongo*, Sotho *lithoko*, Xhosa and Tswana praise poetry, Bahima 'heroic recitations', and so on) are initially baffling. They appear formless, centreless and boundariless. Southern African scholars made valiant efforts to extract form and regularity from the traditions they collected. Damane and Sanders, for instance, expressed a preference for 'poems' which are 'logical and straightforward ... balanced and well-rounded', and observed that though the ordering of stanzas in Sotho praise poetry often appeared arbitrary, 'with a little imaginative effort, it can be seen to follow a definite train of thought' (Damane and Sanders 1974: 36). In line with the principles of orthodox written literary criticism, they strove to smooth out apparent irregularities and fill apparent textual gaps with meaning. *Oríkì* texts contain comments, however, which suggest a different way of making sense of them.

METATEXTUAL CLUES

Perhaps the most immediately striking feature of an *oríkì* performance is its dialogic character. The performer fixes her attention on her subject and insists that he reciprocates. She may throw interjections at him from time to time, demanding that he continue to demonstrate his avid receptivity: for example, 'Làgbàí gbéra fílẹ̀ o dìde' (Làgbàí get up, stand up): 'Ọmọ Abógunrìn ìwọ dà?' (Child of Abógunrìn where are you?); 'Ará Odò Ọrọ̀, ìwọ ni mò ń bá wí!' (Native of the River Ọrọ̀, it's you I'm talking to!). The urgency of her appeal is hard to ignore and listeners do in fact usually pay rapt attention when their own *oríkì* are directed at them in this manner. In the utterance of *oríkì*, the performer is amplifying the subject's persona, filling it out and making his 'head swell' with gratification. By directing to him, in this intensive manner, the public acknowledgement of his distinctiveness and at the same time his successful conformity to the ideal, she is an agent through which his public persona is continually remade. But at the same time, she constructs her own persona as performer within the chant. The more skilful and professional she is, the more strongly she will represent her own pole in the dialogic relation. Ṣàngówẹ̀mí, who made her living from this kind of performance in Òkukù, inserted her own *oríkì* among those of her subjects, representing herself in them as a formidable personality:

Èmi Àbẹ̀ní ń pè ọ́, eégún-inú ọmọ Fákẹ́midé
Nítorí eńlé apá ọ̀tún ò fojúu re wẹni tí ń pe lọ́balọ́ba

> Ìmọ̀ràn ìkà ni tòsì ń gbà
> Àbẹ̀ní, ẹbọ kó jáde n tọ̀kánkán ń rú
> Kùtùkùtù tí mo ríkùn dánà sí ...

> It is I, Àbẹ̀ní, calling you, 'inner masquerade', daughter
> of Fákẹ́midé
> Because the householders to the right don't look kindly
> on a person who salutes all the great ọba
> The ones on the left are planning wicked revenge
> Àbẹ̀ní, the ones straight ahead are making sacrifices to
> get her to leave
> I who from my earliest days had a mind that could follow
> many paths ...

Ṣàngówẹ̀mí represents herself here as abnormally gifted, one who can perform intellectual stunts as a masquerader performs physical ones, one whose powers arouse the envy, fear and hostility of her neighbours so much that they plot on all sides to drive her away (in this culture, the ultimate accolade). She who performs for all the great ọba is calling on her subject to respond. Thus she dramatises and reinforces both sides of the dialogic relation, that exchange which Vološinov described as 'a two-sided act ... determined equally by *whose* word it is and for whom it is meant' (Vološinov 1973: 86). In Vološinov's celebrated image, language is like the electric spark that jumps between the two poles of speaker and hearer; but in the act of uttering *oríkì*, the performer is also actually constituting those poles.

Comments in the *oríkì* themselves show that the dialogic character of the performance is fundamental to a more general notion of social and cultural reproduction. Someone who gives honour where it is due will herself thrive; someone who witholds acknowledgement of others' greatness will lose her own chances to make good:

> Ojú tó rí gbajúmọ̀ tí ò kì
> Towó tọmọ máa réléyun nì sá lọ
> Ọsàn tó rí gbajúmọ̀ tí ò rẹ̀
> Ẹyẹkẹ́yẹ ni ó mọ̀ mu ún
> Ojúù mi rí gbajúmọ̀ mo yọ̀ kì í
> Ire lónìí orí mi àfire

> The eye that sees a man of standing and does not salute
> him [with *oríkì*]
> Both money and children will flee from that one
> The orange tree that sees a man of standing and does not
> shed its leaves [pun on *rè/rẹlẹ̀* to be humble]
> Bad birds will come and suck its fruit
> My eye saw a man of standing, I joyfully saluted him
> May good luck attend me today.

To utter *oríkì*, this passage suggests, is to participate in the maintenance and recreation of a proper disposition of social forces. Only when everyone is

INHABITABLE WORDS

given their due can all thrive.

The reciprocity of this dialogic relation is inseparable from the idea of the social reproduction of the family. *Oríkì* are accumulated as a man matures, and their performance confirms and amplifies his attainment of the enhanced social standing that goes with age. Both his status as a senior man and his acquisition of *oríkì* are seen as being related to the possession of children. One performer said:

> A ì í dàgbà òjè
> Ká má mà lálàjẹ́
> Níjọ́ tá a bá gbó
> Tá a bá tọ́ ni ọmọ ẹni í ń fi kini
>
> We never live to a ripe old age
> Without acquiring some nicknames
> On the day we grow old
> In righteous age, our children will use them to praise us

A man's personality is filled out with experience: and his reputation is established not just by his *having* numerous descendants but by the descendants' attention and regard, encapsulated in their performance of his 'nicknames', i.e. his *oríkì*.

Conversely, it may be suggested that if one pays proper attention and regard to those of senior status, especially by performing their *oríkì*, one fosters one's own social reproduction. Thus one of the most accomplished of Òkukù's women performers, Fadérera, would say, in her *oríkì* chants:

> Ta ni ó mọlé jù mí lọ?
> Ọmọ Awóyẹmí ta níí mọlé ẹni juni lọ?
> ... Mo kini kini
> Mo kìnyàn kìnyàn
> N ò rẹ́ni tí yóò kì mí mọ́
> Fọláwé Wúràọlá ọmọ óò kì mí gbẹ̀san
>
> Who knows my house more than I do?
> Child of Awóyẹmí, who can know a person's house better
> than that person?
> ... I saluted and saluted people [with *oríkì*]
> I saluted person after person
> I found no-one to salute me in return
> Fọláwé Wúràọlá, a child will repay me with salutations.

Gifted with unparalleled knowledge of *oríkì*, she lavishes their performance upon other people. She knows so much more than anyone else that other people are ashamed or unable to respond by saluting her back in equal measure. However, the utterance itself turns into a kind of prayer. Because she has paid honour to others, she in turn will be honoured, by the children that she will bear and bring up to maturity. A mother's recompense is to receive back what she has given, in the form of a good name, an expanded social space, conferred by children. Children, as in the previous quotation, are both the basis of social position and the principal means of its acknowledgement. The dialogic character of *oríkì* performance, then, is seen as productive and effectual. The performance of *oríkì* is equivalent to a bestowal of recognition. By putting a person's *oríkì* in the air one gives oxygen to his or her public standing. And at the same time, one creates the conditions in which this blessing will *go round*: both in the sense of the generational cycle of social reproduction and in the sense that good deeds return blessings upon the doer.

Oríkì, then, participate in the social process by which status is created, acknowledged and maintained. They are inherently sociable, rooted in real social exchanges. This is made evident in the conscious commentary, in *oríkì*, on matters of precedence and protocol. Performers affirm that the mother's lineage must be saluted as well as the father's, for the mother is the originary source of social blessings; they announce that fathers must be given precedence over sons, or that the elder brother must be saluted before the younger:

>Bá à kègbón tán ta ni í kàbúrò?
>Báà ki Bàbáa Fákémidé, ta ní í komo?
>
>If you've not finished saluting the elder brother, who
>   will salute the younger?
>If you haven't saluted the father of Fákémidé, who will
>   salute the child?

In a festive gathering, a performer like Şàngówèmí will salute numerous people, shifting from one to the next as her repertoire, or her subject's patience or money, become exhausted. Each in turn becomes the exclusive focus of her attention, and her performance, taken as a 'whole', ranges over a number of different sets of personal and 'lineage' *oríkì*, clearly distinguishable in the text. But what governs the order of these sets and the length of each is not a formal poetic requirement, but social propriety. This gives us the clue to the apparent centrelessness and formlessness of the chant. Its structure is produced not from purely internal rules governing the relations between elements but also from external, social considerations. This is because a performance of *oríkì* is recognised and celebrated as a species of social action. In uttering *oríkì*, a performer is engaging in a dialogic relationship which is considered to be real in the sense that it conforms to the conventions that govern other dialogic exchanges in social life. The listening subject is the centre of the chant, and on him all the epithets, however disparate, converge.

However, uttering *oríkì* is also a more powerful act than engaging in other forms of discourse. It unlocks the powers inherent in the subject. When these powers are very great - when the subject is an oba or an òrìṣà - dangerous forces are unleashed, which, the singer declares, need to be neutralised by an appeasement before the utterance can continue:

> Kọ́láwọlé Ìbídùnní Ìgbálájọbí Àrẹ̀mú orúkọ mẹ́ta làá pe baba ẹni
> Bọ́ọ pe Oyèkúnlé kólúwarẹ̀ ó fepo sẹ́nu
> Bọ́ọ pe Àrẹ̀mú kólúwarẹ̀ ó fiyọ̀ sétè
> Wọn ò ṣe é fẹnu àtẹ́ pè
>
> Kọ́láwọlé Ìbídùnní Ìgbálájọbí Àrẹ̀mú we call a person's
> father by three names
> If you call Oyèkúnlé, make sure you rub your mouth with
> palm oil
> If you call Àrẹ̀mú, make sure you put salt on your lips
> He's not someone who can be called with an unflavoured
> mouth

Not only are certain personalities more imbued with power and therefore with danger, demanding caution in their invocation, but also certain modes of invocation are more powerful than others. *Oríkì* are more condensed, more capable of eliciting a surge of power between beings, than other utterance; and chanted *oríkì* are more effectual than those merely recited in an ordinary speaking voice:

> A ì wáá kàgbà Ṣèṣú láìkiwì
> Àkànjí Ajíbóyè babaà mi jẹ́ n báọ délé, aráa Kọọkin
>
> You can't salute an elder of Ìṣẹ̀ṣú without chanting *iwì*
> [a style of chanting characteristic of the
> ancestral masquerade cult]
> Àkànjí Ajíbóyè my father, let me go home with you, native
> of Kọọkin

In other words, someone as important as an elder of the royal 'Ìṣẹ̀ṣú' lineage should not have his *oríkì* addressed to him in a conversational manner. His eminence, almost of its own accord, compels the speaker to burst into the more highly-charged, vocally intense *iwì* chant. This suggests that the more elaborated and removed from other registers of speech, the more effectual and 'real' in its impact the utterance of *oríkì* is. Far from putting it in a kind of quarantine, where it is neutralised and immobilised, the intensification of artistry makes the utterance more powerful.

These quotations show that in uttering *oríkì*, the performer is bestowing something on the addressee: recognition, public acknowledgement, and something more, something bordering on actual empowerment. When spiritual beings are addressed, this aspect becomes quite explicit. It is by uttering *oríkì* that the followers of the ancestral *egúngún* masquerade arouse it to action and augment its dangerous force. In the festival of the thunder god Ṣàngó, it is concerted and intensive *oríkì* chanting, accompanied by *bàtá* drumming, that induces the *òrìṣà* to descend and possess his priest in the market place, thus empowering him to perform amazing stunts. It is utterance of the ancestor's *oríkì* at the grave shrine that infuses him with the surge of power needed to spring up, and fly the great and tiring distance that separates him from his descendants.

The empowerment that is effected in and through the utterance of *oríkì*, and the transcendence of states of being that results, are achieved through repeated and extensive salutation. Devotees of ancestral masquerades explain that to animate and activate their *egúngún*, they 'kì í, kì í, kì í', salute and salute and salute it, with *oríkì*. In the excerpt quoted above, Fadérera boasts that she 'saluted and saluted people', 'saluted person after person', until no-one could give back to her what she had given. The repeated verbs *kini kini/ kìnyàn kìnyàn* indicate that what she has in mind is not only greater depth of knowledge, but also a greater ability to keep going. Sheer volume is at issue. The more massive the profusion of attributions a performer can heap on her subject's head, the more enhancement and transcendence she can effect. The following quotation makes the principles underlying the production of an *oríkì* chant quite clear: a performer seeks to create the impression that she could go on forever:

> Máa wí máa wí ní í ṣodó iyán
> Máa rò máa rò ní í ṣorógùn ọkà
> Bẹ́ ẹ ní n wí mo lè wí dọ̀la
> Iṣẹ́ẹ̀ mi ni, òwòò mi ni
> É è sú mi
> É è rẹ̀ mí ...

> 'Speak on, speak on', that's the way of the pestle
> 'Keep talking, keep talking', that's the way of the
>   stirring stick
> If you want me to speak, I could speak until tomorrow
> It's my work, it's my trade
> I never weary of it
> I don't get bored with it ...

In other words, closure and boundaries are the last things the performer wants to achieve. The effectuality of this discourse depends on keeping it open, and keeping it going. It is with this intent that *oríkì* performers borrow materials - from other bodies of *oríkì* but also from other genres including proverbs, songs, Ifá verses, and even riddles - and incorporate them into the chant to supply materials to heap upon the head of their subject. The fatter and more fully-furnished the chant, the more effective it is in swelling the recipient's reputation.

Oríkì chants, then, are both disjunctive and incorporative. By an additive process, epithets of different provenance and with different fields of reference are brought into juxtaposition. The more epithets the performer can get hold of the better. To a skilled performer, all other texts are grist to her mill. With practised sleight of hand she can convert them into attributions. Whatever their origin, their author, their mode of signification and their referent, they can be juxtaposed with other items and made to serve the same attributive purpose. Their primary links within the chant are not to each other but to the subject to whom they are attributed. They co-exist in a relation of equivalence, in the same way that a plurality of names belonging to the same person are equivalent to each other. Because the aim is endlessness and profusion, *oríkì* epithets are not subordinated to an overarching authorial design. Now, this makes possible a sophisticated ideological effect that is both accommodating and potentially subversive. Space will permit me to give only the barest summary here. (A fuller discussion is to be found in Barber, 1991.)

PLURIVOCALITY

Since the items from which a performance of *oríkì* is constructed have independent and often widely separated origins, allude to separate incidents and qualities, and have their own explanatory hinterland without which they yield little meaning, there are gaps between them which, unlike the gaps and silences so brilliantly treated by Macherey (1978), are genetic, belonging to the very mode of existence of the chant, and not the inadvertent outcome of an ideological limit or block. Furthermore, for the same reasons, each item may speak with a different 'voice', some speaking from the point of view of an insider to the group, some of an outsider; some speaking as a young person, some as an elder; some as a male, some as a female. The style of *oríkì* not only permits but actively fosters and supplements both these characteristics. To genetic disjunction it adds extra, grammatical disjunctions that fissure items which are regarded by the practitioners of *oríkì* as single units. To the diverse voices arising from diverse compositional origins, *oríkì* superimpose a continual shifting of pronouns, a modulation and switching of 'speakers' even within semantically unified passages.

Both poles of the dialogic relation constituted in *oríkì* undergo continual changes of position. The living subject of the chant is both the occasion for the performance and its formal centre; but the performer salutes him by surrounding him with named relations. Many of the attributions begin 'Husband of ... ', 'Father of ... ', or 'Son of ... ' Often, the focus of the chant slides from the present subject to one of these relations, usually of an ascendant generation. From saluting a present subject through his ancestors, she modulates to saluting the ancestor himself, evoking his powers and recalling his attributes to life so that he may enhance the living descendant. Behind the shoulder of the apparent addressee are ranks of shadowy others, whose presence *oríkì* can recall. The performer fixes her attention on her subject as if nothing else in the world existed. Yet under cover of this bond, as her chant proceeds, she turns out to be sliding with often almost unmarked transitions from one subject to another. Whether these people are alive or dead makes no difference to the style of address nor to the ease of the transition. They assume in turn the role of addressee, the singer all the while keeping her eyes fixed on the living man before her. Not only this, but the 'you' of the text may shift in specificity. Sometimes 'you' is the actual person on whom the performer fixes her eyes, a named, living, present individual; at other times 'you' becomes a collective or generic representative of a whole lineage; sometimes it seems to be addressed to an individual as embodiment and recapitulation of an ancestor. 'Ọmọ Tóyìnbó, ọmọ Olúlọtán, ọmọ Enípẹ̀ẹ́dé, ìwọ ni mò ń bá wí' (You, child of Tóyìnbó, child of Olúlọtán, child of Enípẹ̀ẹ́dé, it's you I'm talking to): in an address like this, the living individual seems to encapsulate within him the personality of ascendant generations whose place he now occupies.

The 'I' who addresses this shifting subject moves its position and depth even more. From moment to moment the first person singular speaks from a different place.

Sometimes, as in the example of Ṣàngówẹ̀mí's own *oríkì* quoted above, the performer can speak *in propria persona*, as herself, so that the utterer of the text coincides with the 'I' within the text. She may do this to thank a listener for a gift of money, to wish someone well on a festive occasion, to announce her next theme, and so on. From time to time she may elaborate this 'I', as in the example just mentioned - quoting her own *oríkì* to establish a full-blown image of herself as an oral performer. Even in this construction of her own persona, a shift can be observed, from speech coming directly out of her own mouth (*I* Àbẹ̀ní am calling you) to a reference to herself in the third person ('the ones straight ahead desperately wish *she* would leave'). Within this same performance, however, Ṣàngówẹ̀mí's 'I' occupied many other positions: shifting from the voice of an outsider, excluded from the privileges of the lineage she was saluting, to the voice of an insider, affirming that lineage's privileges. As it happens, Ṣàngówẹ̀mí was not a member of the lineage in question; but neither of these voices in the text coincided with Ṣàngówẹ̀mí's own voice. Both represented a constructed position.

Even a chant addressed by one member of a lineage to another, where both are insiders, undergoes the same constant shifts. The 'I' changes position so rapidly and fluidly that normally the switches would not be registered by the listener except as a satisfying quality of overall texture. In an *egúngún* vigil chant performed in honour of a male priest of the *egúngún* masquerade cult by the women of his household, the performers begin with a textual 'I' who is more or less coincident with themselves as utterers of the text. They announce the reason for their vigil and their chant:

> Mé leè sùn o
> Mé leè sùn oorun ń kojú o
> Enígbòórí babaa wa ló béégún ṣiré lọ
>
> I cannot sleep
> I cannot sleep although my eyes are heavy
> Enígbòórí, our father, has gone off with the *egúngún*

Immediately afterwards, however, the text speaks from the point of view of a child of the lineage. Pursuing the theme of the ancestors, with whose propitiation the lineage is so much concerned, the text boasts in the child's voice of a trick he or she plays on his or her mother: the child pretends that its dead father's spirit is demanding propitiation, knowing that whatever food the mother offers at the shrine will also be eaten by the family:

> Kàkà kébi ó pa mí o
> N óò purọ́ fún ìyáà mi
> Màá ní babaà mi gbobì méjì
> Kò ní í kóbì lásán
> Ayérónfẹ́, a kó iyán rúgúdú a ní n fún baba
> Babaà mi ò nìkàn jẹ ẹ́
> Babaà mi mìlàa jẹ ẹ́
>
> Rather than go hungry
> I'll tell a lie to my mother
> I'll say my father wants two kola nuts
> She won't give him kola nuts alone
> Ayérónfẹ́, she'll bring a nice mound of pounded yam and
>   tell me to give it to father
> Father won't eat it alone
> No, father won' t eat it on his own ...

A moment later, the voice modulates to that of a wife of the lineage, boasting of her menfolk's wealth and generosity:

> Bí ọkọ́ mọ̀ mí í kẹ́
> N óò lọ rèé dégbèje aṣọ
> Àìmọ̀ mí í kẹ́
> N óò lọ rèé dẹ́gbẹ̀fà

> Kíkẹ́ tàìkẹ́
> N óò rèé dẹ́gbẹ̀ẹ́dógún
> Enígbòórí, n lọmọ Yáú i fi í dáṣọ ...
>
> If my husband knows how to care for me
> I'll go and buy fourteen hundred cloths
> Not knowing how to care for me
> I'll go and buy twelve hundred
> The moment he takes care of me
> I'll go and buy three thousand cloths
> Enígbòórí, that's how the children of Yáú buy their
> cloth.

There follows a distinctively male voice, a man of the lineage who declares jocularly that if any child of his fails to follow the lineage occupation of masquerading, he will disown its mother:

> Bí mo bá bímọ tí ò ṣe ilàwì òjẹ̀
> N óò ta ìyá ẹ̀ ma wáá fi ṣowó ẹmu ...
>
> If I have a child who doesn't become a singing
> masquerader
> I'll sell his mother and spend the money on palm-wine!

Each of these passages is directed to the same end: amplifying the reputation of the Enígbòórí lineage through reference to the lineage occupational specialisation of masquerading, or to the propitiation of ancestors so closely connected with the masquerade cult, or to the wealth deriving from this specialisation. But the specific point of each passage, and the manner in which it makes its point, depends on our apprehending the gender, age and status of the voice in which it is uttered.

The 'I' of an *oríkì* chant thus moves continually between male and female, adult and child, insider and outsider, specific and generalised persona. It occupies at times the position of the performer herself, at other times shifting completely across to the addressee and speaking in a voice that could be his. The text is all quotations, but they are not like the quotations in *The Waste Land*, identifiable fragments torn from some other context. There is no textual frame or background into which the *oríkì* 'quotations' are inserted; rather, the whole performance slides endlessly around the shifting pronouns, and no voice can be identified as a stable centre, as a starting point or as a frame of reference. Bakhtin (1981: 69) speaks of mediaeval texts where 'The boundary lines between someone else's speech and one's own speech were flexible, ambiguous, often deliberately distorted and confused. Certain types of texts were constructed like mosaics out of the texts of others'. *Oríkì* go beyond what he describes; without either reverence or parody, both of which imply an authorial point of view, they simply are constituted out of representations of the speech of innumerable, shifting others, incorporated into a single performer's utterance. The chant is held together by the suspension of contrasting elements in juxtaposition with each other. As it proceeds, each element asserts itself and then drops out of sight as it is succeeded by another. Each, in turn, is centre stage, just as each subject, for as long as the performer addresses him, is the centre of attention. Though performers are adept at making their materials do different things, according to the nature of the occasion, these materials still retain a certain irreducible independence from the performer's intent and from each other. The performer partially but never wholly imparts to the voices of the text her own inflexions. The juxtaposed voices partially but never wholly enter into relations with each other that open them up by setting them across and against each other. The result is a pervasive ambivalence and a perpetual suspension of resolution.

This allows something very interesting to happen. *Oríkì* chants, as 'praise' poetry, are largely directed toward acknowledging and enhancing the position of the successful in society. Men have more *oríkì*, and are more frequently, publicly and extensively celebrated in them, than women; and 'big men', those who have made a position for themselves by successful recruitment of supporters, have more than lesser men. Everyone has *oríkì*, for everyone has the potential of becoming something in life; but *oríkì* do flow along the dominant conduits of power and influence within the society, legitimating and further enhancing those in positions of advantage. The diverse 'voices' speaking from different points within the social spectrum are coopted to add to the wealth of attributions heaped upon the great. Nevertheless, because they are never *fully* assimilated, the voices of the downtrodden may still momentarily assert themselves. The result is a most profound irony. There is an example in the performance I have just discussed. It includes a passage in which the 'I' is that of a generalised wife of the Enígbòórí lineage, lamenting the exclusion of women from the *egúngún* masquerading which is the lineage men's pride and joy:

> Ará dá obìnrin ni ì í fi i mawo
> Obìnrin ò mọ̀gbalẹ̀
> Ìbá ṣe póbìnrin lè mawo
> Ǹ bá gbénú èkú wèkú
> Ayérónfẹ́ ma gbénú aṣọ ma tún waṣọ
> Ǹ bá sì gbénú agọ̀ so ìlẹ̀kẹ̀ ...

> Women are impatient, that is why they cannot know the secret cult
> Women do not know the sacred grove
> If women were allowed to know the secret cult
> I would wear one masquerade costume after another
> Ayérónfé I would wear one cloth after another
> And inside the costume I would wear beads ...

Women's exclusion from the secrets of the *egúngún* cult is what gives this cult its authority and mystery, for 'the secret' is at the centre of the sacred in Yoruba religious thought, and human collusion in maintaining the secret is indispensable. The women uphold the reputation of the *egúngún* cult, which is the speciality of their husbands' lineage, by expressing in accents of loss and desire their sense of exclusion. Their sorrow and grievance are co-opted - by the women themselves - to fulfil the dominant intent of the performance, which is to salute the Enígbòorí as represented by the male members. But the woman's voice still retains a certain independence, suggesting an alternative point of view. The ambiguity of the text is revealed in the expression *ará dá obìnrin ni ì í fi mawo*. The grammatical construction of this sentence suggests a translation 'Women are impatient/ restless/ unreliable, that's why they can't know the secret' - a male perspective on the exclusion of women. But the performer, Ẹrẹ-Ọ̀ṣun, told me it meant 'Women are fed up/frustrated because they cannot know the secret' - a female perspective.

The passage also reveals a further kind of ironical doubleness. Women assert that they cannot know the secret, but in the same breath they reveal that they do in fact know it: 'I would wear one masquerader's costume on top of another'. *Egúngún* costumes have human beings inside, and this is the 'secret' that women collude in pretending not to know. Because of the continually shifting voices in *oríkì* chants, the performers can go on to give, in the voice of a young boy of the lineage, graphic details of the experience of wearing an *egúngún* costume:

> Àròyé iṣẹ́ bàbáà mi ni
> Ìyáà mi ò tètè mọ̀
> Ó wáá yan èkọ dè mí
> Ó ṣeb'óko ni mo lọ
> Kò mọ̀ pábẹ́ ọdán n mo wà bí ègà
> Tí mo ń ti ń ṣawo ẹnu
> Mọ́ jọ́ọ̀bùn òjẹ̀ ó bá mi rẹ̀kúù mi
> Bọ́bùn òjẹ bá n gbágọ̀ wọ́n á bà mí láṣọ jẹ́
> Eléyùn-un nìí á wáá sorí palagún lábẹ́ aṣọ
> Bí kékeré Ògbórí bá ti gbágọ̀ à mọ́ọ́ yan
> Bí àgbà Ògbórí ti gbágọ̀ á mọ́ọ́ rìn
> Bí kékeré Ìlọ̀kọ́ bá gbágọ̀ yóò wù ọ́
> Enígbòórí, eyín á wáá fun kinkin lábẹ́ aṣọ.

> Vociferous talking is my father's work
> My mother was slow to realise
> She went and bought corn starch loaves to keep for me
> She thought I'd gone to the farm
> She didn't know that I was under the fig-tree like a weaver bird
> Where I was chattering interminably
> Don't let a dirty entertainer wear my *egúngún* costume
> If a dirty entertainer wears my outfit he'll spoil my cloth

> That one has a misshapen head under the cloth
> If a little Ògbórí puts on the costume he'll know how to
> swagger
> If an old Ògbórí puts on the costume he'll know how to walk
> If a little Ìlòkó puts on the costume he will delight you
> Enígbòórí, his teeth will be shining white under the cloth ...

The woman in this scene, the mother, is in ignorance of what her son is really doing. She thinks he's working on the farm, but he is really with his father's band of entertainment masqueraders performing *iwì*, the *egúngún* chant, 'under the fig tree', i.e. in the market. The boy makes a sharp distinction between the *egúngún* costume and the person under it which exposes the 'secret' in unmistakable terms. Because of the multiple, shifting, voices of *oríkì* it is possible for a woman performer to utter words such as these in the persona of a boy. She maintains an appearance of proper collusion in the 'secret' (in her role as a woman, she is like the mother, ignorant of the masqueraders' activities) while at the same time opening a crack in its facade which women as well as men can see through.

The performer thus occupies many different speaking positions. Always maintaining the strong dyadic bond between herself as performer and the recipient of the *oríkì*, she may nevertheless speak from a position within the recipient's own lineage, in words that could appropriately be uttered by himself. She may thus speak simultaneously *as* another person and *to* him, just as she may speak simultaneously as 'herself', the persona she constructs as utterer in the performance, and as representative of many other categories of person: the general public, women as a whole, women of a particular lineage. The 'person' she addresses sometimes coincides more or less with the actual, living man or woman before her, sometimes with a generalised representative of the group, sometimes with other positions in the social map. These positions are never fixed in *oríkì*, and the address slides easily from one position to another. Thus the capacity to open channels and effect a confluence of identities is built into the very composition of *oríkì*, revealing that this is indeed what they are for.

In a text like this, the distinction between 'fictive' and 'real' statements is irrelevant and unworkable. As in the medieval texts so illuminatingly discussed by J.A. Burrow, there is a sense in which textual utterances are prepared to be inhabited by others. 'In many medieval first person poems, the "I" speaks not for an individual but for a type. The speaker is to be understood not as the poet himself, but as a lover, a penitent sinner, or a devotee of the Virgin. Such lyrics offered themselves to be used by any amorous, penitent or devout reader for his own individual devotions, or confession, or wooing; and there is a good deal of evidence that they were indeed appropriated by individual readers in just this way'

(Burrow 1982:61). *Oríkì*, however, offer not a single speaking position which the 'reader' can occupy and appropriate, but a succession of different ones, as a performance continually modulates from one 'I' to another. Anyone with the interest, knowledge and occasion can inhabit the text, appropriating - but never wholly - the succession of 'I's that follow each other through it. An insider in a lineage that owns the formulation 'I grew old, but my beauty did not fade, in Kọọkin' inhabits the 'I' in this utterance in a different way from an outsider who quotes the same words to gratify someone else. The 'real' speaker, the persona of the performer, and the shifting 'I' of the text pass through fluctuating conjunctions and convergences never stable and never fully unified.

In *oríkì*, to summarise, the following features are found. Utterances are juxtaposed without one being subordinated to another. The discreteness of the elements in *oríkì* is heightened by supplementary stylistic disjunctions. The 'I' of the utterance moves continually, speaking with different voices, which are not 'placed' in relation to each other or to the self-presentation of the performer. The text is like a tissue of quotations, but quotation is never distinguished from context - it is *all* quotations - and these quotations modulate fluently and sinuously from one to the next within the prevailing mode of attribution. There is no overall design, no dominant 'authorial voice' in relation to which other voices are calibrated, no framework within which the disparate elements are assigned a determinate place. These features are what keep open the possibility of alternatives. While affirming 'the way things are', *oríkì*-statements contain the seeds of their own opposite. *Oríkì* are the means by which any given state is transcended. It is clear that the withholding of a fixed framework, of a single 'point of view' from which the world can be regarded, is what makes this perpetual motion of transcendence possible. *Oríkì* easily accommodate, indeed their mode encourages, the juxtaposition of opposites. These opposites are contained in one place and held together by a kind of surface tension, the thinnest of skins. Within the transparent integument - 'the 'bag' of *oríkì* into which all kinds of materials are thrown - continual transformations and modulations take place. *Oríkì* never criticise the community's 'orthodoxy', for where there is no heterodoxy, as Bourdieu (1977) suggests, there is no orthodoxy either, but rather an enveloping communal 'doxa' enclosing the whole of experience. But *oríkì* do always hold open, by the oppositions and contradictions embedded in them and deliberately held unresolved and suspended, a tiny 'loop-hole', as Bakhtin (1984) put it: the possibility of things being otherwise.

Oríkì themselves, then, guide us to a view of the text which puts the emphasis in very different places from the mainstream criticism still sustaining the Western written literary tradition and with it the tradition of Anglophone and Francophone African literature. *Oríkì* insist and comment upon their own dialogic character; on their participation in social process, which is represented as being at once empowering and productive; and on the effectuality of elaborated and artful uses of language. Far from putting a text in quarantine, the 'poetic' use of language - heightened and concentrated - and its stylised utterance in the form of a chant, actually adds force to utterance, enabling it to bring about changes of state in the recipients. The language of *oríkì* is often contrived to be difficult, allusive and obscure. As Babalọla, the greatest scholar of Yoruba oral traditions, puts it, '*Oríkì* are full of "half words", which, when they enter the mind of an intelligent person, become whole' (Babalọla 1966: 13; my translation). In other words, the *oríkì* announce their own need for interpretation, for supplementation by the hearer; the difficulties of the language tighten the collaborative dialogic bond between utterer and hearer, and increase the capacity of the utterance to open channels between subjects through which power can flow.

ORAL POETICS/ WRITTEN TEXTS

Oríkì tell us how to apprehend *oríkì*, not how to apprehend Ifá verses, *àlọ́* (folk tales) or myths. The Ifá corpus, at least, has its own hermeneutic devices embedded within it, its own principles of interpretation which have yet to be studied. However, though interpreting Ifá or *àlọ́* is not the same as interpreting *oríkì*, nor is the relation between speaker, hearer and the voices within the text the same, nevertheless the metatexts - the commentary within the *oríkì* texts discussed above - do seem to contain a number of general principles which might form the basis of a broader Yorùbá oral poetics. All the Yorùbá oral genres embody a heightened dialogic relationship in which a proper response from the hearer/s enters into the constitution of the text itself. All are sociable in the sense that they are regarded not as a segregated domain of 'literature' (for which concept there is no translation in Yorùbá) but as an especially potent and pleasurable form of social discourse, set apart in the sense of being more highly valued and more carefully preserved than other speech registers, but nonetheless, grounded in what Vološinov called the 'little speech genres of internal and external kinds' which 'engulf and wash over all persistent forms and kinds of ideological creativity' (Vološinov 1973: 19). And there is a sense in which all of them, though less markedly than *oríkì*, privilege language itself over the achievement of a closed form.

Modern, popular, semi-oral and written forms in Yorùbá also seem to me to share, to a considerable extent, the dialogic, sociable and language-oriented character of oral literary production. One of the most popular modern genres is the neo-traditional chant, using *oríkì*-like formulations but greatly simplified and with greatly increased syntagmatic continuity. These chants offer observations on life, comments on the political and cultural situation, general reflections on morality and behaviour, and so on. They tend to be reassuring rather than original, confirming what the audience already believes rather than challenging it. But they evoke intense delight in listeners, for they appeal to a shared but special and highly valued command of language. The listener participates, sometimes by recognising and mentally completing allusions to proverbial formulations, sometimes by appreciating a novel reinterpretation of a well-known saying, sometimes by following the twists and turns of stylised punning and tonal play. In Yorùbá novels - of which there is already a substantial tradition,[5] usually ignored in discussions of modern Nigerian literature - plots and characterisation, though often lively and strongly drawn, take second place to the authors' celebration of Yorùbá as a medium of expression. What makes these stories enthralling is the endlessly inventive, creative, sophisticated and *knowing* use of language. The writer is in collusion with the reader: the reader, like the listener in an *oríkì* chant, must be able to reconstitute the 'half words' offered by the writer. Yorùbá popular theatre, similarly, is seen by audiences as a repository of linguistic treasures, both archaic *trouvailles* and new coinages. 'Inú eré lèdè Yorùbá kù sí', as one participant remarked; 'It's in the plays that the Yorùbá language survives'. In all these texts, profusion and display are positively valued, and produce an intensity of effect that is highly exhilarating. Embedded in the profusion there are often hints and echoes of what is more strikingly visible in *oríkì*: a pervasive irony arising from the juxtaposition of opposites and alternatives, without an overriding resolution into a single view. All of them, finally, are 'didactic' in a broad and creative sense: that is, they consciously participate in the social reproduction of values, offering the audience or reader a 'lesson' which is often eagerly sought out. 'Others may go to the theatre to laugh', I was told, 'but intelligent people go to pick out a moral that they can use in their lives'. Like the intelligent person in the proverb quoted by Babalǫla, the popular audience thus takes responsibility for its own edification, making whole what comes to it in 'half words'. The poet does 'affirm' things: the performance of these texts is explicitly described as providing models for

---

[5] For comprehensive surveys of Yorùbá written literature, see Babalǫla (1985) and Iṣǫla (1988).

action.

In this sense, the written and semi-written Yorùbá texts do exist in continuum with the great and still thriving oral traditions. The tradition of Nigerian literature written in English, by contrast, is cut off from the vitality afforded by this productive, ironical, dialogic, effectual and sociable celebration of the powers of utterance. Unlike English literature written in England, however, it still has the inestimable benefit of proximity to a living, popular, literary tradition. In Abiọla Irele's view, its 'distinctive mark is the *striving to attain* the condition of oral expression, even within the boundaries established by Western literary conventions'. (Irele 1990b: 63. My italics). In this way, 'the oral tradition continues to function as a fundamental reference of African expression, as the matrix of the African imagination' (Irele 1990a). If this is accepted, scholars of written African literature can no longer afford to relegate oral literature to preliminary chapters of critical works which draw their methodology entirely from modern European written sources. A proper assessment of the relation of written literature to oral requires an oral poetics inspired from within the oral domain.

WORKS CITED

Babalọla, Adeboye. *Àwọn Oríkì Orílẹ̀*. Glasgow: Collins, 1966.

──────. "Yorùbá Literature." *Literature in African Languages*. Eds. B.W. Andrzejewski, S. Pilaszewicz, and W. Tyloch. Cambridge: Cambridge University Press, 1985. 157-59.

Bakhtin, Mikhail. *The Dialogic Imagination*. Ed. Michael Holquist, trans. Caryl Emerson and Michael Holquist. Austin, Texas: University of Texas Press, 1981.

──────. *Rabelais and his World*. Trans. Helène Iswolsky. Bloomington: Indiana University Press, 1984.

──────. *Speech Genres and Other Late Essays*. Trans. Vern W. McGee, ed. Caryl Emerson and Michael Holquist. Austin: University of Texas Press, 1986.

Barber, Karin. "Yorùbá *oríkì* and deconstructive criticism." *Research in African Literatures*, 15 (1984): 497-518.

──────. *I Could Speak Until Tomorrow: Oríkì, Women and the Past in a Yorùbá Town*. London: Edinburgh University Press for the I. A. I., 1991.

Bennett, Tony. *Formalism and Marxism*. London: Methuen, 1979.

Bourdieu, Pierre. *Outline of a Theory of Practice*. Trans. Richard Nice. Cambridge: Cambridge University Press, 1977.

Burrow, J.A. *Medieval Writers and their Work*. Oxford: Oxford University Press, 1982.

Damane, M., and Sanders, P.B. *Lithoko: Sotho Praise Poems*. Oxford: Clarendon Press, 1974.

Eagleton, Terry. *Walter Benjamin, or towards a revolutionary criticism*. London: Verso, 1981.

―――――. *Literary Theory*. Oxford: Basil Blackwell, 1983.

Irele, Abiọla. "Orality, Literacy and African Literature." *Semper Aliquid Novi: Littérature Comparée et Littératures d'Afrique*. Ed. János Riesz and Alain Ricard, Tübingen: Gunter Narr Verlag, 1990. 251-63.

―――――. "The African Imagination." *Research in African Literatures* 21 (1990): 49-67.

Iṣọla, Akinwumi. "Contemporary Yorùbá Literary Tradition," *Perspectives on Nigerian Literature: 1700 to the Present*. Vol. 1. Ed. Yẹmi Ogunbiyi, Lagos: Guardian Books, 1988. 73-84.

Jeyifo, Biọdun. "The Nature of Things: Arrested Decolonization and Critical Theory." *Research in African Literatures* 21 (1990): 33-48.

Julien, Eileen. *African Novels and The Question of Orality*, Bloomington, Indiana: Indiana University Press, 1992.

Macherey, Pierre. *A Theory of Literary Production*. Trans. Geoffrey Wall. London: Routledge and Kegan Paul, 1978.

Ọlatunji, Olatunde O. "The Yorùbá Oral Poet and His Society." *Research in African Literatures* 10 (1979): 179-207.

Pratt, Mary Louise. *Toward a Speech Act Theory of Literary Discourse*. Bloomington: Indiana University Press, 1977.

―――――. "Conventions of Representation." *The Taming of the Text*. Ed. Willie Van Peer. London: Routledge, 1988.

Sekoni, Rọpo. "Oral Literature and the Development of Nigerian Literature." *Perspectives on Nigerian Literature: 1700 to the Present*. Vol. 1. Ed. Yẹmi Ogunbiyi, Lagos: Guardian Books, 1988. 46-52.

Vološinov, V. N. *Marxism and the Philosophy of Language*. Trans. Ladislav Matejka and I. R. Titunik. New York: Seminar Press, [1929] 1973.

Yai, O.B. "Issues in Oral Poetry: Criticism, Teaching and Translation." *Discourse and its Disguises: the Interpretation of African Oral Texts*. Eds. Karin Barber and P. F. de M. Farias, Birmingham: Centre of West African Studies, 1989.

LITERARY THEORY AND AFRICAN LITERATURE
edited by J. Gugler, H.-J. Lüsebrink, J. Martini
Münster/Hamburg 1993, pp. 113-133

A EUROPEAN'S READING OF SOYINKA'S AND OSOFISAN'S THEATRE TEXTS IN 1990

JOACHIM FIEBACH

African arts or texts, like others, are read in specific, historically concrete circumstances that shape the reader's perceiving and understanding. My reading is that of a Central European, more precisely of a German, who has been deeply involved in events in Germany over the past thirty years and who has also been influenced by his African experiences to a considerable extent. My attitudes toward artistic and nonartistic realities rest on a historically dialectical conception that appears to me in many respects to be similar to views expressed in works related to the Birmingham "Culture Studies" project.[1] I understand artistic texts as specific realities in their own right, on their own merit, that is, not as a reflection of something else and yet as phenomena that can and therefore should provide possibilities for critical reflection upon realities outside the artistic texts.

Femi Osofisan's *The Oriki of a Grasshopper* (1986) is a text on the attitudes of a wealthy businessman, a university lecturer and socialist, and the latter's girlfriend and fellow socialist. This is how the author succinctly describes his three characters, Claudius, Imaro, and Moni. The situation and attitudes the text provides are the following. Imaro, the intellectual, has packed his belongings and awaits arrest for his involvement in a student riot that challenged the establishment. The businessman reveals that, by virtue of his social position (power), he has seen to it that Imaro is spared detention, the rough treatment suffered by Imaro's colleagues. Moni is breaking up with Imaro because she reasons that he is too close to the rich to be sincerely devoted to the revolutionary cause. Her brother, Estragon, has been detained and his house has been devastated, but Imaro has been protected by his connections. She does not love him anymore: "I don't want

---

[1] For example Hebdige, 181-244.

to be contaminated." (41) Imaro wants to escape from his ambivalent position and asks for a job in his friend's company. The businessman makes it clear to him that he is not suitable for such employment; it is too late for him to join the non-intellectual, competitive business world. Imaro should remain a university lecturer, for there will be no new generation if the real teachers quit "if no one remains to nurture the fresh minds" (36). Moni cannot stay with Imaro because he is, as she puts it, a wreck (40). He sustains his socialist ideals by depending on capitalists, which is not acceptable to her. Imaro and Moni recall their common past when they jointly dreamed of the revolution for which he was a vigorous campaigner. Groping for dreams that can accord with the contemporary situation untainted, the girl begins a visionary song praising the anti-apartheid struggle, "Cry Amandla!" Imaro joins in when she is singing, "Let Freedom come! To the Forest of thorns and ... grasshoppers" (as she characterizes Imaro). Moni leaves and Imaro ends the song alone, transfixed, according to the stage direction.

Apart from the passages denoting Imaro's prospects of becoming a company man (27-36), there are only a few sequences of events that describe concrete "physical" activities: waiting; the two friends smoking and drinking; the revelation that Imaro was saved by his friend's connections; Moni breaking off her relationship with Imaro. The larger part of the text consists of arguments, reasoned explanations that do not seem to be integral elements of the activities (the situations) in which they are embedded. In regard to their textual structure, they quite often refer to views, dreams, and attitudes that appear to be quite separate from the events denoted or acted out.

The text begins with the presentation of the lecturer's office. The businessman Claudius, a former schoolmate and close friend of Imaro, shows up for a rehearsal of Beckett's *Waiting for Godot*. They cannot start because Estragon, a third man, is missing. They smoke cigars and drink. Claudius tells his friend he had to leave his car and driver behind at the campus gate and walk in. A conversation on essential matters ensues. Imaro, in an attempt to tease Claudius, says he is not behaving according to type and is a disgrace to his class by walking a long way in the dust. Claudius retorts: "So that makes two of us, ehn? Looking at you puffing away at that cigar, and drowning yourself in Chivas Regal. ... Comrade! Revolutionary greetings! *A luta continua*!" (7) After that, in a rather lengthy passage, Imaro ponders his life: "The falsehood of our lives!" As an intellectual he lives in a masquerade: "we intellectuals, whatever labels we give ourselves: We're just as privileged as the rest." Claudius answers: "What's this? A confessional?" And Imaro: "Since I woke up this morning,

I've been thinking. Asking: What's the value of my life?" His self-searching has been sparked by the police raid. All his colleagues were arrested. He is waiting to be taken.

After having explained the situation, Imaro resumes philosophizing: "That's what I'm trying to say! We've been waiting all our lives! You said it just now. We, the so-called intellectuals, we're just professional waiters. ... We wait. We talk. We fiddle with the props. Sometimes even, we relish the left-overs. Like Estragon, nibbling bones." (9) Claudius expresses his choices, his lifestyle, his philosophy of life. He "chose to survive, I chose to live beyond fear, to conquer power. I wouldn't go and stretch out my neck now to talk to rioting students." Imaro and his colleagues had tried to dissuade the students from violence (11). Narrating why and how they calmed down the rioting students, he outlines his philosophy and reveals his recent insights into strategies of transforming society. Students should not let themselves be slaughtered because they are outnumbered (outgunned) by the police and the military. Claudius is giving him the cues.

There follows a remember-the-past role-playing technique that depicts Claudius and Imaro as students defying a civilian minister; they resemble Imaro's students of today standing up to the military rulers. It seems hardly more than a technique to provide new cues for Imaro to externalize his thinking. The former civilian government is gone, but "did poverty go with them? Did exploitation go to the grave?" Imaro delineates the social fabric of today in the indefinite, abstract plural, speaking of "the many" who are opposing each other on differently weighted sides of the barricade: "And the rich now have policemen. They have soldiers, with numbers and uniforms. They make their numerous Luckys go down into the mines and bring out the ore. And then straight into the white ships. Always, always into the white ships." Claudius advises Imaro to unpack his bag; the police won't come for him. Claudius is in a position to save his old friend, and he has spoken to an officer.

At this point Moni, Imaro's girlfriend, enters. Estragon, her brother, has been arrested and his place is in ruins. Imaro explains in the indefinite, abstract plural why the arresters had behaved that way: "Look at them, how little they earn. Their miserable wages. They can't understand why we, so comfortable in our university chairs, can still 'make trouble' as they see it. They get so bitter." (22) Moni is going to leave him. She sees him as Claudius's lap-dog because he is under Claudius's protection and lives comfortably in the rich men's world: "And on Sundays you put on a jersey and accompany them to the squash court. ... God, how I've been deceived! How I loved you! ... All that talk about revolution, war, exploitation, the masses ... but you had built your escape route." (24)

An argument between Moni and Claudius ensues. Imaro steps in: "You're right, Moni. ... I wasn't trying to build myself an escape route. These people, these capitalists you mention, they are indeed too close to me. Maybe I watched them grow up, came to know them so intimately. I know their crimes, but I also know their grotesque fear of poverty, of insecurity, of death." (26) Imaro now wants to quit academia, not the least ("almost to himself") because he wants to ascertain what breaks students after they leave the universities. They come back, if at all, only to show off a Mercedes (27). He wants to get a job with Claudius's company. The role-playing passage already mentioned follows. Claudius winds up the sequence by elaborating on getting rich and staying rich (35). Claudius leaves, and Moni and Imaro continue philosophizing and analyzing the situation.

The arguments and discussions about revolution, campaigning for change, and the unjust social rift appear to be rather loosely connected with what the text conveys as the actual situation in which the characters have to act. Moni appears to be a mere abstraction (a "thought-up" textual construct); she is nothing more than the (abstract) girlfriend who is breaking up with Imaro because of her fixation on the revolutionary cause. There is only one critical event that is concretely connected with her "physical" existence -- the incident that made Imaro pack up and that led to Estragon's arrest. The incident serves as a springboard for Imaro to ponder the basic division in society between the Pozzos and the Luckys, and thus the revolutionaries' predicament in general. Imaro: "What have I achieved? I have talked and talked. Like the others. I've tried to teach my students that we can build a new world. That a brave new world is within our grasp. But to what purpose? Our society has marked us out as eccentric. Worse, as felons! And I am tired. I can't live my whole life as a fugitive." (28) What kind of new world? Why is he a fugitive? According to his own words, he has so far been well situated as a lecturer. It seems as if he yearns to exist in a world of humane, moral generalities and brushes aside, neglecting or even disdaining, the life he is living. "And shout it all to the comrades! Imaro has turned tail and joined them! The tall socialist obelisk has crashed down in the market place of capital, and broken into fragments! ... All because I spoke to Claudius, my friend, at a moment of stress."

Moni: "Rave on, but it's the truth. ... You're their servant! Even if you pretend to see! They take away the others and leave you alone. Untouched. ... You're the Establishment's token marxist, my dear. Nobody will ever touch you. ... Because it's good for them that you are here. Screeching like a cricket, but unable to bite!" (40ff.) The character Moni, for its part, is existent almost only in dreams, in visions of a world outside her own social and/or private realm of relations, interests, desires - if there is any such world at all. It is hardly denoted by the text. She recalls how she saw Imaro in the past: "I first knew you and grew to love you - tall on so many platforms, talking, laughing, waving your arms, specially your arms, affirming. On many nights your voice has come to my pillow, like an echoing dream, your voice urging us not to despair, to rise up and carry the burden of our destiny. Teaching us." Imaro's voice joins her now as she goes on. Both: "We, the young and the gifted of Africa. Of all the black world. We, the educated and the articulate. Rise! Rise up now and shake off your slumber. History waits for our footsteps, for the command of our voices." (38)

The character Moni and probably Imaro too are fond of voices, visions, of abstractions, for that matter, that are not necessarily tied up with their sensuous existence, their physicality. Or to put it another way, they seem to have succumbed to visions, to abstractions, cherishing them, letting them rule over their lives, their actual existence. Moni: "All those beautiful things. Oh, how many words in your voice! And I would reach out and pull it close, I would cuddle your voice jealously, till it turned to endless dreams of hope, of forests shaping into radiant cities, into schools, hospitals, factories and fertile farmlands, of slums yielding place to skyscrapers. ... Aah, is it that same voice I hear now, filled with such dirges of defeat?" (39)

As for Imaro, his predicament seems to stem less from a split personality -- from leading two lives that cannot be harmonized or do not square, therefore defecting from revolution -- than it appears to stem from disillusion, from the confrontation of abstract notions of reality with stark reality. Both characters fail to maintain the "one-dimensional" reservoir of unproblematized dreams they need to sustain their living in a world of ideal visions that appears to be separated from their very existence, or perhaps from any reality outside their "actual thinking." She was (is) in love with voices, probably with the voices' capacity to produce meanings or, more precisely, to signify the much cherished (desired) dream world. This seems to apply to Imaro as well: the final song on Amandla, on the South African reality that is neither his nor her reality, could signify he is formulating a new realm of dreaming that may enable him to carry his "split-personality life" into the future. "To the numerous hands / Pounding without pause / Against oppression." He ends with the vision of a human chain to be -- hand in hand "till / We form a wide ring of wishes" (46). Again wishes, a desired reality, not the one that he has to experience daily.

To compare Soyinka's writing with Osofisan's I should turn to *Season of Anomy*. Ofeyi's milieu, his intellectual background, his endeavors to cope with fighting or even transforming society or unbearable sociocultural conditions are similar to the social situation and to the dreams of Osofisan's university people. And it would be interesting to look at the love stories in both texts (Moni-Imaro, Irisiye-Ofeyi). But I prefer to turn to *Madmen and Specialists*, which, as a drama text, provides a fairer reference for a comparative reading. The text is well known and I need not outline the narrative structure. I am pointing to three sequences of events. On his homecoming the specialist Bero is being obtrusively molested, apparently even physically affected, by the priest's banal chatter and patronizing manner. The story of Bero's father, of the old man's decision to do something about the war is part of the meaningless chatter. The priest narrates that Bero's father, upon receiving a letter from Bero, who had been working in the war zones, all of a sudden stood up and shouted: "We've got to legalize cannibalism." Now the priest wants to know "if he still intends to legalize cannibalism." Bero answers tersely, even harshly to stop the mindless bother: "He does." The priest rambles on: "A stubborn man, once he gets hold of an idea. ... But human flesh." (34) And Bero, taking a decisive step to send him fleeing in consternation, retorts: "But why, Pastor. It's quite delicious."

At this point Bero's sister takes on the priest's role, pestering Bero. She does not believe what he has said, but gets the same answer in a deliberately cruel, cold manner: "Delicious. The balls, to be exact." He warns her sternly not to become concerned with matters outside her little realm "where you're safe. (*Quietly*) Or sane." Bero gives a short description of his father's activities, of his strange enigmatic references to "As." He had served the officers human flesh, and he had tried to stir up the disabled, the victims of the war, to make them THINK! (37) This amounts to challenging the prevailing power structure: "Can you picture a more treacherous deed than to place a working mind in a mangled body?" (37) The supposed-to-be-challengers are at the ready -- they are the mendicants, the running dogs Bero had already sent to his sister's and father's house to spy for him. Bero's sisters calls them "loathsome toads" (39). She is appalled by their antics, their self-abasing "mad" behavior, their cowardice, and their viciously clownlike rebelliousness at the same time. Trying to put an end to his sister's questioning, Bero makes his attitude clear. Why not eat human flesh? "What is one flesh from another? So I tried again. ... It was the first step to power you understand. Power in its purest sense. The end of inhibition." (36) Rationalizing or, more precisely, communicating his philosophy is a means to further, to bolster, to confirm what he experiences, what he actually or "physically" is doing, that is, pursuing at the given moment. It is a means to act as the powerful security chief, as the Specialist who holds others' lives in his hand and who has just returned home to deal with the dangerous threat his father's former activities and his still menacing conception of "As" pose to him and the system he works for.

The Old Man appears at the beginning of Part Two for the first time. He is kept in the cellar of his house under guard of the mendicants, the Specialist's "running dogs." The stage direction reads: "The MENDICANTS are crouched, standing, stooping in their normal postures, humming their chant and listlessly throwing dice. The OLD MAN's attitude varies from boredom to tolerant amusement." The mendicants are the war-crippled whom the Old Man tried to stir into thinking during the war. Now they are playing nasty degrading tricks on him. As Afaa puts it: "He got us into this mess. If there is one thing I can't stand it's amateurs." Bero continues playing debasing games with him. He allows him to write a letter -- but tells him to go to a stationery to buy writing paper although the Old Man's money had been taken away. The Old Man wants to smoke his pipe but does not have a light. Bero offers him cigarettes. Accepting Bero's terms is the only way to get a smoke. He coerces the Old Man into repressing his desire, that is to say into abasing himself. The Old Man sums it up: "Shall I teach you what to say? Choice! Particularity! What redundant self-deceptive notions! More? More?" (48)

The situation concerns not only the confrontation of two antagonistic stances, worldviews. Security chief Bero wants to unveil what his father's "real intentions" were, what "As" is all about, this looming threat to the system, a danger aggravated by the enigmatic nature "As" seems to have. It is not under control, yet control is the basic pillar of the system, and Bero's essential interest in social relations is control. He embodies the very nature of all-encompassing control, he is the Specialist at maintaining the existing power structure and thus has to get any phenomenon within his reach under control. He is the perfect control and power machine. Any particularity, any elusive otherness, that is difficult to control has to be wiped out.

The third event: The Old Man and the mendicants re-present (recall by acting) songs he had taught them. For instance, "Pro patria mourir." In ancient Athens there was not only a quorum but a forum where everyone could gather and co-determine society's policies. Blindman: "That, children, was democracy." Cripple sings to the tune of "When the Saints": "Before I join / The saints above. ... Before I bid / This earth adieu / I want my dues from that damned quorum." (60)

Bero enters and resumes interrogating the Old Man: "So you haven't given up your little tricks." He wants to know about "As," the enigmatic doctrine the Old Man had spread among the victims of the war, the downtrodden, the underdogs, "the playword of your convalescents, the pivot of whatever doctrine you used to confuse their minds, your piffling battering ram at the idealism and purpose of this time and history. What is As, Old Man?" The answer: "You seem to have described it to your satisfaction" (62). "As" appears to be a weapon to combat the powers-that-be, the system that divides human beings into those who hold power and exercise brutal control and those who are controlled. The "piffling battering ram" is directed against the system, or as the system's doorkeeper, the Specialist in maintaining tight, ironclad control, puts it "against the idealism." "Idealism" could be read as the ideological fabric or smokescreen of the system, a term used by Bero himself in another round interrogating the Old Man. The Old Man gives an example what "As" could be. One of the disabled once said: "Let's send our gangrenous dressings by post to those sweet-smelling As agencies and homes. He sat down to compile a mailing list." Then the Old Man understood what "As" was like. Bero retorts disdainfully that the Old Man should look at "your companions -- your humanity." Old Man: "I recognized it. A part of me identifies with every human being." Bero: "You will be disillusioned soon enough." The Old Man: "I do not harbour illusions."

Compared with Osofisan's characters, those who in Soyinka's text dream or who attempt to fight unbearable conditions -- capitalism or Bero's repressive and killing system of "As" -- seem to have entirely different attitudes toward their own situations, a different awareness of the quality (the actual chances) of their views and convictions, in particular of the structures in which they have to act. The Old Man not only tried to stir the downtrodden into thinking about their lot and thus the inhuman cannibalist system but served those in power too -- and human flesh on top of that. He accepts the cigarettes the system's chief security man offers him, in a sense conniving with his (and the underdogs') torturer, a step perhaps unthinkable for the high-minded Imaro, who is morally torn apart, a "wreck," because he socializes with his old friend Claudius, a nicely benign capitalist. Seen this way, the Old Man does not harbor any illusions, and he acts accordingly. He does not hesitate to fight a brutal, cannibalistic system and at the same time to serve its activists human flesh, that is to say, to compromise, to live with the torturers and even to use their ways of dealing with reality. Second, arguments about and over the system and possible changes, the presentation of one's worldview, one's moral stance, spring from the physical confrontation of characters. Reasoning and arguing are "techniques" or "instruments," weapons to further the characters' interests, wants, and tasks. Philosophizing is an act to hurt someone or to defend oneself, to keep oneself alive and to beat the adversary. Seen from this angle, it is a rather profane, a sensuous activity (phenomenon) bound up with and part and parcel of the concrete, the physical or corporal positions (attitudes) of the characters. It is not, as in the case of Osofisan's two high-minded revolutionary characters, an expression of living in a dream world of humane visions, which is the world one actually lives in. Desiring to live in a world of revolutionary dreams is, perhaps, their very existence, their attitude towards life.

What the structure of Osofisan's text thematizes -- or at least signifies to me -- is a propensity to a binary perception of the world. Seen this way, the text is rather closed and/or one-dimensional. Its binary nature seems to leave only two clear-cut -- each excluding the other -- attitudes and/or perspectives imposed on the reader. Accentuating extremely limited choices, the text tends to connote that there is a rather simple world to deal with and that there is little room for movement. The structure and the thematization of Soyinka's text, on the other hand, speaks about constantly shifting and changing perspectives, of intricacy and complexity, of a virtual inexhaustible generation and regeneration of paradoxical movement. The multidimensionality of fluidity connotes in a sense that there are chances and, perhaps, an actual drive to change, to alter things.

Applying Deleuze and Guattari's distinction between the schizophrenic attitude and the paranoid attitude to the Osofisan and Soyinka texts suggests to what extent they may produce different significations:

> Et un type ou pôle schizo-révolutionnaire, qui suit les *lignes de fuite* du désir, passe le mur et fait passer le flux ... je ne suis pas des vôtres, je suis éternellement de la race inférieure, je suis une bête, un nêgre. Les honnêtes gens disent qui il ne faut pas fuir, que ce n'est pas bien, que c'est inefficace, et qu'il faut travailler pour des réformes. Mais le révolutionnaire sait que la fuite est révolutionnaire, *withdrawal freaks*, a condition d'entrainer la nappe ou de faire fuir un bout du systeme. Passer le mur, dût-on se faire nègre a la manière de John Brown. George Jackson: 'Il se peut que je fuie, mais tout au long de ma fuite je cherche une arme!'

And:

> Le paranoïaque machine des masses, il est artiste des grands ensembles molaires, formations statistiques ou grégarités, phénomènes de foules organisés. ... On dirait que, des deux directions de la pysique, la direction moléculaire qui va vers les grands nombres et les phénomènes de foule, et la direction moléculaire qui s'enfonce au contraire dans les singularités, leurs interactions et leurs liaisons a distance ou de différents ordres, le paranoïaque a choisi la premiere: il fait de la macro-physique. Et que le schizo au contraire va dans l'autre direction, celle de la micro-physique, des molécules en tant qu'elles n'obéissent plus aux lois statistiques; ondes et corpuscules. Flux et objets partiels qui ne sont plus tributaires des grands nombres, lignes de fuite infinitésimales au lieu des perspectives de grands ensembles. ... L'un est un investissement de *groupe assujetti*, aussi bien dans la forme de souveraineté que dans les formations coloniales de l'ensemble grégaire, qui réprime et refoule le désir des personnes; l'autre, un investissement de *groupe-sujet* dans les multiplicités transversales qui

portent le désir comme phénomene moléculaire, c'est-à-dire objets partiels et flux, par opposition avec les ensembles et les personnes. (329-30, 332-33)

What Osofisan's text is almost obsessively conveying, the necessity to change, appears to be contradicted by the text itself, by its binary structure and the binarily structured realities of society and the individual it signifies. Using Deleuze and Guattari's notions and terms, the text appears to be "paranoid" by neglecting and suppressing the desires and wants of "singularities," by depreciating the concrete, the "physicality" of the individual (the singularity). Moni and Imaro are constantly repressing their desire, their inner selves. The abstractions -- that is, the poor masses, the many rich men, the "herd" -- appear to be "idolized" or, at least greatly "foregrounded" by Moni's and Imaro's attitudes. Readers can easily construct them as cemented by Claudius's urging Imaro to remain the craving-for-the-revolution intellectual. Soyinka, on the other hand, created a "schizoid" text whose preferences cannot be easily pinpointed, whose perspectives are always changing, whose very structure speaks of multidimensionality. What it may signify appears to be highly elusive, and hence it is a text "on the run," "becoming" (Deleuze and Guattari's "Becoming"). It may connote transformation, perhaps even fundamental societal change. It speaks strongly of the particular, the singularities, the concrete, and of "physicality" focusing on desires, tracing their "line of flight" (Fluchtlinien). Seen from this perspective, Osofisan's text, which almost desperately thematizes liberation (revolutionary change), looks rather conservative. It speaks of the suppression of desires, thus of the individual's (the singularity's) self-denial, of his or her psychical and intellectual self-mutilation or self-effacement -- perhaps of rigidification.

Soyinka's text could be read as a subversive phenomenon brimming with vibrant moves, rebellious activities, maybe even lust for change. It speaks of the struggle to emancipate desires, of productive power as an agent in the shaping of social relations and in the determination of the individual's attitudes. Without identifying with Deleuze and Guattari's reading of societal mechanism and history in general, I point to their conception of desire as *the* productive force:

Si le désir produit, il produit du réel. Si le désir est producteur, il ne peut l'être qu'en réalité, et de réalité. ... L'être objectif du désir est le Réel en lui-même. ... Comme dit Marx, il n'y a pas manque, il y a passion comme 'être objet naturel et sensibel'. Ce n'est pas le désir qui s'étaie sur le besoin, c'est le contraire, ce sont les besoins qui dérivent du désir: ils sont contre-produits dans le réel que le désir produit. ... Le désir se tient toujours proche des conditions d'existence objective, il les épouse et les suit.

The poor and the dispossesed know

> que le désir a 'besoin' de peu de choses, *non pas ces choses qu'on leur laisse, mais ces choses mêmes dont on ne cesse de les déposséder*, et qui ne constituaient pas un manque au coeur du sujet, mais plutôt l'objectivité de l'homme, l'être objectif de l'homme pour qui désirer c'est produire, produire en réalité. Le réel n'est pas impossible, dans le réel au contraire tout est possible, tout devient possible. ... Les révolutionnaires, les artistes et les voyants se contentent d'être objectifs, rien qu'objectifs: ils savent que le désir étreint la vie avec une puisance productrice ... (34-35)

It is, for example, the desire of the mendicants (e.g. the Blindman) to get their share of the sensuous world's riches and/or to get a segment of that "damned quorum" that constitutes the productive potential of Soyinka's text in regard to conveying the possibility of change.

The reading would itself be one-dimensional if I stopped at the point of looking at textual structures and whatever they may signify and ignored the historical contexts, the sociocultural realities from which the texts emerged and therefore were meant to reveal in their significations. Reading a text without trying to take into consideration the sociocultural realities in which it is embedded or toward which it is directed in the first place could constitute just another binary, manichean approach. The actual relationship between reader and text is, "unconsciously," a three-tiered one (Mukarovsky), at least. My reading, that is, my perception of a text, includes my understanding of the sociocultural situation at a given place and time. It is an expression of the way I relate to the world, the manner in which I interpret the world. It necessarily comprises my experience and thus has great bearing on my construction of Nigerian and African realities. I try to look at myself from the outside, to objectify my perspective thereby, and enable me to criticize it.

I know quite well that Osofisan's texts have in general been widely received as complex. They thematize the necessity of societal transformation and revolution, and their structures speak of permanent movement, of intricate multidimensionality, not least in their affinities to Brecht's dramaturgy. Imaro's speeches elaborate this thematically. As far as the signification by dialogue is concerned, the intricate play of paradoxes and ambivalences can hardly be overlooked. And I assume the Nigerian intellectuals -- who else reads Osofisan's works or attends their theatrical production? -- the intellectuals who are leftist-leaning or who share the leftist commitment Osofisan expresses, in all probability have read his text as a major emancipatory or even revolutionary statement over the past fifteen years.

In contrast, Soyinka's plays, *Madmen and Specialists* included, have rather reluctantly, rarely unequivocally, been considered essentially rebellious, liberating texts. Osofisan commented in an interview in 1982, "To Soyinka history is cyclical, human beings are cannibals who only need a little respect from fate and the tragedy goes on." Achebe and Soyinka alike "are not on the side of the oppressors. But they are haunted by change. They don't believe in change, instead they get tragic about it and say Oh God, so this is fate."

In 1977 Biodun Jeyifo posited that Western critics see in "Soyinka plays, with eminent justification, Western bourgeois individualism incarnate." In contrast, "A militant has described *The Chattering and the Song* as the most revolutionary play ever written and produced in Nigeria." Osofisan's play may be said "to dramatise the following questions: how are revolutionaries made; of what stuff are they made; in what consists the rightness and authority of their cause? It is, of course, necessary to add that these are extrapolations from the play. Even overtly didactic theatre, of which *The Chattering and the Song* is not an example, makes its points or proves its theses in the intricacies of dramatic action." And in 1978 Jeyifo remarked that the East African sights

> are focussed more sharply on all the means of liberation, as much from foreign and domestic oppression, as from the systems of thought and the mystifications of reality inherited from previous ages unencumbered by the problems of the present epoch... Thus, we so often find a positive optimistic confidence in the possibility and necessity of progress and resolution in East African drama, while generally in West African drama, what we often confront is disillusionment or irrationalist pessimism. To date, and as far as I know, only Osofisan, Sowande and Omotoso of the West Africans have dared to believe in, and represent revolutionary alternatives to the alienations and contradictions of the semi-colonial and new-colonial societies of black Africa. (48, 52, 62)

Gerald Moore suggested in 1981 that Osofisan's symbol, the god of divination, Orunmila, the "bringer of knowledge," was the guiding spirit for *The Chattering and the Song*:

> Cette oeuvre doit donc apporter la preuve que l'usage qu'il fait lui-même de mythologie et du rituel... est plus dynamique, plus orienté vers l'avenir que l'utilisation par Soyinka de héros solitaires prenant leurs inspiration en Ogun... Il est vrai que les personnages de Soyinka semblent souvent sur le point de se laisser aller à un déspoir et à une colère démoniaque... Malheureusement, la fin de la pièce est gachée par la platitude de l'Hymne des fermiers qui est censé exprimer les valeurs du nouvel ordre révolutionnaire. (32)

Osofisan's texts of the 1970s may support the appraisal of the early 1980s. There are structural aspects of *The Chattering and the Song* (1976), *Morountodun* (1979), and *Once Upon Four Robbers* (1980) that speak of ambivalence, sensuousness, and of changing perspectives and of openness.

Sandra L. Richards points to Osofisan's fascination with the dilemma-tale structure, with the riddle as accentuated by the metaphor "The riddle begins anew" introducing *The Chattering and the Song*. Referring to an event of the play within the play when the character Yajin rushes forward to interrupt the characters' playing of a scene at the Alafin's court, she argues that the organic, "closed" flow of the "fictive" world gets destroyed. The interruption would be a first instance of "the eruption of an unplanned, 'real' event into the system of the fictive realm." The sequence of events produces "contradictory meanings" Richards compares Osofisan's plays to traditional dilemma tales, and suggests that there are similarities between *The Chattering and the Song* and the ambivalent, highly fluid, multidimensional attitudes of the trickster deity Eshu. "Rather than offering prescriptions, he structures the 'conclusions' of many of his plays like traditional dilemma tales in which viable options may not be immediately apparent, and the assembled community arrives at a possible critical interpretation only through the free-flowing interchange of ideas outside the fictive realm of art." (286-87)

Although Richards's reading tends to a certain extent to blur the structural elements that work against the openness of the texts, it appears to be valid if applied to the ending of *Morountodun* and, in particular, of *Once Upon Four Robbers*. In *Morountodun* the director addresses the audience, emphasizing that everything presented in the play is for "your entertainment" and that the play may be different tomorrow (may produce different significations?). The text ends with an image that seems to be rather enigmatic, indicating the possibility of various contradictory perspectives: Moremi and Tibuti are looking at each other "in harsh spotlight." What does that mean, the legendary, historical figure Moremi facing the woman Titubi, who in the play spied on the revolutionary farmers' movement she joined? It could be inferred from the image that "The Riddle begins anew" in a different situation and, perhaps, taking an entirely different course (79).

The end of *Once Upon Four Robbers* could be read as a dilemma-laden passage signifying a historical situation that does not offer an acceptable (humane?) solution. The robber Hasan is confronted by his brother, the sergeant, who has to bring him to trial for his crimes. The situation gives the soldier an insight into the cleavage-troubled society. He is on the side of the affluent people who keep the impoverished masses in slavery. The robber Major: "But man is so fragile, so easy to kill. Especially if he robs and lies, if he wantonly breaks the law. Serg, today that law is on the side of those who have, and in abundance, who are fed and bulging. ... But tomorrow, that law will change. The poor will seize it and twist its neck." (63) There is no imminent solution to the social problem. The epilogue leaves it to the audience to opt for execution of the robbers -- or for what? If the audience decides to free the robbers, according to the stage directions the robbers immediately resume their trade, victimizing the audience. If the audience decides otherwise, it inflicts capital punishment on the robbers and becomes part of the execution. Rendering a judgment can be a troubling experience.

On a closer look it is mainly the "macroform" -- for instance, the constant shifting from role playing to storytelling and/or singing and vice versa, the change from role enacting to doing a play within a play and/or audience-addressing and back -- that might speak of the ambivalence, of the multi-layeredness, of the intractable shifting of perspectives and hence of permanent movement. It is the complex "macroform" that Soyinka first demonstrated in *The Road* and *Madmen and Specialists* and then continued with *Opera Wonyosi* in 1977.

A rather different picture is manifest when it comes to the structural elements that may be called "molecular," that is, to the characters as "actants," as signifiers whose attitudes (talking and/or behaving, Brecht's concept of gestus would be appropriate) make up substantial aspects of the respective texts. They are presented as rather one-dimensional, as activists in a more or less binarily structured textual reality. There is the group of the honest, the morally intact, and in particular those who have insight into societal mechanisms (social injustice, class divisions, brutal oppression of the poor) and who strive for fundamental change. The dividing line in *The Chattering and the Song*, for instance, runs between Sontri, Yajin, and Lele, on the one hand, and Mokan, the intruder and informer, the vicious agent of the ruling system. In *Once Upon Four Robbers* the robbers' moral or human virtues as adversaries or even enemies of the system are immensely enhanced by presenting them as people who possess a kind of insightful class-consciousness, who sharply grasp societal mechanisms, and who act collectively in defending themselves. They appear to be highly idealized criminals. Even after one of them, Major, has cheated on the others, they try to rescue him from execution. They carry on with their thievery but do not engage in killing and promise to abstain from cruelty. From this angle, the text presents a rather closed, binarily structured world made up of one-dimensionally-behaving groups.

Closure or one-dimensionality appears to have originated, at least to a certain extent, in the projection of penetrating self-reflection and of deep insight regarding societal mechanisms upon the "actants", who represent (signify) the victims and/or opponents of the ruling system. It is their philosophical arguments that make Osofisan's texts look revolutionary or that convey the sweeping revolutionary analysis of society that was absent from or only partly addressed in Soyinka's works. Olu Obafemi appraised

Osofisan in 1982: "Like his contemporaries, he aims to propose a socialist ethical perspective for Nigeria by first reawakening the people's consciousness to a reality beyond the decadence of the present. There are dangers inherent in such a commitment. As these young play-wrights are aware, one of the grave dangers is that artistic depth might be sacrificed for political content; that the writers might resort to sheer propaganda as in the farmers' Anthem in *The Chattering and the Song*." (133)

Obafemi points to a crucial aspect of Osofisan's works: the preponderance of verbalization, of overemphasis on the "actants'" utterances, their propensity for argumentation and reasoning. Propaganda is a mode of verbalizing "rational" attitudes and views; it tends generally to give prominence to the abstract. This may easily translate into foregrounding abstraction in literary texts and in accounts of "historical events." It is a way of preferring the abstract (semantics) over the concrete, the sensuous body, the corporal substratum, the signified over the signifier. The body can thereby more easily appear to be separable from the mind. Desire is neglected or primarily conceived of only as yearning to argue, to reason. The Moni-syndrome, as sketched above, is an epitome of to what extent the neglect of desire -- of the sensuous foundation of the individual's and society's existence -- and actual attitudes can lead to fixating on abstraction, or seen from another angle, fixating on the word and hence on the predominance of argumentative rationality. And this, in turn, may result in the individual's self-denial, in giving up claims on his or her very sensuous existence, as practiced in the case of sacrificing the body to thinking. Moni's obsessive concern for the revolutionary cause appears to me, for example, as just another mode of bowing to the overriding significance of the word.

Giving up desire, or the body's essential wants, is tantamount to knuckling under to the all-encompassing claims of the superiority and control of reason. Both phenomena are modes of colonizing desire, of the actual suppression of the "molecular entities" by other forces. Such forces could be identified as Lyotard's (1979, 30ff.) "Grands Récits" or, in other words, as the claim on supremacy and the actual dominance of abstractions as societal strategies (the revolutionary cause). The epilogue to *The Chattering and the Song* presents a case in point. It stresses that the individual has to dissolve, has to give up self in the collective. The individual has to abandon his or her particularities in order to pursue the revolutionary cause and -- above all -- has to comply with the objective march of events, which is just another version of the all-encompassing "Grands Récits" or colonizing abstractions that demand the individual's, that is to say the body's, total submission. It is a phenomenon that can be grasped and "handled" only by thinking and verbalization.

From such a perspective sensuous activities like singing and dancing seem to be of secondary importance. The staunch revolutionary character Lele, in a sense a one-dimensional "actant," and his girlfriend, Funjola, will be the "shuttle in the loom" -- that is, bodies entirely devoted (subjugated) to the revolutionary cause. They "shall order the world in fresh designs" if "we dance as one" (56). Lele: "What is a single man in revolution? Once a movement begins, in the search for justice, it will run its course, without those who serve to spark it off. History will not remember us." (53) The pattern of thinking or attitude that separates Moni from Imaro seems to be the pattern at the root of Imaro's predicament: self-denial, the negation or suppression of sensuous concreteness. The repression of physical wants and desires, the self-effacement of the individual, spring from and at the same time cause the rather binary understanding and acceptance of societal mechanisms and of the individual's insignificance in history. Textual structuring is a translation of this attitude into literary and theatre works. And so is the projection of one's own interests onto other social groups -- the intellectuals' interests onto farmers, the lecturer's onto students. The intellectuals do not actually suffer what they think the farmers suffer. But they project their wants or, more precisely, their desires to change the world onto the farmers' movement, which is referred to only verbally and hence does not play a role as a "sensuous actant," a signifier in the actual unfolding of the text.

Soyinka's texts are different in these respects. In *Madmen and Specialists*, arguing, reasoning, and verbalizing are inseparably connected to actual deeds and accordingly to the desires and wants of the "actants." History as an "objective phenomenon" and relations between the individual and society are tackled and evaluated with regard to what they do and to what they mean to the individual, to his or her physicality. The emphasis is on the wants and interests of the single body, on "singularities." It seems to be this realism or this sensuousness that have been labeled "bourgeois individualism." Focusing on the sensuous entity does not, however, preclude essential aspects of history coming into sight or decisively influencing the single body's situation. It is, rather, a different perspective on the interrelationship between these two phenomena, resting on a perception of things as basically ambivalent, in permanent flux, and even as impenetrably complex. It is this perspective that translates into Soyinka's textual structures, and it is most profoundly thematized by his *Bacchae of Euripides*.

The liberating explosion of hitherto repressed desires and sensuousness engendered by Dionysos is inseparably intertwined with the attempt at revolutionizing the ironclad hierarchical regime of Pentheus's

Thebes. The slave leader's thirst for sensuous pleasure, his fascination with wine and nature, is just another aspect of his desire for social freedom, for getting rid of the shackles of slavery. The process of liberation itself is Janus-faced, a tricky paradox as epitomized by Dionysos's attitude. He is both the gentle and the cruel god, the liberator of repressed desire and shatterer of the slave system who does not hesitate to make his followers barbaric killers. There is no "propaganda" or, more precisely, any mere verbalization, no referring to an abstraction as the final solution to all problems at the end of Soyinka's texts; rather, there is the connotation of open-ended, paradoxical, almost intractably ambivalent history. And the course of events -- Pentheus's self-strangulation because of his paralyzed thinking and his mother's murdering her own son -- hints at the intricate and at times enigmatic results individuals produce at terrible costs by pursuing their cherished ends and/or living out their desires. The blood spurting from the head of Pentheus is at the same time the wine on which the socially differentiated (antagonistic) Theban society feasts.

The revolutionary alternative that perhaps could change the murderously unjust world of ruthless laissez-faire capitalism is put in perspective in *Opera Wonyosi* -- but as one of many possibilities within a complex textual structure, and one that may produce the signification "within an intricate historical process." It is hinted at by only one "actant," a signifier who appears just in one event. Jenny Leveller, the roomcleaner, voices in a song her desire to change her lot and thereby realize the Leveller movement's revolutionary aspirations since the seventeenth century. There is no obtrusively verbalized, abstracted projecting of the vision onto other groups and/or characters. This presentation of a wide range of different signifiers or "actants" renders the multidimensionality and intractable complexity of the signified, that means of history, more adequately. Openness thus serves as a "barbed hook" to prevent the text from "closing up," from becoming rigid.

Referring to Lyotard's (and Deleuze's) critique of abstractions such as the "Grands Récits" I should not go so far as to identify with all their views and tenets. In the late 1960s, prompted by the agonizing contradictions and the failures of the socialist project of the traditional Left and in particular of its attempted realization in socialist countries all over the world, this critique may now tend to become a new form of totalization excluding any "Great narration" that might emerge as part of new, entirely re-worked alternatives to the socio-economic and cultural-ecological crises human civilization is rapidly heading for. Brecht's theatre and, in a different way, Heiner Müller's texts do not bear out that sort of "totalizing critique" which Lyotard's reading of Brecht's dialectical theatre may suggest.[2] An artistic phenomenon should be examined in regard to its role or function, or to the significations it might produce in specific historical contexts. The historicity of creating works of art and of reading them, that is, of perceiving texts, should be uppermost.

Seen within the historically concrete situation of Africa, and Nigeria in particular, it is more the totalizing emphasis on (the desire for) revolutionary possibilities than the notion of or the hope for societal alternatives as such that appears to have driven Osofisan to "embrace" abstractions and thus to produce some texts that can signify one-dimensionality and binarity in spite of structural elements that are meant to counteract "closure" (as in *Once Upon Four Robbers, Morountodun,* and other plays). His idealizing characters and the characters' "obsession" with abstractions (the revolution, the antagonistic society at large, and so on), the dominance of verbalization, seem to compensate for the lack of a concrete, "sensuous" revolutionary movement or even of the dim historical prospects a (Marxist or socialist) revolutionary alternative might have. There has been no situation in Nigeria for the past twenty years that could have held out realistic chances to change society fundamentally as longed for and verbalized by Osofisan's characters, and apparently by Osofisan himself and a small group of radical intellectuals in the 1970s and the early 1980s. This is not to say that the social divisions and enormous failures of Nigerian society were not visible and painfully palpable. On the contrary. There have been quite a few rebellious activities of farmers and such other strata as students, caused by the cleavages and aimed at doing away with essential elements of the antagonistic system. Even the Nigerian press, which is mostly controlled by the representatives of the very forces that sustain the status quo, has been elaborating the basic problems day by day. But there has been no societal force in sight to further the fundamental, grand transformation of unbearable realities the Left and Marxist intellectuals have been yearning for.[3] What the Zaria students experienced in attempting a critical "theatre for development" might give an idea of the insuperable obstacles that thwart even programs for modest evolutionary remedies. They described their Bomo-project in 1980 as follows: "To refuse to offer bribe proved impossible, to team up did not work, neither violence nor importunity worked. We then asked what their (the peoples', J. F.) next

---

[2] See Lyotard (1980).

[3] As to dominant attitudes of larger sections of Nigerian society, see for instance Lloyd.

line of action would be. The answer was a frustrating 'Forget it'." The students' conclusion: "Again, as in the case of the University, the bureaucracy ensures defeat for any element of *evolutionary* change which some might attempt to introduce into the system -- simply through incompetence, inefficiency and 'normal procedures'." (Creative Writers Workshop, 43, 49)

Karin Barber's analysis of Yoruba popular theatre hints at the paradoxical and difficult-to-define attitudes, the wants and the worldview of the "common man," the people whom Osofisan refers to as the victims and the potential revolutionary force. The robber-chief of the Lere Paimo Company's production *The Secret Is Out* was very different from the noble, insightful robbers Osofisan presented, and he was the favored central character, a much adored figure. He wielded a "hidden attractivenes." Although he "is held up as an awful example of a wicked man, he stands head and shoulders above all the characters for wit, charisma, and the kind of daring cynicism much admired in traditional Yoruba culture." (Barber, 1982, 449)

The problems of Osofisan's dramaturgy as far as it purported to generate, or is regarded as generating, open-ended, multidimensional textual structures (see Sandra Richards) and the predicament of his intellectuals Imaro and Moni (the predicament of leftist intellectuals at large?) seem to result from underestimating fundamentally ambivalent and simultaneously productive desires, wants, and aspirations. Or from a different vantage point, the problems appear to have been engendered by a rather abstract reading of societal processes. Thus, until the mid-1980s, the "actants" of Osofisan's plays that present a revolutionary stance stress that the individual should deny himself or herself in the interest of the abstractions "transformation of society" and "revolutionary movements in history." The fixation on abstractions seems to make the "actants" ignore the very realities, that is, the sensuous substratum, the "material" foundation of history. Again, Karin Barber on the role of these elements or of experience as an opposite to abstract thinking in African "popular arts," the means in the arts that are produced by people who are integral parts of the masses and who convey their attitudes quite adequately ("attractively"): "In the first place, the views that ordinary people express may be 'false consciousness' (a concept not without its own problems) but they are also *their* consciousness: the people's arts represent what people do in fact think, believe, and aspire to." And: "What is needed... is an approach that recognizes that popular arts have their own conventions through which *real experience* is transformed, articulated, and made communicable." (Barber, 1987, 8, 38)

It is, rather, the insistence on singularity and hence on sensuousness, on the working of desire that is at the same time a destructive force (Ogun-Dionysos) that may have enabled Soyinka to hold up the vision of the alterability of realities, and thus of socioeconomic actualities as well. He presents textual realities that apear to be more open-ended.

I would like to suggest a general conclusion. It is the heavy thematization and accordingly the verbalization of the necessity of revolutionary change, of societal mutability, that appears to be at the root of Osofisan's propensity until the mid-1980s to "close" some of his texts. He thereby presents rather "unsensuous" textual realities that may induce a perception of history as a rather "unsensuous" reality, despite the lavish ostentation of sensuous elements (dance, music, metaphoric language that is beautiful in part).

Soyinka's texts, although somewhat conservative and esoteric at first and second glance, appear to be more apt to further critical perception, more likely to contribute to shaping "subversive" and, perhaps, even "liberation-geared" attitudes. They do not foreground self-negation of the individual but try to delineate the tricky working, the ambivalent production (destruction and production at the same time) of the concrete, of the desires and wants of the "molecular individuals." The reading I have presented here does not apply to all the works Femi Osofisan has produced so far -- and I do not know what surprises he holds in store for us. My "construction," my specific historical perception of the texts under discussion does not extend to his works since the mid-1980s. Texts such as *Another Raft* that keep thematizing alternatives to the existing catastrophic social realities tend to help produce a different picture of the individual's desires and of the inseparable intertwining of the individual's body (physicality) and his or her striving to implement visions of emancipation and social change. But tracing the trajectory of Osofisan's oeuvre is a topic for another day.

WORKS CITED

Barber, K. "Popular Reactions to the Petro-naira." *Journal of Modern African Studies* 20 (1982): 431-50.

───────. "Popular Arts in Africa." *African Studies Review* 30 (1987): 1-87.

Creative Writers Workshop. "Popular Drama at A.B.U., Zaria." *Okella: A Journal of Creative Writing* 1 (1980): 37-51.

Deleuze, G., and F. Guattari. *L'Anti-Oedipe*. Paris: Les Editions de Minuit, 1972.

Hebdige, D. *Hiding in the Light*. London: Routledge, 1988.

Jeyifo, B. *The Truthful Lie*. London: New Beacon Books, 1985.

Lloyd, P.C. *Power and Independence. Urban Africans' Perception of Social Inequality.* London: Routledge and Kegan Paul, 1974.

Lyotard, L.-F. *La Condition postmoderne*. Paris: Les Editions de Minuit, 1979.

———. *Des Dispositifs pulsionels*. Paris: Christian Bourgeois Editeur, 1980.

Moore, G. "La mise en cause des Titans de la littérature." *Le Monde Diplomatique*, Dec. 12, 1981.

Obafemi, O. "Revolutionary Aesthetics in Recent Nigerian Theatre." *African Literature Today* 12 (1982): 118-36.

Osofisan, F. *The Chattering and the Song*. Ibadan: Ibadan University Press, 1977.

———. *One Upon Four Robbers*. Ibadan: Bio Educational Services, 1980.

———. "Interview." *Daily Times* (Nigeria), Nov. 27, 1982.

———. *Morountodun and Other Plays*. Ibadan, Longman, 1982.

———. *Two One-Act Plays*. Ibadan: New Horn Press, 1986.

———. *Another Raft*. Lagos, Malthouse Press, 1988.

Richards, S.L. "Toward a Populist Nigerian Theatre: the Plays of Femi Osofisan." *New Theatre Quarterly* 3 (1987): 280-88.

Soyinka, W. *The Road*. London: Oxford University Press, 1965.

———. *Madmen and Specialists*. London: Methuen, 1971.

———. *The Bacchae of Euripides: A Communion Rite*. London: Methuen, 1973.

———. *Season of Anomy*. London: Rex Collings, 1973.

———. *Opera Wonyosi*. London: Rex Collings, 1981.

OUSMANE SEMBENE ET IBRAHIMA LY:
L'ENGAGEMENT POLITIQUE DE L'ECRIVAIN DANS LES SOCIETES POSTCOLONIALES AFRICAINES

MAGUEYE KASSE

Les états africains, indépendants pour la plupart après 1960, ont constitué et constituent encore des objets d'étude autour de leur histoire passée et présente, des voies d'émancipation politique, sociale et culturelle qu'ils ont empruntées. La colonisation francaise, pour certains de ces pays au sud du Sahara, a profondément marqué cette histoire. Les discussions, les controverses et les interrogations autour de ces voies ne manquent pas. En effet, trois décennies d'indépendance nominale ont marqué des étapes importantes dans un développement très souvent remis en question au regard de ses résultats pas toujours convaincants. Des problèmes nouveaux ont surgi dans cette période, mettant à nu des impasses et aggravant même des situations, par ailleurs catastrophiques. Des valeurs morales nouvelles sont apparues pour chasser des valeurs de référence.

Le rêve d'une Afrique traditionnelle sécurisante ne peut plus servir d'exutoire dans le meilleur des cas. Dans le pire, une référence constante à celle-ci est idéologiquement chargée et sert d'alibi pour perpétuer des injustices flagrantes. La référence au passé colonial ne suffit plus à expliquer les énormes problèmes auxquels l'Afrique Noire est confrontée. La colonisation a eu des effets catastrophiques durables, mais les responsables de l'arriération de L'Afrique sur beaucoup de plans, ne sont plus exclusivement hors du continent. Ce dont il s'agit, en dernière instance, c'est la question du legs colonial et de sa gestion. Cette question de nature existentielle, revêt une caractéristique particulière à la lumière d'un bilan à dresser. Ce bilan tourne autour du choix des moyens mis en oeuvre pour, en se libérant de la tutelle coloniale, se développer. Rappelons quelques aspects sans nous y attarder outre mesure. L'éducation, l'école et la formation sont un baromètre pour mesurer le degré de maîtrise des connaissances, de la maîtrise des faits principaux de l'histoire africaine, les possibilités réelles et scientifiques de compréhension des valeurs culturelles de référence. Le taux de scolarisation et d'analphabétisme est une pierre de touche dans cet édifice du savoir et une aune à laquelle on peut mesurer les progrès accomplis par les sociétés africaines dans les directions ci-dessus indiquées.

Il est une vérité que l'on se plait à souligner: Plus sans doute en Afrique que partout ailleurs, la littérature que l'on qualifie "d'africaine" à défaut d'un meilleur concept et toutes les manifestations qui s'apparentent à l'art, sont nées d'un besoin irrésistible de comprendre les situations traversées par l'Afrique Noire, de la perception de la nécessité d'une transformation qualitative et d'une volonté de faire participer le maximum d'acteurs. Sans que cette mission que s'assigne la littérature produite en Afrique Noire soit largement partagée par l'ensemble des auteurs africains, il y en a cependant très peu qui ne s'en réclament pas, peu ou prou. La ligne de partage passe souvent par le degré d'implication dans les batailles sociales.

Nous partons du fait que la littérature part et prend sa source dans les réalités sociales, économiques et culturelles. Le regard porté sur ces réalités et la réflexion que ce regard suggère prend donc appui sur le vécu et est directement prise de position. Celle-ci est d'autant plus claire que le vécu est chargé et sa fécondité est fonction de la valeur des moyens utilisés pour la faire partager. Il nous revient en mémoire le célébre texte de Brecht sur les *cinq difficultés pour écrire la vérité*. Il faut du courage pour aller à la recherche de la vérité, il en faut pour la diffuser après l'avoir découverte et il faut de la ruse pour la populariser. Ce faisant, comme le remarquait Georg Lukács à propos de Brecht, il faut provoquer des crises salutaires.

Chez les deux auteurs que nous avons priviliégiés dans le cadre de cette étude, la prise de conscience, c'est à dire l'accès à la vérité de situations insupportables, conditionne la prise de position et le jeu de l'écriture, qu'elle soit littéraire, filmique ou de théâtre. Cette écriture se sert de moyens stylistiques en fonction des publics visés et en tenant rigoureusement en compte leur état d'esprit réel et surtout avec une grande capacité d'adaptation. C'est ainsi que la langue d'écriture, médium d'emprunt et pendant longtemps objet de controverses que l'histoire a tranchées, dans le choix porté sur elle, avait donné par anticipation la réponse à la question de la place des langues nationales dans les batailles culturelles et politiques. La revendication de la place qui doit leur revenir est juste dans son principe, mais il s'agit du moment approprié pour en faire un cheval de bataille à côté de revendications de portée plus fondamentale. C'est à travers une claire perception de l'ordre du discours que Sembène par exemple a concilié, sans qu'ils s'excluent mutuellement, le langage littéraire et le langage cinématographique. Dans un entretien qu'il nous a accordé Sembène revient sur cet aspect:

> C'est cela le problème: comment faire de l'oeuvre d'art un outil de prise de conscience .... Non, il (le passage de la littérature au cinéma) n'est pas gratuit, il évolue parce que l'écriture est "amorphe", il est statique. Le lecteur est dans son coin, tranquille, il réagit intérieurement, tandis qu'au cinéma, si tu observes le public, il bouge, je veux dire, tu sens la salle bouger, il y a une espèce d'onde, de courant, enfin une sorte de vibration qui passe et tu peux savoir si le public adhère ou non au film.

Dans l'approche littéraire donc, la question des étapes et de leurs exigences respectives revêt une grande importance qui conditionne en retour les niveaux de perception et de réaction potentielle. Il faut, en plus, préciser que le cadre dans lequel évolue la littérature est semé d'embûches dont la plus considérable est la dualité partout présente entre société de tradition orale, qui passe progressivement à l'écrit avec ses valeurs en constante mutation, et société ou embryon de société moderne avec ses contradictions propres. L'approche littéraire des types de problèmes qui affleurent à ce niveau est tributaire de la perception de la manière dont ces problèmes se croisent, se superposent, dans une dialectique des contradictions. Chez Sembène et Ly, ce phénomène est intéressant à observer dans la mesure où leurs littératures respectives sont porteuses de projets de société qui se complètent selon les exigences nées du développement de la société à chaque étape. En cela aussi, ils demeurent des écrivains réalistes. Leur projet de société est une utopie concrète. En posant la question de l'Indépendance immédiate dans *l'Harmattan* qui, par ailleurs, réunit tous les problèmes qui seront abordés ultérieurement, Sembène était en adéquation avec son temps, *les Bouts de bois de Dieu* (1960) de même que *O pays, mon beau peuple* (déjà en 1957) reprennent le thème en ajoutant la dimension anti-raciste et de classe et tracent les voies possibles de la libération africaine, action des travailleurs et de leurs alliés. La mise en scène au théâtre *Les Bouts de bois* en 1984 donne un cachet actuel à cette problématique. Cette libération est fortement connotée par l'époque qui a vu grandir les oeuvres, époque sans doute marquée par le conflit idéologique entre le capitalisme, son succédané la voie africaine du socialisme ou authenticité, et le socialisme et la compréhension qu'on en avait. La vie de Sembène, ses prises de position ne laissent planer aucun doute sur ses choix.[1]

---

[1] Gëstu: "Question: 'Mais est-ce que tu n'a pas peur d'être taxé de communiste, de marxiste?' Sembène: 'Mais pourquoi! Je m'en réclame et me taxe de l'être, c'est enfoncer une porte ouverte. La question, c'est, comment en tant que marxiste, rallier

Avec ses deux romans *Toiles d'araignées* et *Les Noctuelles vivent de larmes* et sa disparition prématurée en 1989, Ibrahima Ly est moins connu de la critique littéraire. Né a Kayes au Mali en 1936, Ly a eu une courte vie qui l'a profondément marqué. D'abord ses études en France qui l'ont conduit à diriger l'une des plus prestigieuses organisations d'étudiants africains: la Fédération des Etudiants d'Afrique Noire en France-FEANF. Cette organisation par sa nature anti-colonialiste et anti-impérialiste a joué dans la prise de conscience des étudiants africains des années 60 jusqu'au milieu des années 70 et dans l'affirmation du nationalisme positif de beaucoup d'élites et de dirigeants politiques africains, un rôle de premier plan. La fidélité de Ly ensuite aux nobles idéaux de la FEANF de même que son engagement politique lui ont valu l'arrestation, la torture dans les prisons de son pays et l'exil à Dakar où il a enseigné les mathématiques à l'université. Les séquelles de son séjours en prison n'ont sans doute pas peu contribué à sa mort prématurée. *Toiles d'araignées* y apporte un témoignage bouleversant. Dans ce roman Ly règle la question de sa mutation en tant qu'intellectuel par une sorte d'adresse à l'égard de ses semblables:

> Vous n'êtes pas francs, vous les intellectuels. Qui êtes-vous? Des flamboyants. Jeunes, ils ne servent à rien. Etudiants, ils font le beau, avec des fleurs rouges étincellantes. Tout le monde les aime, les admire. Ils font de belles promesses. Adultes, ils sont inutiles ... (254)

Amilcar Cabral a utilisé dans les années 70 une formule qui n'a pas toujours été bien comprise: "Intellectuels africains, il faut vous suicider (dans les masses)". Chez Ly comme chez Sembène, il s'agit d'un suicide, c'est à dire d'un dépassement dialectique: appropriation du savoir sans lequel rien n'est possible pour s'en servir rationnellement. Une rupture donc plus concrète, contrairement à *L'Aventure ambiguë* de Cheikh Hamidou Kane, double négation de ce qui a produit l'homme, c'est à dire son milieu, en le soumettant au feu de la critique constructive, et rupture avec le milieu d'accueil, le savoir occidental et son aliénation. Cette double rupture apparait nettement chez Sembène et Ly dans chacun de leurs héros. La vision étroite et nostalgique de la société traditionnelle est aussi aliénante que la volonté d'adaptation à une société dont on ne perce pas l'essence. Du fait de leur nature respective de classe, elles ne laissent aucune place à l'épanouissement intégral de l'Homme. La rupture qui conduit à l'identification de l'Homme et de sa place passe par le procès de l'Etre et du Paraître. "L'oeuvre d'art pousse à la réflexion, elle n'est pas la solution de la vie" confie Sembène en faisant référence à *La Mère* de Gorki. Les éléments constitutifs de la maturation du facteur subjectif suivent

---

davantage de monde à notre bannière, c'est-à-dire des gens qui ne partagent pas mes opinions, mais qui, au fond d'eux-mêmes, reconnaissaissent la probité d'un artiste'." (14)

pratiquement le même processus que chez Brecht avec le "Verfremdungseffekt". Cette distanciation cependant porte en germe les éléments du changement reconnu comme nécessité objectivement ressentie. Les conditions sociales d'existence à elles seules ne conduisent pas à cette rupture qualitative. Pendant longtemps, Sembène s'est refusé à s'identifier au changement à travers ses personnages. L'exacerbation des conflits y conduit cependant. C'est la réponse à la question que se pose le héros du film *le Mandat*, ou des dépossédés de *Xala*: Qui changera tout cela? Moi, toi, vous, nous: Cette Masse devient plus concrète chez Ly dans *Les Noctuelles*

> Cela changera
> Qui conduira ce changement?
> La jeunesse cultivée de ce pays! (199)

Dans le mouvement de prise de conscience, nous avons parlé de la quête de la vérité et du courage qui en est la condition. Ceci est illustré par la confrontation avec sa propre histoire. Dans *Ceddo*, film à peine osé dans le contexte d'un pays à 90% de musulmans, Sembène retrace l'histoire de la notion de sacré dans les religions révélées, leur confrontation avec les sociétés traditionnelles antérieures. Chacune se sert de l'homme à des fins d'exploitation au nom de l'esclavage. En brisant le mythe de la religion, Sembène force à réfléchir en actualisant. Le rôle dévolu à tous les guides spirituels a été de tout temps exorbitant, les sociétés modernes renforcent cette caractéristique. Cette confrontation accouche d'une position plus radicale encore chez Ly "Les adeptes des mânes des ancêtres aidaient à la capture des infidèles. Les musulmans prenaient le relais en organisant la vente sur les marchés locaux et l'acheminement vers les côtes et à travers le désert. Les chrétiens faisaient le reste." (79) L'une des premières tares de nos sociétés traditionnelles, dont les principales caractéristiques se sont perpétuées jusqu'à notre époque, est la règle de la soumission, à une croyance, à l'éducation, à la gérontocratie, à l'adaptation et donc à l'écrasement des plus faibles. "Importer un Dieu, c'est toujours choisir l'esclavage: première vérité dont les conséquences sont lourdes." (46) "Une gérontocratie ne peut engendrer que des esclaves. Pour dominer le jeune, le vieux doit le domestiquer, le dresser comme on dresse un cheval ou un éléphant. Le vieux n'a jamais incarné la sagesse. C'est un leurre. La générosité, l'enthousiasme, le sens du sacrifice ne sont pas dans ce qui périclite et fait des efforts désespérés pour survivre." (47) La troisième vérité qui vient en complément des deux premières est la mesure exacte, propre à Sembène et Ly, de la place et du rôle dévolu à l'argent depuis son introduction dans les sociétés africaines. Synonyme de pouvoir, il occupe une fonction de perversion, désacralise, en les dépassant, des valeurs, pour en instaurer d'autres, déshumanise et ronge le corps social comme un cancer. Le traitement de ce thème chez Sembène et Ly est particulier dans la mesure où ils introduisent tous deux un élément d'appréciation, qui, historiquement explique la nature de classe du pouvoir et de l'argent: les sociétés africaines attendent toujours leur Révolution Bourgeoise. L'argent a produit des bourgeois oisifs, non productifs, qui ne comprennent le rôle de l'argent que comme satisfaction de besoins crées et suscités de manière artificielle. La gabegie, la corruption, y compris du sacré, et la concussion ont remplacé le rôle productif de l'argent. Les bourgeoisies africaines sont apparues dans les valises de la colonisation, elles se sont développées en classe parasitaire. Elles ne sont pas apparues historiquement, leur action obère tout développement réel. Elles exercent une fonction pernicieuse de destruction des restes des valeurs positives et leur influence idéologique s'exerce à tous les niveaux, insidieusement en imposant ses modèles, ou ouvertement par la violence. L'argent est destructeur de valeurs comme la solidarité, le respect de soi, donc des autres; il n'est pas synonyme de bonheur puisque réalisé sur la souffrance des autres. *Niiwaam* (1988) de Sembène illustre bien cette fonction du déplacement du centre de gravité des valeurs, du choc entre l'univers de la campagne et l'érection artificielle de la ville qui n'obéit à aucun impératif de développement. Ly revient sur l'aspect et le souligne: "L'argent est la parole faite pour tous. C'est lui qui crée la société dans laquelle il doit circuler comme la navette dans la chaine ou le fer de la houe dans le champ ... " (150) L'ensemble des faits et gestes de la société portent une marque vénale: "Le fétiche ne vaut que par la salive qui l'a crée et sans laquelle il n'est qu'une poupée. Le bénédiction s'achète et se mérite." (150) La société impose donc ses règles qui se drapent du manteau de l'ancienne pour mieux écraser, les Yoro, Mariama, Niélé, Solo, Haadi de Ibrahima Ly, une chaine de vies écrasées parce que ces êtres purs refusent de se compromettre, ils remettent tout en question. C'est leur drame et la note d'espoir pour un autre avenir. C'est le même cheminement que Sembène avait tracé et qui se perpétue dans un engagement plus radical.

Ces approches littéraires des problèmes de nos sociétés, dans leur absence de compromis chez Ly par exemple où le style assome par le choix du vocabulaire et la précision du terme, reflètent la complexité des problèmes qui servent de matière à la littérature. L'aliénation gagne du terrain pour l'observateur averti, le choix des moyens les plus appropriés semble aujourd'hui relativement limité pour sortir des impasses de toutes sortes. La crise du système vécue par la plupart des états africains est manifeste à plusieurs niveaux, la littérature se trouve devant de nouveaux défis à relever: faire davantage prendre conscience. Quand on parcourt le paysage littéraire et artistique de certains pays comme le Sénégal, on est frappé de constater que ce qui apparaissait comme l'apanage exclusif d'auteurs comme Sembène ou Ly tend progressivement à être partagé largement. Même si les styles et les approches diffèrent parfois sensiblement, il n'en demeure pas moins qu'ils traduisent tous un ensemble de préoccupations quant au devenir des sociétés. On les qualifie certes pas de littératures engagées, bien que certains aspects rappellent les thèmes de la littérature engagée, ils suggèrent cependant la nécessité de la réflexion profonde. En cela Sembène et Ly sont des précurseurs dont l'approche des sociétés semble incontournable. Les problèmes en Afrique Noire sont tels que le doute s'installe très souvent sur les possibilités réelles d'en sortir. Les programmes d'ajustement structurels avec leurs impitoyables conséquences pour des gens déjà si démunis, sont venus renforcer la paupérisation. Le nouvel ordre économique mondial se fait attendre, la spirale de l'endettement atteint des sommets vertigineux, le chômage des jeunes évoque des lendemains chargés de violence. La question cardinale aujourd'hui demeure: Que faire? par quel bout faut-il entreprendre un travail de redressement? C'est par cette question, suggérée au départ qu'il faudrait conclure: Les perspectives qui s'ouvrent n'apparaissent pas, pour l'instant du moins, porteuses d'avenir. La littérature se trouve ainsi devant de nouveaux champs d'investigation pour aider à une nécessaire maïeutique. L'engagement de l'écrivain n'y suffit plus, mais il y joue un rôle, par ailleurs irremplacable, surtout dans le processus de l'éducation, de l'ancien vers le nouveau, dans la mise en exergue de la place importante qui revient au travail créateur et honnête, valeur qui semble aujourd'hui perdue.

OUVRAGES CITES

Ly, Ibrahim. *Toiles d'araignées*. Collection Encres Noires. Paris: L'Harmattan, 1982.

———. *Les Noctuelles vivent de Larmes*. Collection Encres Noires. Paris: L'Harmattan, 1988.

Sembène, Ousmane. "A bâtons rompus avec Ousmane Sembène: Entretien réalisé par Maguèye Kassé le 14.10.1986." *Gëstu* 4 (1988): 8-14.

LITERARY THEORY AND AFRICAN LITERATURE
edited by J. Gugler, H.-J. Lüsebrink, J. Martini
Münster/Hamburg 1993, pp. 143-161

POLITICS AND VALUE IN SOUTH AFRICAN LITERATURE: SOME THOUGHTS ON RECENT INTERVENTIONS BY ALBIE SACHS AND NJABULO NDEBELE[1]

DAVID MAUGHAN BROWN

INTRODUCTION

Early in 1990, extracts from a paper titled 'Preparing Ourselves for Freedom', written by Albie Sachs for an ANC In-house Seminar on Culture, were published in the *Weekly Mail* in an atmosphere of intense political excitement occasioned by the almost simultaneous announcement by President De Klerk of the unbanning of the ANC. Sachs's is a deliberately polemical intervention whose most striking proposition is that members of the ANC 'should be banned from saying that culture is a weapon of struggle' (Sachs, 1990: 1). Sachs's paper, which goes on to advocate a broadening of the range of permissible subject matter for South African writing, has occasioned intense debate among South African cultural workers and academics from both ends of the ideological spectrum. The drama of the political moment and Sachs's standing as a legendary ANC exile, on the point of returning to South Africa maimed in an assassination attempt by agents of the apartheid state, have perhaps conspired to distract attention from the fact that Njabulo Ndebele has been arguing a similar case, in far greater detail and with far more theoretical cogency, for the better part of the last decade.

The 1980s saw the eclipse of Black Consciousness as a major

---

[1] This paper was wirtten in May 1990 while I was in Britain on sabbatical leave undertaking a research project with the financial assistance of the Institute for Research Development of the Human Sciences Research Council, whose assistance is hereby acknowledged. Opinions expressed in this paper and conclusions arrived at are those of the author and are not necessarily to be attributed to the Institute for Research Development or the Human Sciences Research Council.

determinant of South African literature; the elaboration of Ndebele's theoretical argument in support of a more inclusive subject matter and a greater complexity of approach in South African literature; and, if *Staffrider* can be taken as representative, a recuperation of 'standards' and an effective strikingback of the literary convention so radically threatened by Mothobi Mutloatse's often quoted:

> We will have to *donder* conventional literature: old-fashioned critic and reader alike. We are going to pee, spit and shit on literary convention before we are through; we are going to kick and pull and push and drag literature into the form we prefer (Mutloatse, 1980: 5).

Given the immediacy of the political moment and the stir that Sachs's paper has caused, this seems an apposite juncture for a tentative consideration of some of the theoretical issues raised by Sachs's and, more importantly, Ndebele's essays. Alhough the immediate occasion for this essay is the need to examine the road ahead for cultural production, theory and criticism at a crucial turning-point in South African history, its broad concerns with such issues as 'protest literature', 'relevance', the ascription of 'literary' value and the democratization of cultural production, are obviously widely applicable to literature elsewhere in Africa. I should make it clear from the outset that I have a high regard for both the writers whose essays are discussed in this paper and am embarking on this discussion very much in the spirit of the comment with which Ndebele concludes 'Redefining relevance':

> These observations, it should be stated, are put forward not as laws, but as possible guidelines by which our writers can conduct a debate and bring to bear further analysis on the tasks of writers and the role of their art in the unfolding revolution in South Africa. The tasks themselves are immense and challenging. I believe a vigorous discussion of them will, in itself, be a significant act of freedom (Ndebele, 1989: 51).

ALBIE SACHS: 'PREPARING OURSELVES FOR FREEDOM'

In arguing that members of the ANC should be banned from saying that culture is a weapon of struggle - an assertion which he sees as 'not only banal and devoid of real content, but actually wrong and potentially harmful' (1990: 2) - Albie Sachs takes as his starting point the question whether 'we have sufficient cultural imagination to grasp the rich texture of the free and united South Africa that we have done so much to bring about' (Sachs: 1). Sachs sees the identification of cultural production with the struggle as harmful in three main respects: firstly, it results in 'solidarity criticism' whereby artists are not pushed to improve the quality of work which is required only to be politically correct; secondly, it narrows the range of themes to the point where ambiguity, contradiction, and all that is 'funny or curious or genuinely tragic' is excluded; thirdly, it results in a line-up of characters who are entirely good or entirely bad. Sachs highlights what he sees as the inappropriatenes of a theoretical position, which he admits to having himself previously espoused with 'solemn formulas of commitment', by contrasting art with a 'real instrument of struggle':

> In the case of a real instrument of struggle, there is no room for ambiguity: a gun is a gun, and if it were full of contradictions, it would fire in all sorts of directions and be useless for its purpose. But the power of art lies precisely in its capacity to expose contradictions and reveal hidden tensions - hence the danger of viewing it as if it were just another kind of missile-firing apparatus (1990: 2).

By contrast with black South African music, which 'ignores apartheid and establishes its own space', Sachs sees South African literature as obsessed by the oppressors, 'completely shut in by apartheid' (1990: 3) and devoid of any account of the new consciousness being developed by the oppressed. Sachs regrets the fact that ANC poetry is never about love and asks 'What are we fighting for if not the right to express our humanity in all its forms, including our sense of fun and capacity for love and tenderness and our appreciation of the beauty of the world?' (1990: 3). Sachs concludes his essay by calling for the recognition that artists 'have certain special characteristics and traditions' and suggesting that the ANC should not be prescriptive about culture but should strive rather 'to write better poems and make better films and compose better music and ... get the voluntary adherence of the people to our banner' (1990: 9).

Sachs's sentiments are impeccably democratic in their concern for the people's right to choose, and one would obviously want to endorse his vision of a unitary, non-racial and democratic South Africa. But, in spite of the euphoria with which his intervention has been greeted (see for example the letter by Brenda Cooper, *Weekly Mail*, 23/2/90: 12) there are a number of problems, on both the theoretical and expository levels, with this essay:

(i) Perhaps most seriously, Sachs's call for a moratorium on the identification of culture as a weapon of struggle, however deliberately tendentious, constitutes a peremptory dismissal of a very substantial body of cultural theory, to which the major African contributors have obviously been Fanon, Cabral and Ngugi. To cite just one example, one has only to look to the present situation in Natal to see the pertinence of Cabral's assertion:

> In order for culture to play the important role which falls to it in the framework of the liberation movement, the movement must be able to preserve the positive cultural values of every well-defined social group, of every category, and to

> achieve the confluence of these values in the service of the struggle, giving it a new dimension - the national dimension. Confronted with such a necessity, the liberation struggle is, above all, a struggle both for the preservation and survival of the cultural values of the people and for the harmonization and development of these values within a national framework (Cabral, 1973: 49).

However impatient Sachs may be with the literature produced by those who uphold the maxim, it is self-evidently not true to say, in the face even of this single quotation from Cabral, that the statement that 'culture is a weapon of struggle' is 'devoid of real content'. Sachs may regard the assertion as 'banal' but before his dismissal of it can have theoretical validity he needs to engage with Cabral, Fanon and Ngugi, among others, on a theoretical level and counter their far more substantial and fully developed arguments to the contrary.

(*ii*) None of the three characteristics of South African literature which Sachs cites by way of justification for his proposition is an inevitable outcome of art's being seen as an instrument of struggle. Critical response, the range of themes treated, and the mode of characterization adopted are in no way necessarily limited by an overdetermining theoretical concept of culture as a weapon of struggle. What should be at issue, what is at issue for Ndebele, is not so much the theoretical concept itself as the historical conditions which have determined the narrowness with which that concept has generally been interpreted within South African culture.

Marga Holness's account of Angolan poetry produced by the founders of *Message* suggests the possibility of a different outcome to the process of cultural production, in spite of broadly similar historical conditions of oppression and in spite of a determining view of culture as a weapon of struggle:

> Poetry became the principal means by which they struck roots among the people, writing for the people, making of the despair and suffering of the people on the sterile lands and in the shanty towns the material of poetry, rediscovering a land and customs which had been deformed in the distorting mirror of the oppressor, and creating a modern national literature which gave voice to the people's aspirations (Quoted Amuta, 1989: 186).

(*iii*) Taking its precise historical context into account, and viewing such formulations as 'the free and united South Africa that we have done so much to bring about' as symptomatic, it is difficult to avoid interpreting Sachs's intervention as implying that the incipient negotiations between Government and ANC signal the demise of apartheid, that this brings an end to the struggle, and that the time is therefore ripe for extricating cultural production from the regrettably subordinate role it has played to politics by reasserting its rightful role as an expression of the richness and fullness of individual life. There is nothing in the essay to suggest that the struggle does not end with the dismantling of apartheid and should extend, to use Cabral's formulation, to freeing the national productive forces from all kinds of foreign domination (Cabral: 43). If this is an accurate inference it would presumably account for the readiness with which Sachs is prepared to discard a body of cultural theory developed largely by socialist theorists like Ngugi and Cabral.

(*iv*) Sachs's denial of culture's status as a 'weapon' by analogy with the characteristics of 'real instrument(s) of struggle' is problematic. Firstly, the argument is unconvincing in its use of the analogy. To expose contradictions, art has to direct itself (or 'aim') at those contradictions; if it self-contradictory it will not succeed in its aim. Self-contradiction is not generally regarded as one of the hallmarks of 'great' art. Literary production will inevitably embody contradictions, and the producers of complex works may well harness contradictoriness to their cause, but if art sets out to 'expose contradictions and reveal hidden tensions' the contradictions must, in the first instance, be inherent in what is being written about, or targeted, rather than in the instrument itself. However 'rich' and 'complex' a work of art may be, there is obviously a limit to the leeway allowable to ambiguity if successful communication is to be achieved in the pursuit of exposure and revelation.

Secondly, and more fundamentally, this analogy posits a separation between the cultural and political realms which has worrying implications. Sachs criticises ANC drama, poetry and painting for 'never acknowledging that there is bad in the good, and, even more difficult, that there can be elements of the good in the bad' (1990: 2). ANC cadres have been involved for some years in killing the 'bad' in whom there are elements of the good - necessariy so in the political circumstances, and presumably with Sachs's approval, however reluctant. To imply that killing people with elements of the good in them is a necessary evil, but that it is not acceptable to write about them as if they had no elements of good in them, is to place cultural practice in stark contradiction with political practice. Literature assumes the aspect of a redeeming conscience in a realm seemingly divorced from politics.

(*v*) Sachs's central categories of 'art' and 'literature' remain unproblematized, as does the concept of 'literary value' which underpins the call to 'write better poems'. 'Value' for Sachs is not transitive, as it is, for example, for Eagleton, for whom 'it means whatever is valued by certain people in specific situations, according to particular criteria and in the light of certain purposes' (Eagleton, 1983: 11). Nor, to use a different formulation, is it 'radically contingent': 'All value is radically contingent, being neither an inherent property of objects nor an arbitrary projection of subjects but, rather, the product of the dynamics of an economic system' (Smith, 1983: 11).

When Sachs talks about 'better' poems whose criteria is he judging by? Who would the poems be 'better' for, and why would they be 'better'? In a situation of violent political conflict such as that pertaining in Natal at present, where in the past four years well over 3000 people have been killed and tens, if not hundreds, of thousands of people made homeless, it would be patently absurd to castigate the writers who are publishing poems about the conflict in *Echo* for the narrowness of their thematic focus and for not writing poems about making love.[2] This perhaps underlines the point that Sachs's concerns can afford to rise to the surface once the fighting is perceived to be over.

NJABULO NDEBELE: 'PROTEST' AND RELEVANCE.

(i) Summary

In turning to Ndebele, it seems necessary to try to give a brief summary of the argument as it is developed over the course of the three major essays - 'Turkish Tales and Some Thoughts on South African Fiction' (1984/1988a), 'The Rediscovery of the Ordinary: Some New Writings in South Africa' (1985) and 'Redefining Relevance' (1989a) - before proceeding with a discussion of some of the theoretical issues raised by these essays. It will be readily apparent from my summary just how closely Sachs's concerns overlap with Ndebele's. It should be made clear from the outset, however, that Ndebele's are very full, very tightly argued essays to which it is impossible to do justice in a summary.

The major part of 'Turkish Tales and Some Thoughts on South African Fiction' consists of reflections about South African fiction sparked off by a reading of Yashar Kemal's *Anatolian Tales*. Ndebele argues that in an oppressive society like South Africa social conditions tend to enforce overt tendentiousness in subject matter, 'commitment' comes to be defined in terms of the level of explicit political preoccupation literature displays, and this leads to fiction built around the interaction of surface symbols - 'symbols of evil on the one hand, and symbols of the victims of evil on the

---

[2] *Echo* is a weekly supplement to the Pietermaritzburg *Natal Witness*, directed mainly at a black audience, which publishes a 'Poets' Corner' in which many poems written about the Natal conflict have appeared.

other' (1988a: 329) - which presents an analysis of the South African experience which can only be superficial and politically counter-productive:

> All these symbols appear in most of our writings as finished products, often without a personal history. As such they appear as mere ideas to be marshalled this way or that in a moral debate. Their human anonymity becomes the dialectical equivalent of the anonymity to which the oppressive system consigns millions of oppressed Africans. Thus, instead of clarifying the tragic human experience of oppression, such fiction becomes grounded in the very negation it seeks to transcend (1988a: 329).

Because the analysis underlying this depiction of South African society is primarily a moral one, its interest, by Ndebele's account, lies in the exposure of social evil; this by-passes the need to analyse the social processes leading to that evil and leads to 'indictment' rather than 'knowledge'. Where the writing of fiction is concerned, this is seen as producing a conflict between the aim of storytelling, categorized as 'creative writing', and that of imparting social information, identified as 'journalism' (1988a: 330). The imparting of social information by those who are not in control of the process of gathering and interpreting that information, which has almost invariably been the case with black writers in South Africa, frequently leads to 'sloganeering' (1988a: 331). The result is that 'the average African writer ... produces an art of anticipated surfaces rather than one of processes' (1988a: 332) which has little chance of transforming the consciousness of readers because the only demand being made on their faculties is one of recognition.

For Ndebele the remedy lies, at the technical level, with acceding to 'the demands of the craft of fiction'. These demands consist in 'a more than casual view of the relationship between fiction and society, or between artistic information and social information' and in grappling with such basic aspects of 'art' as: 'setting, conflict, credible characterisation, consistent narrative point of view, the complexities of fictional language and time' (1988a: 333). Ideologically, Nbebele advocates a stance which stresses social or historical process as a condition for meaningful knowledge acquisition and will thereby encourage in writers 'a more explanatory approach to fiction' whereby individual events can be situated 'within an explainable totality of social meaning' (1988a: 333).

Ndebele develops the argument of the 'Turkish Tales' essay in 'The Rediscovery of the Ordinary: Some New Writings in South Africa' published a year later. Here, taking his cue from Barthes's phrase 'the spectacle of excess', he sees the history of black South African literature as a highly dramatic and demonstrative 'representation of spectacle' occasioned by the 'brazen, exhibitionist openness' of South African oppression (1985: 143).

Ndebele takes a La Guma short story, 'Coffee for the Road', as paradigmatic, and concludes of it that: 'Subtlety is deliberately unintended. What is intended is spectacular demonstration at all costs. What matters is what is seen. Thinking is secondary to seeing. Subtlety is secondary to obviousness' (1985: 147). At the same time, he argues that either to denounce the writing as unartistic and too political, or to defend it on the grounds that everything in South Africa is political anyway, would be equally to miss the mark, because 'the writing validates itself in terms of its own primary conventions and its own emergent, complex system of aesthetics' whereby, for black South African readers, the value of this literature lies in the readers' recognition of 'the spectacular rendering of a familiar oppressive reality' (1985: 148). Ndebele identifies the characteristics of the spectacular as follows:

> The spectacular, documents; it indicts implicitly; it is demonstrative, preferring exteriority to interiority; it keeps the larger issues of society in our minds, obliterating the details; it provokes identification through recognition and feeling rather than through observation and analytical thought; it calls for emotion rather than conviction; it establishes a vast sense of presence without offering intimate knowledge; it confirms without necessarily offering a challenge. It is the literature of the powerless identifying the key factor responsible for their powerlessness. Nothing beyond this can be expected of it (1985: 149-50).

This essay concludes, however, that the convention of the spectacular has run its course and, to illustrate this, Ndebele gives an account of three short stories (his own stories published in *Fools and Other Stories* [Ndebele, 1983] would have been as good, if not better, as examples) which he sees as having broken with this tradition of spectacle. The first of these is commended for moving away from merely documenting oppression 'to offering methods for its redemptive transformation'; for its dispassionately analytical approach; and for 'rediscover(ing) the ordinary' which, as the opposite of the spectacular, is 'sobering rationality ... the forcing of attention on necessary detail'. 'Paying attention to the ordinary and its methods', we are told, 'will result in a significant growth of consciousness' (1985: 152).

This growth of consciousness is clearly perceived as having a political dimension. Ndebele declares that 'the overwhelming injustice inherent in the South African social formation is something that cannot be ignored under any circumstances ...' (1985: 155). The 'ordinary', rather than the spectacular, should be the focus of the writer's political contribution precisely because it is the day-to-day lives of people which constitute the content of the struggle (1985: 156). Ndebele cites Lenin's comment on the need for the revolutionary class to have the capacity 'to take the mass revolutionary actions that are strong enough to smash (or break up) the old government' and argues that:

> The new literature can contribute to the development of this subjective capacity of the people to be committed, but only on the basis of as complete a knowledge of themselves and the objective situation as possible. The growth of consciousness is a necessary ingredient of this subjective capacity (1985: 156).

The essay concludes with the ringing assertion that 'no civilization worth the name will emerge without the payment of disciplined and rigorous attention to detail' (1985: 157).

Ndebele's argument receives its fullest theoretical exposition in his 1989 essay 'Redefining relevance'. Here he identifies 'an epistemology in which reality is conceived purely in terms of a total polarity of absolutes' - itself a product of the nature of South African oppression - as the impetus behind the continued writing of protest literature in South Africa after the genre has 'run its course' (1989a: 40). Where to know is to know how badly one has been treated, the articulation of grievance can produce a rhetoric which comes to dominate the consciousness of the oppressed to the exclusion of the critical attention to the concrete social and political details of that oppression which is necessary for any constructive engagement with it. However valid the moral response may be, not only can the articulation of protest be seen, ironically, to be the index of powerlessness, but the dominant mode of perception, in failing to transcend its own limitations, 'can become part of the oppression it sought to understand and undermine' (1989a: 43).

Turning specifically to literature, Ndebele acknowledges that protest writing had the effect of sharpening the moral sense, which might have been the only effective way to validate and maintain the sense of legitimate political opposition, but sees it as having outlived protest politics - whose effective end he sees as being signalled by the founding of the Black Consciousness Movement - and, in so far as objective conditions no longer justified or supported an entirely emotional or moral attitude, as having turned into a 'pathology' (1989a: 44).

With the growth of the economy and industrialisation in the 1970s, Ndebele sees new forms of power as having accrued to the oppressed, leading to new perceptions of what was politically possible, and generating what Ndebele sees as the 'greatest challenge of the South African revolution', namely:

> the search for ways of thinking, ways of perception, that will help to break down the closed epistemological structures of South African oppression .... The challenge is to free the entire social imagination of the oppressed from the laws of perception that have characterised apartheid society. For writers this means

freeing the creative process itself from those very laws. It means extending the writer's perception of what can be written about, and the means and methods of writing (1989a: 45).

Ndebele identifies the root cause of 'the rather slow growth of South African literature', seen primarily in its limited range of explorable experience ('tragically limited in comparison to the complex structure of the oppression itself' [1989a: 47]), as being South African writers' failure to grapple with the theoretical demands of cultural production once a general consensus about commitment had been achieved. (1989a: 46) His account of the role of the artist in the new South African society is predicated on a clear distinction between the propagandist who aims at immediate action, and whose intentions are entirely practical, on the one hand, and, on the other hand, the artist, who is interested in 'delayed' rather than immediate action, and whose spurs as 'artist' are only won via the engagement of irony in the necessary process of reflection through which the relationship between politics and art is mediated.

Arguing that the South African State's strategies for domination have diversified to take advantage of a complex industrial society, and that this demands a greater complexity of response on the part of the oppressed, Ndebele concludes that:

> relevance, for the post-protest South African writer, begins, as it should, with the need for the seizure of state power; but for the writer, this need also fragments into a concern with an infinite number of specific social details which are the very objects of artistic reflection; and it is such social details which constitute the primary reason why the struggle occurs in the first place (1989a: 48).

At the political level the writer is called upon to contribute to the consolidation of the new-found power of the oppressed, resulting from their key role in the economy, by consolidating consciousness of that power at all levels of society. This will, again, be achieved primarily by 'a freeing of the imagination in which what constitutes the field of relevance is extended considerably' (1989a: 48):

> The operative principle of composition in post-protest literature is that it should probe beyond the observable facts, to reveal new worlds where it was previously thought they did not exist, and to reveal process and movement where they have been hidden (1989a: 50).

(II) CRITIQUE

The three essays I have tried to summarize here represent the most sustained, and much the most influential, theoretical intervention in South

African literary studies over the past decade. There are, however, a number of features of Ndebele's theoretical argument which should perhaps give one pause before it is accepted as the foundation on which can be built 'a rigorous, responsible and illuminating radical criticism, one in tune with the "terrible beauty" of our times, which is able to push forward the frontiers of our literary and intellectual culture' (Ndebele,1989b: 35).

The political philosophy underlying Ndebele's poetics very explicity endorses 'radical change' and 'revolution' - seen in the light of Lenin's analysis (1985: 156) - rather than reform. This is evidenced most explicitly in Ndebele's reference to 'the development of a dangerous predisposition to reform rather than to radical change' (1989a: 43). His advocacy of the analysis in fiction of the whole range of social being, and his sustained critique of protest literature derive their primary impulse from a commitment to political change: 'radical change relies on continuous critical engagement with reality ... an uncritical rhetoric of protest can easily impair the capacity of the oppressed to think strategically' (1989a: 43). The whole project of Ndebele's critical and theoretical writing over the past decade can be seen to be driven by the desire for a 'revolutionary' transformation of South African society, which is perceived as being possible 'only with the contribution of the oppressed themselves as decision makers', and as being realizable in fiction only 'if the writer genuinely believes in the oppressed, in the first instance, as makers of the future' (1989: 46, 50).

Where literary theory is concerned, Ndebele perceives his own radicalism as being in marked tension with, firstly, 'the political school of criticism', which is characterised as prone to being exasperated by a 'seeming lack of direct political consciousness' on the part of a fictional character (1985: 154), and, secondly, with that section of 'the radical intellectual movement' from which 'the demand for a surface art emanates' (1988a: 336). It is worth dwelling for a moment on this perceived tension because it would appear to derive from a defensiveness on Ndebele's part with respect to his own practice as a writer of fiction, and, in particular, with respect to the relationship between his own 'radical' theoretical position and that which underpins mainstream liberal-humanist aesthetics.

In the particular instance quoted above Ndebele's reading appears itself to construct 'the demand for a surface art' which it finds in Michael Vaughan. Vaughan comments that Mtutuzeli Matshoba's stories dispense with the 'whole liberal preoccupation with individual interiority, and hence with subtle and elaborate characterisation' because 'characterisation establishes individual specificity and separateness, which is not functional to Matshoba's project' (quoted Ndebele, 1988a: 333). Ndebele interprets

Vaughan as implying that 'a writer's concern with subjectivity in character development may amount to a bourgeois or liberal escapism into an ethos of individualism' (1988a: 333). He admits that Vaughan doesn't, in fact, say this, but that doesn't prevent him from transforming what Vaughan does say, which is descriptive rather than prescriptive, into a 'demand for surface art'. A year later this 'demand' has been further embellished: 'Even the progressive side has been domesticated by the hegemony of spectacle. For example, it will lambast interiority in character portrayal as so much bourgeois subjectivity' (1985: 150).

The major tension between Ndebele's radical political stance and the theoretical approach to South African literature elaborated in his essays lies with his acceptance, without apparent interrogation, of many of the categories, and much of the value system, of liberal aesthetics. The point is not so much that the categories and value system, with their preoccupation with individual sensibility and consequent overtones of elitism, are necessarily devoid of any validity, but rather that a radical and self-reflexive criticism would evidence a consciousness of the need to subject them to theoretical scrutiny.

Thus, for example, one finds Ndebele employing such formulations as 'basically, the demands of the craft of fiction are that ...' and 'the world of fiction demands that the writer grapples with some of the following problems which are basic to his art ...' (1988a: 333). In what sense does 'fiction' make its own transcendent and unchanging 'demands' independent of the contingent value ascribed to it by its producers and readers? The assumed immutability of the 'demands' of the genre in the face of changing historical circumstances would seem to imply a concept of culture as static, which implicitly undercuts a project designed specifically to encourage a dynamic cultural response to unfolding events. Formulations such as these can on occasion be found to be bearing the burden of key points in the overall argument: 'All the writer needs to understand is that he [sic] can only be genuinely committed to politics through a commitment to the demands of his art' (1988a: 338). The effect of such formulations is to naturalize and make transcendent the hegemonic demands of dominant groups of critics and literary theorists at specific historical moments.

The clearest example of this is to be found in Ndebele's call for interiority in the rendering of 'bad' characters:

> Is it useful, in the quest for a transforming social understanding, for a writer to always portray such characters as finished products: unaccountably vicious, cruel, malicious, fawning and greedy? Obviously not. And here, the maturity of the writer is called for, since he is called upon to be narratively fair-minded even to those he socially abhors. The point is that attempting to understand the villain in all his complexity does not necessarily imply a political acceptance of him. On

the contrary, it intensifies political opposition even more ... . We cannot wish away evil; but genuine art makes us understand it. Only then can we purposefully deal with it (1988a: 335).

The formulation whereby the writer 'is called upon', in a process reminiscent of both Joan of Arc and Althusser, obscures the fact that the interpellation is actually coming from a body of historically specific critical opinion to which Ndebele himself obviously subscribes. The category of 'maturity' similarly naturalises a transitive value-judgement: 'maturity' is a condition achieved by a process of growth which reaches its culmination when the views of neophyte and elder reach perfect coincidence. Attempting to understand the villain in all his complexity does not, as Ndebele rightly says, imply a political acceptance of him or her - what it does imply is the acceptance of an aesthetic with an identifiable intellectual history and an uncertain record as an intensifier of political opposition.

This is not simply a matter of quibbling with terminology in the interests of intellectual disputation. To focus attention on Ndebele's use of terms like 'maturity' is to point to symptomatic usages rather than merely 'inaccurate expressions' (Ndebele, 1989b: 32). Ndebele's assertions have far-reaching implications for both literary theory and practice. The difficulties of establishing the extent to which fiction ever intensifies political opposition are manifest, and must be particularly so within a paradigm which looks to individual sensitivity for the validation of cultural production. This is not the place for a critical ranking of political novels in terms of their likely success at intensifying political opposition, but it is worth remarking in passing that Ndebele's assertion would lead one, for example, to expect Bloom's *Transvaal Episode* to rank more highly than Vieira's *The Real Life of Domingos Xavier*, Ngugi's *A Grain of Wheat* to rank more highly than *Petals of Blood* and his Gikuyu novels, and La Guma's *Time of the Butcherbird* to rank more highly than *In the Fog of the Season's End*. In each case it seems highly improbable to me that the novel which attempts to interiorize its villains is the one most likely to intensify political opposition. Indeed, in the case of La Guma - who, it will be recalled, provided Ndebele's exemplum of the 'spectacular' - the attempt to understand Meulen in *Time of the Butcherbird* leads to the negation of the rationale for Murile's political action, which comes to seem quite arbitrary, and leads ironically to the killing of Meulen and Stopes being the most striking example of the 'spectacular' in all La Guma's fiction (La Guma: 1979). What seems to be at issue here is the untested assumption that the criteria for evaluation developed within an aesthetics of individual sensibility will be equally applicable to the cultural production emanating from mass political struggle.

Ndebele clearly accepts the category of 'genuine art' as absolute and maintains very firm generic distinctions, such as that between 'fiction' and 'exposition' (1985: 149). He accepts the concept of 'universal experience' and incorporates it among his criteria of literary evaluation (1988a: 335). He endorses the elevation of the 'artist' above the rest of humankind in terms of the claim Henry James stakes to 'fine' intelligence on the basis of the '... very obvious truth that the deepest quality of a work of art will always be the quality of the mind of the producer. In proportion as that intelligence is fine will the novel, the picture, the statue partake of the substance of beauty and truth' (1988a: 339). And he privileges the 'writer' over the critic: 'The role of literature in this situation is not an easy matter ... . However, writers rather than critics, are likely to provide the ultimate direction' (1990: 23). In a poetics strongly reminiscent of Wordsworth's 'emotion recollected in tranquillity', Ndebele sets up an opposition between 'indignation' and 'understanding' (1988a: 324), lays stress on delayed ('art') as against immediate ('politics') action, and sets high store by 'the sobering power of contemplation' (1985: 150). The writer's immediate aim is held to be:

> a radically contemplative state of mind in which the objects of contemplation are that range of social conditions which are the major ingredients of social consciousness. Exclusion of any on the grounds that they do not easily lend themselves to dramatic political statement will limit the possibilities of any literary revolution, by severely limiting the social range on which to exercise its imagination (1989: 48).

The ultimate aim is 'a civilization based on the perfection of the individual in order to permit maximum social creativity' (1985: 150):

> The aim is to extend the range of personal and social experience as far as possible in order to contribute to bringing about a highly conscious, sensitive new person in a new society. This, it seems to me, is the function of art in, and its contribution to, the ongoing revolution in South Africa (1989a: 50).

Highly conscious and sensitive people are what any progressive movement would strive to produce, but these are transitive terms. The notion that Great Literature extends the personal and social experience of the reader and thereby contributes towards the perfection of the individual by producing highly conscious, sensitive new persons is precisely what has provided the rationale for the highly conservative critical practice that has dominated South African English studies for the past forty years, and signally failed to usher in a new society in the process. While it is undoubtedly important to extend the social range on which the imagination can be exercised, a 'literary revolution' would seem to involve rather more than that.

The critical question is, of course, precisely what the highly conscious new persons are going to be conscious of. In the context of 'ongoing revolution', and bearing in mind the track-record of cultural projects aimed in the first place at the development of individual sensibility, it would seem important to be explicit about the need for the 'highly conscious, sensitive new person' to be conscious of more than his or her high consciousness. Any revolutionary cultural project in the South African context would need to be conscious, in particular, that there is more to the struggle for liberation than the ending of statutory race discrimination.

A 'literary revolution' would have, for a start, to hold up for examination the exclusive concepts of the 'writer' and 'standards' which pervade liberal aesthetics. Pietermaritzburg's *Echo* poets, responding to the burning down of their homes or the brutal political killing of family or friends, attempting in the process to make a cultural intervention in the endemic conflict in social circumstances wholly unconducive to 'a radically contemplative state of mind' and far more conducive to indignation than 'understanding', will be less well served by an exclusive concept of the 'writer' than by an inclusive one, such as that articulated by Mothobi Mutloatse: '[The poet] could be a street-cleaner, migrant worker, night-soil remover or anything. He simply feels moved to articulate his experience and present it artistically. Any person can do that, if only he perseveres' (quoted Cullinan, 1980).

Whatever Ndebele's own practice may be, and I have no doubt that as President of the Congress of South African Writers he is very active in the encouraging of young writers, his theoretical intervention has, in at least one crucial area, had the effect of narrowing, rather than broadening the base of cultural production. I refer to the magazine *Staffrider*, of which Ndebele has said in interview:

> *Staffrider* has been part and parcel of the spread of a democratic culture. It was instrumental in the process whereby more and more people in this country were enabled to have an effective say on the social, cultural and political affairs affecting them ... even the most inexperienced writers were given the opportunity to articulate their experiences and views. This was important and the unevenness in the quality of the voices is the direct result of the non-elitist democratic orientation of the magazine. It gave large numbers of young writers and artists the opportunity to be exposed to the broad South African public. As far as this is concerned *Staffrider* fulfilled its role very effectively.

> However, in line with my belief in the spirit of self-criticism and self-evaluation, I believe this should also be applicable to *Staffrider*. Thus, while we are engaged in harnessing the necessary sophistication of conceptual, organisational and political means to effectively oppose apartheid, *Staffrider* too must come to terms with this. It has to focus on the fine points of writing, engage in the great cultural and political debates and help to crystallise the role of cultural workers and progressive intellectuals in this country (Ndebele, 1988b: 345).

This passage seems to me to reveal very clearly the tension between the democratization of cultural production and the maintenance or recuperation of 'standards' which lies unresolved at the heart of Ndebele's theoretical argument. Ndebele gives no indication as to what social, political or cultural changes have taken place which make it no longer necessary for more and more people to be enabled to have an effective say on the social, cultural and political affairs affecting them. Self-criticism and self-evaluation would tell *Staffrider* that it had fulfilled its role very effectively, which Ndebele admits. Neither in this interview, nor in the essays, does Ndebele theorize the 'focus on the fine points in writing' in a way which accommodates it to an evidently approved 'non-elitist democratic orientation'. Moreover Ndebele here gives his seal of approval to a movement away from that non-elitist democratic orientation. Where *Staffrider* was concerned that consisted in the replacing of a publishing ethos encapsulated by Kirkwood's 'Nobody wanted the kind of editorial policy that comes from the top: "We've got a policy. We've got standards. If you fit in with this policy, come up to these standards, we'll publish you"' (Kirkwood, 1980: 22) with one based on Christopher van Wyk's: 'I also insisted that a system of literary merit be adopted' (van Wyk, 1988: 166).

Van Wyk recognizes, in the interview from which this quotation comes, that 'a literary and cultural magazine does not necessarily exist to display the best writing in a particular society (and) serves basically as a forum or meeting place', and acknowledges that one of *Staffrider's* main purposes 'was to encourage new writing in South Africa'. But he also makes it abundantly clear that it was on the strength of Ndebele's theoretical arguments that *Staffrider* was felt to 'require critical intervention and long-term strategies which would replace the reactive protest writing with a more profound imaginative engagement with the South African reality' (van Wyk,1988: 167). In so far as the most visible empirical effect of Ndebele's theoretical approach has been a 'critical intervention' which has served to restrict the forum and impose quality controls on people's 'effective say on the social, cultural and political affairs affecting them' that approach could arguably be seen as less radical in its effects than the one it replaced.

As South Africa moves towards non-racial democracy, there is surely a need for a theoretical approach to African literature which theorizes the democratization of cultural production in the South African context. This should not be read as a 'demand for surface art': Ndebele's search for perfection is admirable, as is Sachs's desire for 'better' poems. Nobody would deny writers the right 'to reflect on their own practice' or to 'hanker after the enhancement of their craftmanship' (Ndebele, 1989b: 32). The point is that the decision as to where cultural 'perfection' lies - the supreme accolade in the ascription of what is always transitive value - and what constitutes 'better' poetry must, like other decisions, be opened to those who are in other respects acknowledged as the 'makers of decisions' and the 'makers of the future'. It seeems unlikely, for example, that the audience for worker's theatre in South Africa over recent years would be as ready to write off that cultural production as Sachs appears to be.

There are a number of obvious issues involved in the democratization of literature. These would include: (i) interrogating the status of 'the writer' - all those who write are writers; (ii) demystifying the categories of 'Art' and 'Literature' and thereby making them available to all; (iii) demystifying the status and role of the 'critic' and 'teacher'; (iv) accepting the 'radical contingency' of literary value; (v) promoting collaborative cultural production as an acceptable alternative to individual cultural production; (vi) encouraging community participation in the production, distribution and consumption of cultural products; (vii) recognizing that political as well as aesthetic implications attach to denying the validity of utterance on the basis of purely formal considerations; (viii) recognizing that what 'merits publication' depends very much on particular social and historical circumstances. Under some circumstances the psychological and political benefits for writers of the recognition accorded by publication, in terms of empowerment and the validation of experience, must be allowed to outweigh an exclusive consideration of the 'fine points of writing'.

The struggle in South Africa will not end with the dismantling of apartheid, democracy and 'democratization' will have little meaning without a fundamental restructuring of South African society. For those engaged in cultural debate in a context in which, after centuries of the most ruthless and exploitative oppression, representatives of a white racial minority are about to embark on negotiations in the hope of winning the collaboration of a black middle class and thereby maintaining their position of privilege, it is salutory to bear in mind Peter Widdowson's observation that bourgeois criticism has 'so constituted "Literature" as to reproduce and naturalise bourgeois ideology as '"literary value"' (Widdowson,1980: 140). In these terms, 'literary value' unless radically interrogated, 'correlates closely with the values of bourgeois liberal-humanism in general, and substantially helps to underpin it.'

I have been trying in this paper to identify what seems to me to be a fundamental tension between the radical politics on which Ndebele's essays are based and the more conservative aesthetics underpinning his cultural programme. That Ndebele is commited to a radical transformation of South African society is not in question, even if his essays do not explicitly endorse the anti-imperialist thrust of a Cabral or an Ngugi. At the same time virtually every feature of what Anne McClintock has identified as the 'presiding liberal aesthetic faith' in South Africa up to the 1970s can in some measure be identified in Ndebele's essays. She lists the articles of this faith as follows:

> individual creativity, immanent and 'universal' literary values, unity of vision, wholeness of experience, complexity of form, refined moral discrimination untainted by political platitude, irony, taste, cultivated sensibility, and the formal completion of the work of art ... (McClintock, 1980: 612).

This is not to suggest for a moment that the argument of Ndebele's essays is thereby invalidated. The main thrust of that argument, relating, firstly, to the need to broaden the range of social experience regarded as the legitimate subject-matter of cultural production, and, secondly, to the desirability of greater analytical rigour and more attention to detail in the writer's approach to that subject-matter, seems to me to be unanswerable. The idea is not to denounce or 'demolish' (Ndebele: 1989b: 33) Ndebele's highly cogent thesis. But, as the basis for a radical criticism, which will be able to reach beyond the dismantling of apartheid and contribute on the cultural level to the struggle for the kind of liberation envisaged by Cabral and Ngugi, it may be that a more self-reflexive, and more explicitly democratically oriented, theoretical approach will be needed, which will subject received aesthetic categories to a more testing scrutiny than is apparent in the essays by either Ndebele or Sachs looked at here.

WORKS CITED

Amuta, Chidi. *The Theory of African Literature*. London: Zed, 1989.

Cabral, Amilcar. *Return to the Source*. New York: Monthly Review Press, 1973.

Cullinan, Patrick. "Comment." *The bloody Horse* 2 (1980): 5-8.

Eagleton, Terry. *Literary Theory: An Introduction*. Oxford: Blackwell, 1983.

Kirkwood, Mike. "*Staffrider*: An Informal discussion," *English in Africa* 7.2 (1980): 23-31.

La Guma, Alex. *Time of the Butcherbird*. London: Heinemann, 1979.

Mutloatse, Mothobi. Introduction to *Forced Landing*. Johannesburg: Ravan, 1980.

Ndebele, Njabulo S. *Fools and Other Stories*. Johannesburg: Ravan, 1983.

―――. "Turkish Tales and Some thoughts on South African Fiction." *Staffrider*, 6 (1984): 24-25, 42-48.

―――. "The Rediscovery of the Ordinary: Some New Writings in South Africa." *Journal of Southern African Studies* 12 (1985): 143-57.

―――. "Turkish Tales and Some Thoughts on South African Fiction" reprinted in *Ten Years of Staffrider*. Ed. A.W. Oliphant and I. Vladislavic. Johannesburg: Ravan 1988a, 318-40.

―――――. "The Writer as Critic and Interventionist." *Ten Years of Staffrider*. Ed. A.W. Oliphant and I. Vladislavic. Johannesburg: Ravan: 1988b, 341-46.

―――――. "Redefining relevance." *Pretexts* 1 (1989a): 40-51.

―――――. "The Ethics of Intellectual Combat." *Current Writing* 1 (1989b): 23-35.

―――――. "Liberation and the Crisis of Culture." *Southern African Review of Books*, 3, (3 & 4) (1990): 22-3.

Sachs, Albie. "Preparing Ourselves for Freedom." Unpublished mimeo. Extracts published as "From Solidarity to Artistic Freedom." *Weekly Mail* (Johannesburg), February 2 (1990): 23.

Smith, Barbara Herrnstein. "Contingencies of Value." *Critical Inquiry* 10 (1983): 1-35.

Widdowson, Peter. "'Literary Value' and the Reconstruction of Criticism.'" *Literature and History* 6 (1980): 138-50.

QUESTIONNEMENTS ET MISES EN PERSPECTIVE

HANS-JÜRGEN LÜSEBRINK

I. QUESTIONNEMENTS

L'extériorité permet, souvent, l'ouverture de perspectives inattendues et neuves. Ainsi ce colloque qui se proposait d'interroger les rapports entre littérature africaine et théorie littéraire, a fini par focaliser ses questionnements, de manière insistante et parfois radicale, sur la spécificité même du discours théorique, sur son statut, sa forme et ses enjeux. Interroger les discours théoriques contemporains à partir des littératures africaines, c'est-à-dire de littératures non-européennes et fortement ancrées, jusqu'à nos jours, dans des formes de communication et des traditions culturelles orales, a amené à reconnaître le fait que les théories en cause étaient toutes d'origine occidentale, et de par-là - peut-être - inadéquates à la compréhension et à l'interprétation de cultures et de littératures non-occidentales.

B. Jeyifo est certainement allé le plus loin dans cette perspective en constatant que le discours théorique dominant qu'il considère comme un "idiome spécialisé" ou un "jargon", est exclusivement de provenance occidentale et marqué par un haut degré de canonisation ("exclusively Western, high-canonical provenance"). Il souligne, en effet, le puissant impact des discours théoriques produits dans les *centres* intellectuels du monde occidental - du marxisme au déconstructivisme en passant par le structuralisme et la sémiotique - sur l'interprétation des littératures provenant de la *périphérie* des sociétés du Tiers-Monde où ils ne sont pas seulement reproduits et imités, mais également appliqués à des situations culturelles et des formations littéraires fondamentalement différentes. Cette reconnaissance d'une différence - qui incite à repenser les discours théoriques sur les littératures africaines - va bien au-delà du simple constat de diversité, mais conduit à mettre en cause, comme le postule E. Julien dans la conclusion de sa contribution, les significations occidentales des notions de "Littérature" et de "Théorie".

En même temps, les débats du colloque ont insisté sur le fait que tout discours théorique implique un pouvoir: pouvoir sur le sens du texte, mais aussi puissance des institutions détentrices du discours interprétatif et théorique. Ces questions se posent, en effet, avec une singulière acuité au sujet de littératures nées dans le sillage des conquêtes coloniales et des projets d'acculturation occidentaux, et produites sur la base de structures de dépendance qui demeurent fortes non seulement sur le plan politique et économique, mais également sur le plan culturel et linguistique. Peut-on appliquer les théories du structuralisme littéraire, nées dans un contexte intellectuel précis, celui du Paris des années soixante, et pensées quasi exclusivement à partir d'analyses de textes littéraires *européens* des 18e, 19e et 20e siècles, aux littératures africaines, sans les repenser à fond? Que peut vouloir dire le concept de "Champ littéraire" forgé par Pierre Bourdieu pour les littératures africaines? Peut-on parler de "Champ littéraire" à l'égard de littératures produites dans des cultures où la culture écrite et ses institutions restent, dans la grande majorité des cas, marginales par rapport aux cultures orales traditionnelles, d'une part, et d'autre part par rapport à l'influence croissante de la "nouvelle oralité" des médias radiophoniques et télévisés? Faut-il penser le "champ littéraire" en Afrique par conséquent sous une autre forme à structure au moins tripartite embrassant également la scène de l'exil, politique, mais aussi économique pour certains, - généralement parisien pour les auteurs francophones ou londonien pour les écrivains de langue anglaise - et dont l'importance n'a cessé de croître depuis l'aube des indépendances africaines au début des années soixante? Et que peuvent signifier les théories, essentiellement nordaméricaines et nées dans le contexte des années quatre-vingt, de "post-histoire" et de "déconstructivisme", pour les littératures d'un continent braquées avec insistance sur son histoire et ses réalités politiques et sociales actuelles? Peut-on, enfin, transposer des théories psychanalytiques du texte aux littératures de l'Afrique Noire où les structures familiales - et donc l'inconscient collectif (Collomb 1976) - sont fondamentalement différentes de celles de l'Occident? Les débats du colloque ont incité à se poser ces questions de base et à repenser quelques-uns des cadres théoriques susceptibles d'être appliqués aux littératures africaines. La prise de position de R. Bjornson en faveur des approches du "New Historicism" (G. Geertz, J. Clifford) et sa critique poussée des théories déconstructivistes en vogue surtout aux Etats-Unis tracent une possible voie de réponse qui implique en même temps le postulat que toute théorie littéraire appliquée aux littératures africaines doit constituer également une théorie de la culture (englobant l'ensemble des systèmes symboliques d'une société). La position de E. Julien emprunte une autre direction et plaide pour un comparatisme littéraire qui part de la situation coloniale constitutive - avec ses implications culturelles, politiques et mentales - comme soubassement socio-culturel de toute interprétation de textes littéraires africains, et propose, à travers l'exemple de la mise en parallèle de *La Vie d'un boy* de Ferdinand Oyono et de *l'Immoraliste* d'André Gide, un paradigme d'analyse pouvant servir de modèle.

Enfin, le sens même de la notion de "théorie", de son contenu, de sa fonction et de son statut, a été discuté et mis en cause. B. Jeyifo attaque, dans sa contribution, avec virulence les 'étalages' du supermarché théorique actuel dans les universités européennes et nord-américaines qui lui semblent "carnavalesques". Il propose de distinguer entre "Theory" et "Theorism", ce dernier constituant essentiellement un "jargon" hautement spécialisé, fonctionnant à l'intérieur d'institutions relativement closes et détaché largement de toute tentative d'interprétation de textes littéraires concrets. Les littératures africaines, avec l'importance qu'elles accordent à la représentation fictionnelle des réalités sociales et politiques du continent, constituent ainsi un défi à certaines évolutions du discours théorique occidental, d'autant plus que nombre d'écrivains africains (tels O. Sembène, Ngugi Wa Thiong'o, H. Lopes, Mongo Beti) tiennent, dans des interviews, essais et préfaces, eux-mêmes un discours théorique qui souligne l'ancrage social et historique de leurs oeuvres.

II. JALONS DE PERSPECTIVES

Le double objectif d'une grande partie des écrivains africains désireuse de se référer aux réalités sociales et politiques de leur continent (ce qui n'est pas identique avec une volonté de représentation 'réaliste') et de s'adresser en même temps à un large public - tel O. Sembène qui s'est considéré comme "la voix de son peuple" (Sembène 1977) ou Henri Lopes affirmant dans une préface qu'"il faudrait que chaque Congolais lise ce livre" (Lopes 1985, 5) - se trouve en contradiction fondamentale avec les réalités socio-culturelles de la diffusion du livre dans l'Afrique contemporaine. Le prix élevé des livres, le taux d'analphabétisme des populations atteignant dans nombre de pays plus de 30%, et un réseau de bibliothèques publiques et de librairies très insuffisant expliquent la diffusion extrêmement restreinte de la littérature africaine, sous la forme de *livre monographique imprimé*, sur le continent africain.

Mais à côté de cette voie de diffusion majeure, par le livre monographique et sa lecture, certes dominante en Europe et en Amérique du Nord, existent d'autres formes de réception littéraires, peu étudiées jusqu'ici, mais capitales en Afrique: la diffusion, d'abord, de textes littéraires par la presse (feuilleton, résumé, compte-rendu), la radio et, surtout, à travers des anthologies scolaires; la diffusion, ensuite, du message de l'auteur, mais également de son style et de son écriture, à travers des lectures publiques, des conférences, et surtout des interviews dans la presse écrite, à la radio et à la télévision ce qui explique que l'impact de certains auteurs - comme Ousmane Sembène au Sénégal, Célestin Manga au Cameroun ou Jean-Marie Adiaffi et Amadou Koné en Côte d'Ivoire - dépasse très largement les circuits de diffusion de leurs *livres* imprimés et les publics de lecteurs corrélatifs; et, enfin, certains textes littéraires imprimés ont atteint, à travers l'adaptation au théâtre et à l'écran (cinéma, télévision), des publics non-lettrés, tels *Le Mandat* et *Xala* d'Ousmane Sembène mis à l'écran ou la nouvelle *Sarzan* de Birago Diop adaptée au théâtre.

D'où une double conséquence, sur le plan méthodologique, pour toute étude portant sur *l'impact social* des littératures africaines écrites: l'analyse du *rôle social* de l'auteur, de son image et de ses formes d'intervention publiques, de l'interview télévisée aux ouï-dires traversant l'espace public; l'analyse, également, de la *dissémination textuelle de l'oeuvre*, des citations dans la presse et à la télévision jusqu'à sa publication sous forme de feuilleton ou sa diffusion comme pièce radiophonique et morceau d'anthologie.[1]

Le constat effectué par Abiola Irele (1990) soulignant que la littérature orale, sous ses différentes formes, constitue l'intertexte majeur des littératures africaines écrites, est à la fois pertinent et provocateur. Il implique, en effet, pour toute recherche, notamment d'orientation sociocritique et sémiotique, visant à scruter le potentiel sémantique du texte analysé, la connaissance approfondie de l'intertexte culturel et des langues africaines parlées par l'auteur, dans sa pratique quotidienne, et les personnages qu'il met en scène. Marquées par le clivage, hérité de l'époque coloniale mais caractéristique pour la grande majorité des cultures africaines (avec des exceptions majeures comme la Tanzanie), entre langue européenne de l'écriture et langue parlée, entre langue officielle (de l'administration, de l'école, de la presse et des institutions culturelles et littéraires) et langue dominante de la communication quotidienne, les littératures africaines en langues africaines sont profondément empreintes d'une *structure de traduction*: traduction d'une réalité linguistique, mais

---

[1] Voir sur ce point Ricard (1987) et Lüsebrink (1990).

traduction également d'un système de références culturelles que tout écrivain africain laisse transparaître, de manière plus ou moins explicite et étendue, par l'utilisation de termes en langues africaines, expliqués ou non en bas de page par des notes, la citation de savoirs culturels ou encore la traduction directe et immédiatement perceptible d'expressions, de proverbes ou de formes de dialogues à partir de langues africaines. L'écrivain ivoirien Ahmadou Kourouma est certes allé le plus loin possible dans cette direction en créant, dans ses deux romans *Les Soleils des Indépendances* (1968) et *Monnè, outrages et défis* (1990), une écriture 'biculturelle', constamment marquée par la diglossie français/malinké, infligeant ses lois grammaticales et lexicales à la langue française utilisée comme langue *d'écriture* de base (Koné 1992). Malgré des travaux pionniers de ces dernières années, comme ceux d'Amadou Koné (1984), de Werner Glinga (1990), de Karin Barber (cf. son article dans le présent volume), de Samba Dieng (1989) et de Papa Samba Diop (1992), l'analyse systématique de l'intertextualité orale des littératures africaines écrites, et sa nécessaire théorisation en sont encore à leurs débuts. Celle-ci devrait comporter en particulier le relevé et l'étude systématique des toponymes, patronymes et occurrences en langues africaines dans les textes écrits en langues européennes, de leurs fonctions et de leur espace sémantique (connotations, codes culturels)[2] ainsi que la mise en rapport des genres littéraires écrits et ceux des littératures orales dont des travaux comme notamment ceux de Jean Derive (1986, 1990) ont commencé à étudier, pour des aires culturelles et linguistiques précises, le système.

L'intertexte occidental des littératures africaines écrites, beaucoup mieux connu notamment en ce qui concerne les genres du roman et du théâtre (cf. Kane 1982; Makouta-Mboukou 1983; Ricard 1986; Fiebach 1988), reste encore largement à explorer à l'égard de ses rapports avec la littérature coloniale, ses institutions, ses formes littéraires (cf. Mouralis 1984 et dans le présent volume) et ses discours sociaux (presse, textes officiels, textes ethnographiques, livres scolaires etc.). Le *processus d'autonomisation* des littératures africaines écrites, entre le début des années vingt et la fin des années soixante qui virent l'émergence d'auteurs comme Kourouma et Ouologuem, se caractérise en effet par une *structure de la réplique* et du *contre-discours*. Celle-ci fait constamment référence aux discours coloniaux tout en les récusant et en les transformant, de manière plus ou moins explicite et radicale. L'étude des interdépendances entre

---

[2] Voir sur ce point la thèse de Papa Samba Diop (Université de Bayreuth 1993, 2 vols.) portant sur l'intertexte culturel africain de l'ensemble de la production romanesque sénégalaise, de 1920 à 1990, et comportant également un volume de glossaire commenté (Diop 1993).

discours colonial et littératures africaines naissantes poursuivie dans le présent volume par E. Julien et B. Mouralis, celle des préfaces de romans africains, de l'époque coloniale jusqu'aux indépendances, entreprise par Bokiba (1991), l'analyse comparatiste des discours européens et africains sur les "Tirailleurs sénégalais" (Riesz/Schultz 1990) ou encore l'étude des versions multiples, dans les littératures orales et écrites, de La Fontaine jusqu'à des textes africains et caraïbes, de la fable "Le meunier, son fils et l'âne" (Riesz 1993), tracent à cet égard des voies de recherche possible et peut-être exemplaires. L'approche intertextuelle s'avère particulièrement fructueuse pour des textes d'une grande complexité d'écriture tels les romans *Le Devoir de violence* (1968) de Yambo Ouologuem et *Monnè, outrages et défis* (1990) d'Ahmadou Kourouma. Véritables 'machines textuelles', ils citent, réécrivent, pastichent et transforment, entre autre à travers les registres de la satire et de l'ironie, aussi bien un intertexte colonial occidental multiforme que des références aux littératures africaines écrites en français et en arabe (notamment les chroniques de Tombouctou) et aux littératures orales, notamment les épopées de l'Ouest africain.[3]

Le caractère souvent 'manifestaire', engagé et politique de nombreux ouvrages littéraires africains, surtout des deux premières générations d'écrivains africains, ont conduit à privilégier, dans les études critiques, les approches thématiques et idéologiques, au détriment de l'analyse des formes esthétiques. Face aux travaux multiples concernant les idéologies mises en place par la production romanesque africaine ou certains thèmes (représentations de la femme, de la figure du dictateur, de la ville etc.), les études relatives à des genres spécifiques (autobiographie, genres dramatiques et poétiques) sont relativement rares, mis à part le roman. La poésie africaine écrite, extrêmement prolifique entre la fin des années trente et le début des années soixante, souvent publiée dans des périodiques africains[4], est peu étudiée, en dehors de quelques grands auteurs, notamment Senghor, et peu explorée à l'égard des formes esthétiques et des genres (de provenance aussi bien occidentale qu'africaine) employés. Cela vaut également pour le théâtre africain dont l'étude des *genres esthétiques* se trouve largement négligée par rapport à l'analyse des thèmes et celle de certains grands auteurs (Soyinka, Dadié, l'Ecole William-Ponty, Cheikh A. Ndao, e.a.).

L'évolution des différents *genres littéraires* dans les littératures africaines écrites montre, en effet, une scission croissante entre 'genres

---

[3] Voir à propos de Ouologuem Koné (1987); Wolitz (1973); Mouralis (1984a).

[4] Voir sur ce point le chapitre "Textes poétiques" dans Lüsebrink (1994).

scripturaux' (roman, nouvelle, essai) et 'genres semi-oraux' (théâtre, poésie) caractérisés, de plus en plus, par le recours aux langues africaines ou des formes d'écriture et de performance bilingues. Cette évolution comporte également un défi pour les approches sociologiques ou sociocritiques des littératures africaines: dominé, jusqu'à présent, très largement par une sociocritique visant l'étude du social et du politique *dans* le texte littéraire et constituant ainsi, en définitive, beaucoup plus une 'thématique sociale du texte' dans la lignée des travaux e.a. de Claude Duchet, de Jacques Leenhardt ou de Lucien Goldmann, l'ancrage social de la littérature africaine dans le champ social et littéraire a été, en définitive, peu étudié.[5] Le déclin de la poésie africaine écrite depuis le début des années soixante - à commencer par le recul considérable du nombre des poèmes *publiés* - est certes lié, en partie, à une déconnection croissante du champ littéraire et du champ politique qu'avait réunis, à travers de multiples périodiques servant de supports de publication, la poésie militante des années quarante et cinquante. L'éclosion d'un théâtre populaire, bilingue ou entièrement en langues africaines et pour lequel le support de l'écrit a de moins en moins d'importance, en Tanzanie, mais aussi en Côte d'Ivoire (notamment le "Théâtre Koteba"), au Togo (les "concert-partys") et en Afrique du Sud, a ainsi fondamentalement modifié la fonction sociale du théâtre comme institution et marginalisé les établissements théâtraux calqués sur le modèle occidental, comme le Théâtre Soriano à Dakar.

Si les institutions occidentales (européennes et dans une moindre mesure nord-américaines) de consécration et de canonisation littéraires - éditeurs (de prestige et 'valeur symbolique' extrêmement inégaux), prix littéraires, universités - continuent à jouer un rôle primordial au sein des différents champs littéraires africains, le rôle des institutions *locales* n'a cessé de croître depuis les années trente, et notamment depuis l'africanisation des curricula littéraires de l'enseignement entre la fin des années soixante et le milieu des années soixante-dix.[6] Si la réception critique des littératures africaines en Europe commence à être relativement bien connue, notamment pour les cas de l'Allemagne et de la France, le fonctionnement du champ littéraire dans les différents pays du continent africain même, en particulier en ce qui concerne le discours critique (évolution, objets, discours, agents) et de la circulation scolaire des auteurs

---

[5] Voir des jalons de cette perspective dans les travaux de Bernard Mouralis ainsi que dans Ricard/Riesz (1992) et Bjornson (1991).

[6] Voir sur ce sujet Mouralis (1984), 108-116 (chapitre "le contenu des programmes"), Lüsebrink (1990), 234-242, Ogden (1982), Huannou (1984), Futcha (1984), Lindfors (1990) et Ntonfo (1991).

africains, reste assez peu étudié. Des auteurs comme Abdoulaye Sadji (Senegal), Boury Ndiaye (Senegal), Bernard Dadié (Côte d'Ivoire) et Felix Couchoro (Togo), par exemple, ont eu un succès, une notoriété une présence infiniment plus grands dans les champs littéraires de leurs pays qu'à l'étranger, malgré l'édition de certains de leurs ouvrages en France.

Au lieu de prôner une 'Théorie africaine de la littérature' qui serait à construire, à partir de la nécessaire reconnaissance de l'altérité culturelle et linguistique des sociétés africaines, j'aurais plutôt tendance, à l'issue de nos débats, à parler d'un *transfert de modèles et de concepts théoriques*: 'Transfer' non pas au sens d'une simple application de modèles et de concepts théoriques occidentaux, mais au sens de 'transformation' et de réemploi. Le transfert du concept de "champ littéraire", par exemple, signifierait e.a. de ne pas confiner sa définition[7] au domaine de l'écrit et de l'imprimé, mais d'intégrer également l'ensemble des pratiques culturelles et littéraires orales; celui du concept de "genre" impliquerait, pour sa part, de distinguer systématiquement, pour l'ensemble du système des genres littéraires africains, entre genres écrits (ou scripturaux), genres oraux et genres semi-oraux, avec des circuits de diffusion spécifiques.

Les communications et débats de notre colloque montrent enfin, au-delà de la grande diversité des approches, des interrogations et des objets analysés, que la sociologie de la littérature devrait occuper, au sein de tout questionnement théorique et de toute recherche sur les littératures africaines écrites, une place centrale, incontournable, du fait de la volonté de la grande majorité des écrivains africains de se définir par rapport aux préoccupations fondamentales de leurs contemporains, et d'ancrer ainsi leurs oeuvres dans les réalités sociales et politiques de leur époque: mais elle devrait passer d'une approche sociocritique trop souvent axée sur l'étude de la thématique sociale du texte et l'objectif de circonscrire le reflet du social et du politique *dans* le texte, à une sociologie de la littérature proprement dite. Celle-ci implique l'analyse du champ littéraire dans son ensemble, de ses agents et de ses institutions, du système esthétique des genres littéraires qu'il met en place, de ses rapports avec d'autres formations du discours social (et où les discours ethnologiques et historiographiques sont particulièrement importants pour les littératures

---

[7] Voir par exemple la définition de Pierre Bourdieu dans Bourdieu (1991), 4-5: "Le champ littéraire est un champ de forces agissant sur tous ceux qui y entrent, et de manière différentielle selon la position qu'ils y occupent (soit, pour prendre des points très éloignés, celle d'auteur de pièces à succès ou celle de poète d'avant-garde), en même temps qu'un champ de luttes de concurrence qui tendent à conserver ou à transformer ce champ de forces."

africaines) et, enfin, des "habitus" (Bourdieu) sociaux, mentaux et culturels qu'il génère, représente et met en circulation à travers l'oeuvre littéraire.

OUVRAGES CITES

Bjornson, Richard. *The African Quest for Freedom and Identity. Cameroonian Writing and the National Experience*. Bloomington/Ind.: Indiana University Press, 1991.

Bokiba, André Patient. Le discours préfaciel, instance de légitimation. L'exemple du Cameroun. *Etudes littéraires* 24.2 (1991): 77-98.

Bourdieu, Pierre. Le champ littéraire. *Actes de la Recherche en Sciences Sociales* 89 (1991): 4-46.

Collomb. "Le fou, problème du développement." *Africa* 80. 15 avril (1976): 43-45.

Derive, Jean. *Fonctionnement sociologique de la littérature orale*, thèse pour le doctorat d'Etat, Université de Paris III, 3. vol. 1986.

————. "L'oralité africaine ou "la littérature en kit" Réflexions sur l'apport de l'étude de l'art oral africain à quelques problèmes théoriques de la littérature générale. *Semper aliquid novi. Littérature Comparée et Littératures d'Afrique. Mélanges offerts à Albert Gérard*. Ed. János Riesz et Alain Ricard. Tübingen: Gunter Narr (1990): 227-38.

Diop, Papa Samba. "Les bouts de bois de Dieu" d'Ousmane Sembène. In Gilles Dorion, Franz-Josef Meissner, János Riesz (ed.) *Französisch heute - Le Français aujourd'hui. Festschrift für Jürgen Olbert*. Frankfurt: Moritz Diesterweg (1992): 449-65.

————. *Archéologie littéraire du roman sénégalais*. Habilitationsschrift. Universität Bayreuth, 1993, 2 vols.

Duchet, Claude. *Pour une sociocritique ou variations sur un incipit*. Paris: Larousse, 1971.

Fiebach, Joachim. *Die Toten und die Macht der Lebenden: zur Theorie und Geschichte von Theater in Afrika*. Wilhelmshafen: Heinrichshafen, 1986.

Flutcha, Innocent. La littérature africaine dans l'enseignement secondaire au Cameroun: une portion congrue. *Recherche, Pédagogie et Culture* 68 (1984): 36-39.

Glinga, Werner. *Literatur in Senegal. Geschichte, Mythos und gesellschaftliches Ideal in der oralen und schriftlichen Literatur*. Berlin: Reimers, 1990.

Huannou, Adrien. *La littérature béninoise de la langue française, des origines à nos jours*. Paris: ACCT-Karthala, 1984.

Irele, Abiola. The African Imagination. *Research in African Literatures* 21 (1990): 49-67.

Kadima-Nzuji, Mukala. *La littérature zairoise de langue française (1945-1965)*. Paris: ACCT-Karthala, 1984.

Kane, Mohamadou. *Roman africain et tradition*. Dakar: Nouvelles Editions Africaines, 1982.

Koné, Amadou e.a. *Du récit oral au roman*. Abidjan: Ceda, 1984.

————. *Bilinguisme et écriture du français: Ecrire deux langues à la fois*. In Gilles Dorion, Franz-Josef Meissner, János Riesz (ed.) *Französisch heute - Le*

Français aujourd'hui. Festschrift für Jürgen Olbert. Frankfurt: Moritz Diesterweg (1992): 440-48.

Lindfors, Bernth. "The Famous Author's Reputation Test: An Update to 1986." *Semper aliquid novi. Littérature Comparée et Littératures d'Afrique. Mélanges offerts à Albert Gérard.* Tübingen: Gunter Narr (1990): 131-44.

Lopes, Henri. Préface. In: Maxime Ndébéka, *Soleils neufs*. Yaoundé: Editions Clé, 1969.

Lüsebrink, Hans-Jürgen. *Schrift, Buch und Lektüre in der französischsprachigen Literatur Afrikas. Zur Wahrnehmung und Funktion von Schriftlichkeit und Buchlektüre in einem kulturellen Epochenumbruch der Neuzeit.* Tübingen: Niemeyer, 1990.

——. *La conquête de l'espace public colonial. Prises de parole et formes de participation d'écrivains et d'intellectuels africains dans la presse à l'époque coloniale.* Paris: L'Harmattan, 1994.

Makouta-Mboukou, Jean-Pierre. *Introduction à l'étude du roman négro-africain d'expression française.* Dakar: Nouvelles Editions Africaines, 1983.

Mouralis, Bernard. *Littérature et développement: essai sur le statut, la fonction et la représentation de la littérature négro-africaine.* Paris: Silex, 1984.

——. Un carrefour d'écritures: "Le devoir de violence" de Yambo Ouologuem. *Recherches et Travaux. Bulletin (Université de Grenoble)* 27 (1984a): 75-92.

Ntonfo, André. Littérature et enseignement au Cameroun. Problématique d'une politique culturelle. *Etudes Littéraires* 24.2 (1991): 51-64.

Ogden, John. The Africanization of the curriculum in Gabon. *The French Review* 6 (1982): 855-61.

Ricard, Alain. *Livre et Communication au Nigéria. Essai de vue généraliste.* Paris: Présence Africaine, 1975.

——. *L'invention du théâtre. Le théâtre et les comédiens en Afrique Noire.* Paris: L'Age d'Homme, 1986.

——. *Naissance du roman africain: Félix Couchoro, 1900-1968.* Paris: Présence Africaine, 1987.

Riesz, János, et Joachim Schultz (Eds.). *Die "Tirailleurs sénégalais." Zur bildlichen und literarischen Darstellung afrikanischer Soldaten im Dienste Frankreichs. Présentations littéraires et figuratives des soldats africains au service de la France.* Frankfurt: Peter Lang, 1989.

Riesz, János, et Alain Ricard: *Le champ littéraire togolais.* Bayreuth: African Studies Series (vol. 23), 1992.

Riesz, János. Les littératures d'Afrique Noires vues du côté de la réception. *Revue de Littérature Comparée* 1 (1993): 9-19.

Sembène, Ousmane. Interview avec Erika Schork. *Afrika* 18 (1977): 18-19.

Wolitz, S.J. L'art du plagiat - ou une brève défense de Ouologuem. *Research in African Literatures* 4.1 (1973): 130-41.